CW00431237

DUNSTAPLELOGIA

THE

DUNSTAPLELOGIA

The early Victorian
History of Dunstable

CHARLES
LAMBORN

Dunstaplelogia
first published 1859

This edition, with new preface and
index, published
November 2002
by the Book Castle,
12 Church Street,
Dunstable,
Bedfordshire,
LU5 4RU

ISBN   1 903747 25 2

Printed by Antony Rowe Ltd.,
Chippenham, Wilts

Preface

2002

By John Buckledee
Editor of The Dunstable Gazette

IT was a time when a smallpox epidemic spread through Dunstable, when skylarks netted on the Downs were still being cooked in their thousands as a gourmet delicacy, when a new and vigorous Rector organised a drastic renovation of the neglected Priory Church.

The mournful booming of bitterns living alongside Wellhead brook could still be heard from as far away as the Five Knolls and people in the town centre might still see glow-worms gleaming in their gardens.

Charles Lamborn, a Dunstable schoolmaster, recorded all this in his book, the Dunstaplelogia, which first appeared in booklet form in 17 instalments throughout 1859.

Now this facsimile of his early Victorian history of Dunstable has been published by the Book Castle of Dunstable as another in its series of rare books about the town.

Inside this volume you will find the name of the last person to be held in the town's stocks in West Street, as well as the name of the man punished on the post of the hotel near the crossroads for deserting his family.

There are descriptions of how boys from the Free School, in what is now called Chew's House, would use oyster shells to build grottoes on street corners to commemorate St James's Day.

There is also a description of boys from the same school taking part in a curious ceremony to mark Dunstable's boundaries. A hole would be dug in an appropriate spot on the edge of town in which a boy would be stood on his head – and then receive a slap on the seat!

Charles Lamborn's book was announced in the

Dunstable Chronicle, the predecessor of the present Dunstable Gazette, on January 29, 1859.

In that issue an advertisement said simply:

Will be published on Tuesday next, February 1st, price 2d, No 1 of the

DUNSTAPLELOGIA.

A view of Dunstable Priory Church, from a Photograph, taken expressly for the occasion, will be issued with the first number.
May be had by order, of J. Tibbett, "Chronicle" Office, Mr T.C. Johnson, Post Office, Dunstable, and of Mr Barton, Toddington.

The slim booklets, each inside a paperback cover which had a different colour for each part, continued for 17 separate issues... a total outlay of 2s 10d for purchasers of the complete series. Townsfolk were, perhaps, encouraged to persevere with their collection by the odd decision of the printer to end a booklet in mid-sentence whenever space ran out on the final page!

But this all fell into place later when purchasers could assemble the parts into book form. The result was a substantial and useful record of Dunstable's story as it was understood at the time.

Bound copies of the Dunstaplelogia are extremely scarce and some of these have pages missing where the original purchasers missed an issue. The individual booklets are even rarer. So for many people this complete facsimile edition will be the first opportunity to read one of the earliest efforts to recount the history of Dunstable in some sort of scholarly order.

Charles Lamborn, in his introduction, mentions two previous publications calling them (rather disparagingly): "The notes put together by Dunno and Derbyshire, in illustration of their respective poems".

This is a reference to Dunno's Originals (that curious and eccentric mixture of local history, anecdotes and poems written by William Nicholls in 1821, 1822 and 1823) and to a collection of poems and a brief history of Dunstable produced by George Derbyshire, parish clerk of Dunstable, in the early 1850s.

The first complete edition of all nine parts of Dunno's Originals (only five were issued in the author's lifetime) was published by the Book Castle in 2001. Next year, if all goes well, there will be another in this series of reproductions, this time of the History of Dunstable written by W. H. Derbyshire (George Derbyshire's son) in 1872 and 1882.

The W.H. Derbyshire volume incorporates most of his father's material (and also complains, incidentally, that some of this had been copied, without acknowledgement, into the Dunstaplelogia).

Clearly, there was a flurry of interest during Victorian times in learning about Dunstable's past. This was being very much encouraged by the activities of the printer, James Tibbett, who had become an influential figure in the town.

Mr Tibbett began his business career as a trader, selling newspapers from beneath an umbrella in Dunstable market. He eventually purchased a shop in High Street South, in part of the building which now houses the Moore's department store. He bought a small printing press as one of his many enterprises, and this part of his business particularly prospered. It developed over the generations into Index Printers, whose large factory once covered the site at the rear of the shop which is now occupied by Dunstable Health Centre.

James Tibbett founded the town's first newspaper, the Dunstable Chronicle, in 1855. That same year he collected together the five published booklets of Dunno's Originals and reprinted them as one volume, borrowing the Dunno woodblocks from William Nicholls' son in order to do so. Then, in 1859, he printed the Dunstaplelogia as a part-work (using, incidentally, Dunno's woodblocks once again to provide a page of illustrations).

The production methods of the time account for the printing gremlins which modern readers might find peculiar. Tibbett would have set up each page using individual pieces of type which, when assembled, were inked and used to print single pages on a flat-bed press. Once this was done, the type would be disassembled and placed back in boxes in alphabetical order ready for use again on the next publication. So once a page was completed, it would be expensive and very inconvenient to set it all up again. This is why you find (on page 186) a poem by George Derbyshire with an apology for its omission from pages earlier in the book. Similarly, it is startling to find (on page 207) Jas Tongue's observations on the decline of stage coach traffic occurring, without any link, immediately after a piece about a Bible Study group. Mr Tongue's statistics were in full flow on page 143 and that is where the later paragraphs should occur – if only the printer could reset the intervening 64 pages!

The present facsimile edition faithfully reproduces the 1859 edition with, of course, all its idiosyncrasies.

Charles Lamborn, who had taught at the Sunday and Day schools which had been established in what is now the parish hall on Church Green (next to the Priory Church), had been working on the Dunstaplelogia throughout 1854 and 1855. He was aided by his "esteemed friend" Alfred T. Smith, who in 1855 was in charge of over 100 day scholars at the same school (page 162).

Lamborn penned the preface to his volume in 1857. But by that time his life had changed considerably.

He had moved to take charge of the British School in West Street, Dunstable, which had been founded (in 1843) to provide children with an education which, although Christian, would be non-sectarian.

This school began in a room in the Baptist Chapel in West Street but moved to the newly built Temperance Hall, on what would become the corner of Victoria Street, in 1845. Then it made the mistake of extending the premises to accommodate 200 children and thus incurred a debt which it struggled to repay. It is not clear at what date Mr Lamborn became involved in this (an advertisement was published in 1854 giving his name as the British School master) but in March 1855 the school was forced to close.

Mr Lamborn then found himself having to earn a living as master of two industrial schools in nearby villages where the pupils had to pay their way by producing straw plait for the local hat trade before receiving some form of elementary education. The Dunstaplelogia goes into great detail about the methods used in creating the plait which at the time was the basis for Dunstable's principal industry. So Charles Lamborn wrote his published introduction to his book from the Industrial School, Northall, and the title page of the original booklet described him as "late head master of the British School, Dunstable" as well as being a "popular lecturer in natural philosophy".

This was changed when bound copies of the collected booklets were put on sale. In these Mr Lamborn was described instead as a "member of the Architectural and Archaeological Society for the county of Buckingham".

Back in Dunstable, James Tibbett was having an aggravating time as a newspaper proprietor. He had fallen out in the most public and vitriolic fashion with his formidable editor, W.H. Derbyshire, (the same man who produced that other history of the town mentioned earlier) and had been forced to dismiss him. The disagreement seems to have been over the publication of some readers' letters which the proprietor wanted left out, and the omission of some letters which the proprietor wanted included. Tibbett closed the Chronicle in 1860, complaining later that being responsible for a public paper "leaves one open to many petty annoyances and vindictive feelings".

However, James' son, Daniel, set up his own printing business in High Street North (on a spot which is now part of the entrance to the Quadrant shopping centre) and in February 1865 founded another local newspaper, the Dunstable Borough Gazette, which is still going strong today.

The significance of this to the story of the Dunstaplelogia is in the design of the masthead, or title piece, of both the Dunstable Chronicle and the original Dunstable Borough Gazette. Both included an identical piece of artwork: an elaborate and ornate version of the arms of Dunstable which includes the motto Justitia Omnibus Fiet (Justice to all be done). The same engraving appears as an illustration in this book (facing page 44) and its origin greatly intrigued that other eminent Dunstable historian, Worthington Smith, who had made a detailed study of Dunstable's arms.

In May 1906 Smith wrote in the Gazette: "Where did this motto come from?...I can find no trace of it except at first in Lamborn's book. Did he, a schoolmaster, invent it? It is very likely. He certainly was no herald, as the heraldic description as given by him is faulty, it is incorrectly punctuated and the word 'or', which means gold, is printed 'on'. Lamborn copied this description, without acknowledgment, from Dunno's Originals (Part One) who although he has 'or' right, has his punctuation incorrect".

Until recently, it was not easy to view early copies of the Chronicle, and Worthington Smith seems to have been unaware that the motto first appeared on a newspaper mast-head rather than in Lamborn's book. But it is intriguing to wonder whether Lamborn really did create this significant part of Dunstable's tradition. He was certainly proud of his classical knowledge. In what he calls the glossary and index to Dunstaplelogia he gives the Latin derivation of some of the words he uses (Dunstaplelogia, you will note, means dun, a hill, stapel, a market, and logos, discourse). And he seems to have worked quite closely with James Tibbett. His book includes an elaborate description of a shepherd's stick (page nine) which is the previously unpublished continuation of a text from Dunno's Originals to which Tibbett may have had access.

The illustration of the arms of Dunstable (with the mistake in its caption which so irritated Worthington Smith) is one of a number of beautiful engravings which adorn the Dunstaplelogia and which, at the time, were sold separately as well as part of the book. They were based on pictures by James Tibbett Junior, Photographic Artist, who advertised "Photographic Portraiture by the Collodion Process – which possesses so many advantages over the Daugreotype (*sic*)". In 1859 he was publicising alterations and improvements to his portrait gallery in the Chronicle office "where you may obtain a warranted life-like likeness, taken in a few seconds, in any weather, in a style that cannot be surpassed...Open from nine till dusk. Dark dresses preferable".

Charles Lamborn lived in Cross Street, Dunstable – an area which was almost entirely demolished to make way for the present car park in the north-west quadrant of the town.

His book, almost incidentally, gives the flavour of what the town was like in his time. He remarks on seeing glow-worms in a garden at Cross Street, and seeing two Golden Crests knocked down by a stone as they flew on waste land in West Street between Cross Street and Icknield Terrace (page 258).

He describes the dismal booming of bitterns, rare birds which once lived among the sedges of the Wellhead brook (which rises near the present entrance to the gliding club). Their calls, like the uninterrupted bellowing of a bull, could be heard as far away as the Five Knolls (page 265). He tells of the onset of smallpox in 1853, when "death on his pale horse, beginning in Church Street, hurried many of the adult population to their long resting place". Lamborn (page 222) describes in detail his ineffective visit to the old lodging house for travellers during the course of the epidemic: his horror at the experience is palpable. And it is impossible not to be affected by his obvious grief at the early death of Miss Brown, of Dunstable Park, an "amiable and prudent young lady".

The descriptions of life in Victorian Dunstable are perhaps the most interesting part of Lamborn's book but there needs to be a word or two of warning here for anyone who might mistake the Dunstaplelogia as being a definitive history of the town. There has been so much additional research since Lamborn's time that his revelations about more ancient eras are very likely to have been amplified or corrected by later historians and archaeologists such as Worthington Smith, Thomas Bagshawe, Bill Twaddle, F.A. Fowler, James Dyer, Joyce Godber, Les Matthews, John Lunn, Nigel Benson, Omer Roucoux, Joan Curran, Joan Schneider and Vivienne Evans.

For example, the reference to Dunstable once being called "Forum Diannae" is now known to be based on a notorious forgery which misled a generation of historians. There is certainly no tunnel from the Priory Church to the High Street and Lamborn's persistent spelling of the town's name as Dunstaple was not typical of his time. The site of the Friary has now been excavated, considerable research has been done about the route of the Watling Street, and much has been learned about the Roman name of the town and about Saxon occupation nearby.

Today, we probably know more about Roman Dunstable than we do about Charles Lamborn! There was little written about him while he was in Dunstable and after the disaster of the closure of his school he moved away from the town and seems to have been forgotten. Luckily for those of us today who are wondering who he was, he left one significant clue – his membership, as mentioned in some bound copies of his book, of the prestigious Architectural and Archaeological Society of Buckinghamshire. The list of members has been preserved, and his name appears among the society's records in 1860, the only person of that surname in the society.

The next year, the society published a detailed article by Charles Lamborn about antiquarian discoveries in Bierton, the village near Aylesbury. The 1861 census in Bierton records him as living in that village and describes him as a schoolmaster. There is no-one else of that name in the region and it seems conclusive that Charles Lamborn, the school-master of Bierton, is the same Charles Lamborn, the school-master who had once lived in Cross Street, Dunstable.

If this is accepted, then much more information emerges from records in Buckinghamshire about Lamborn's life.

He was born at St Pancras in London in around 1820. His father, also named Charles, was variously described as a house painter or a house decorator.

Young Charles received a good education and by 1844 he was working as a schoolmaster at Wing near Leighton Buzzard. In December that year he married his first wife, Mary Woodman, at Wing Parish Church. She was 20 years older than him, born in Wing, and the daughter of Vere Woodman, also a schoolmaster. The village school at Wing was not opened until 1850, so they were teaching privately or at one of the numerous straw-plait schools in the area.

Why Charles and Mary came to Dunstable is not clear, but there were many straw plait schools in the town. He certain-ly became a prominent member of the Priory Church con-gregation, and eventually took charge of its Sunday School in what is now the parish hall.

His big chance came when he was made headmaster of the British School in West Street but, clearly, this was not a suc-cess. When a public meeting was called in 1855 to discuss ways of relieving its debts, only three people attended and the school closed. Lamborn wrote, somewhat sadly, that "the order of Divine Providence" had directed his steps to anoth-er sphere of labour.

That meant making his living by teaching in two plait

schools in the Northall area, but this was becoming a dis-
credited method of educating youngsters and life would not
have been easy.

But he now began writing the Dunstaplelogia, and penned
his introduction to the book two years later, in 1857. There is
a poignant reference in the Dunstaplelogia (page 241) to his
nostalgic return visit to Dunstable to attend a Wesleyan
bazaar on Whit Monday in 1859: "On this sunny June morning we travelled through the chalky gorge and entered this
world-esteemed locality..."

As 1859 is the year his booklets were belatedly appearing,
it is interesting to note that even at that late stage he was still
adding to the manuscripts (part 15 of the 17 was advertised
in the Dunstable Chronicle in August 1859). But the passage
of the book, referring to the bazaar, is very puzzling. It is
written as though he were a stranger to the town and its
church, rather than the author of a learned work which must
have been causing some local comment.

By 1871 Mary had died. Charles Lamborn, still described
as a schoolmaster, is recorded as living at Cedar Villa,
Bierton. With him there is Price Maria Wyatt, unmarried, a
farmer's daughter from Barrett Lodge in Wing. The 1871
census calls her a schoolmaster's housekeeper but that same
year she and Charles were married, returning to his family
home at St Pancras for the ceremony at Christ Church. On
the marriage certificate Charles is called a "commission
agent".

It was Price Maria's first marriage and, at 61, she was ten
years older than her husband. Her death is recorded in the
Bucks Herald of Aylesbury in November 1881.

In that year, Charles was described as a retired schoolmaster. In 1883, still in Bierton, he is described in the parish
register as a poultry breeder and assistant overseer.

He married for a third time on October 19, 1885, at
Aylesbury Parish Church. On the certificate he calls himself
a retired schoolmaster and gives his age... 65. It was the first
time on any of his marriage certificates that he had written
down that particular detail – the words "full age" had previously been enough. His wife, a widow, was Martha Holland
Rowswell, aged 50, daughter of William Frederick East,
gent. In 1887 and 1891 he is recorded in local directories as

living at 2 Victoria Street, Aylesbury, and described as
as an "assistant overseer (Bierton)" – Victoria Street is
quite close to Bierton village. The couple subsequently
moved to Southend in Essex where Charles died of a
cerebral haemorrhage on July 19, 1894. His death certificate describes him as a retired schoolmaster, aged
75, and says that his widow, M.H. Lamborn, was present at his death in their home at 12 Albert Road.

We have to read between the lines of Lamborn's
book to gain an impression of his life in
Dunstable. He seems to have been an earnest,
joyless man whose stern morality was certainly more
typical of his time than today and was in complete contrast to that other historian, the fun-filled Dunno.

There's little sympathy evident in Lamborn's view of
the "undeserving poor" in Dunstable workhouse or the
desperate drunks in the travellers' lodging house, and it
clearly does not occur to him that he might have done
something more to help. And his apparent involvement
with the Priory group of visitors who met every
Wednesday to acquire skills in the Holy Scriptures "for
the conviction of the gainsayer, the instruction of the
ignorant, the comfort of the feeble-minded, the healing
of the backslider..." might not have endeared him to
everyone.

Even his undoubted admiration for Miss Brown of
Dunstable Park is expressed in the most prudent
way...she was a woman who was beloved and respected "for her good sense, amiable manners, retired
virtues and correct taste... ever ready to give a helping
hand to every good institution and to send relief to the
poor."

We should not mock such a respectable attitude, but
it IS significant that when Lamborn's school was failing and a public meeting was called to try to rescue the
situation, only three people attended. He was not popular.

His seriousness also makes us wonder about some of
the idiosyncrasies of his text. Why does he launch into
such a long story (page 110) about a young highway-

man's theft of twenty guineas, and tell it in the style of a fiction-writer? Perhaps this had been a particularly successful script for one of his "lectures in natural philosophy" which he wanted to preserve in print. And does he really mean it when he describes the commander of the Dunstable Volunteer Corps as the "noble and gallant leader" (page 164)? An initial thought is that he was poking fun at a pompous part-time soldier, whose only feat was to prevent a popular prizefight from taking place on the Downs. But such irony is unlike Lamborn.

We should realise that it was advisable, in the Dunstable of 1857, for a young author to tread very carefully. Lamborn's gentle praise for the achievements of Mr Hopcroft, his predecessor at the British School, would have been written with the knowledge that Mr Hopcroft had been insulted by the considered refusal of the West Street Baptists to allow him to take charge of their Sunday School. And he avoids becoming embroiled in the bitter controversy surrounding the Dunstable Reformer, a newspaper which had been set up by W.H. Derbyshire to attack the owner of the Chronicle (James Tibbett).

The Rev Frederick Hose, to whom Lamborn dedicates his book, was a formidable character who could be an implacable enemy (there is a remarkable document in existence written by Alfred P. Wire, a master at the church school in the 1870s, describing the Rector as "selfish, unscrupulous, unpopular and vindictive").

With such combative characters around it is understandable that Lamborn merely hints at scandals: "This tale is no fiction... his name was mentioned to the writer but prudence still forbids it being made public".

That is quite frustrating because now, perhaps, we will never know. But these nuggets of information make Dunstaplelogia a treasure-trove for future historians. With the text readily accessible at last, some more of its little mysteries will surely be unravelled.

John Buckledee
August 2002

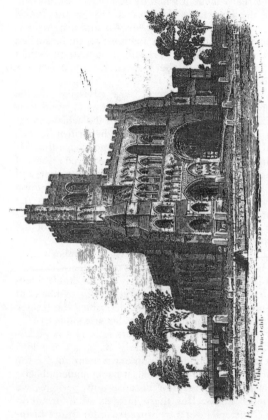

Pub.d by J.Tibbett, Dunstable.

From a Photograph.

P.TODD.sc.

DUNSTABLE PRIORY CHURCH.

THE

DUNSTAPLELOGIA:

WHEREIN IS SET FORTH, THE

ORIGIN, MANNERS, CUSTOMS, TRADE

AND PROGRESS,

OF THE

TOWN OF DUNSTAPLE,

WITH NUMEROUS ILLUSTRATIONS,

AND THE ANTIQUITIES CONNECTED THEREWITH

DURING THE

ROMAN AND SAXON PERIODS,

WITH MANY TRANSLATIONS FROM THE ORIGINAL LATIN;

BY

CHARLES LAMBORN,

LATE HEAD MASTER OF THE BRITISH SCHOOL, DUNSTAPLE, AND

POPULAR LECTURER IN NATURAL PHILOSOPHY.

DUNSTAPLE:

PRINTED AND PUBLISHED

BY JAMES TIBBETT, "ALBION" PRINTING OFFICE, HIGH STREET.

1859.

DEDICATION.

TO THE REVEREND FREDERICK HOSE, M.A.,

RECTOR OF DUNSTABLE.

REV. SIR,

While a Parishioner of yours, I was permitted to enjoy much of your kindness and instruction, and though my best services could ill repay the same, yet I became intensely attached to your Ministry and Township. When therefore, in the order of Divine Providence, my steps were directed to another sphere of labor, I keenly felt the separation, and thereupon set myself about the compilation of the present work, which will exhibit much that is instructive, in the past and present condition of this interesting scene of your ministerial labour.

Having completed the same, I beg to lay it before you and the people of your charge, as a lasting expression of gratitude and affection.

I am,

Reverend Sir,

With sentiments of sincere devotion,

Your ever faithful and most obliged Servant,

CHARLES LAMBORN.

3

Contents

4

Illustrations

THE INTRODUCTION.

COURTEOUS READER,

Having read those interesting sketches
of History relative to Dunstaple, in the Beauties of England,
and the notes put together by Dunno and Derbyshire, in
illustration of their respective Poems, I could not but feel it
was a serious omission in the literature of the Town, that no
one had endeavoured to collect and arrange in their Chronological order the scattered fragments of the past. Consequently
in the years 1854—5, in company with my esteemed friend
Mr. A. T. Smith, C.M., I visited most of the spots indicated,
and took measurements of those not previously ascertained,
and examined those already given; and where the variations
were but trifling, I have chosen to follow those already received
as correct; and where the matter was one of conflicting
opinion, I have preferred the decisions of the most approved
Antiquarian authors.

In the preparation of this work I have borrowed largely
from Old England, Saxon Chronicle, Sharon, Turner, and
others; and my thanks are due to W. B. Farr, Esq., for his
indefatigable research amongst the ancient works in the British
Museum; as also to many kind friends in the town, who have
not only cheerfully responded to my numerous inquiries, but
for their kindness in devoting so much valuable time in re-
viewing and perfecting my manuscript. Nevertheless, after all
my research, many points remain unapproached; and any

letters left for me at the Publisher's, tending to supply that which is defective, will be accepted with many thanks and receive every attention in future editions.

I will conclude these introductory observations with the story of Momus, whom Jupiter sent to convey his favor to men. Alighting upon the earth, he exclaims, " Come hither, ye happy mortals, great Jupiter hath opened to your benefit his all-gracious hands. 'Tis true he made you somewhat short-sighted, but to remedy that inconvenience, behold how he has favored you !" So saying, he unloosed his portmanteau, when an infinite number of spectacles tumbled out, and were picked up by the crowd with all the eagerness imaginable. There was enough for all ; every one had his pair ; but it was soon found that these spectacles did not represent objects to all men alike : for one pair was purple, another blue, one white, another black ; some of the glasses were red, some green, and some yellow, in short there were all manner of colors, and every shade of color. However, notwithstanding this diversity, every man was charmed with his own, believing it the truest, and enjoyed in opinion all the satisfaction of reality.

To apply this to the present work. I have striven myself to get a clear and distinct view of the object in pursuit. I have got as near as possible in order to be quite correct, and yet in the general scramble I may have picked up a blue pair of spectacles, while others have the green, and thus my eyes may have deceived me : I hope therefore, that those who see differently, will admit that they also may with equal unconsciousness on their part be laboring under a similar delusion. Should I therefore be supposed to have erred, and mistaken blue for green, or green for blue, I trust that those who know how easily these tints may be confounded with each other, will excuse the failing, and favor me with the same generosity they receive at my hand.

Your's faithfully,
C. L.

Industrial School,
Northall, 1857.

DUNSTAPLELOGIA.

THE CELTIC PERIOD.

ACCORDING to a very ancient tradition which although not possessing scriptural authority, is grounded upon Scripture, the Cymri, as they are still called in their own language, are descended from Gomer, the common ancestor of all the Celtic tribes, Britain having fallen to their lot when the islands of the Gentiles were divided among the children of Japhet, every one after his tongue, after their families, in their nations.

The original inhabitants of the locality upon which Dunstaple now stands were a people called Cassii, and spread themselves but sparingly over the counties of Beds. Bucks. and Herts., and proved to be no mean combatants with the powers of Rome.

Perhaps there is no spot where the relics of the earlier inhabitants of our land can be better

traced in their consecutive order, or more advantageously studied, than on the Downs, within a
mile from the present town of Dunstaple; and
yet although referred to by antiquarians, the order
of their succession through very distant periods
of time, has not been distinctly pointed out : this
deficiency I shall endeavour to supply.

Within this area are portions of two British
trackways, called Via-Vitellina, which ran from
Richborough in Kent, to Chester ; and the Via-
Icenorum, from Norwich to Dorchester, which
the Chronicles record were begun by King Dun-
wallo, was finished and perfected by his son
Belinus.   Contiguous to the roads are the
evidences of the aboriginal British stations, consisting of simple holes for residences formed in
the chalk, with numerous tumuli, or burial-places
of that people.

First then, are the most ancient British stations
and trackways just mentioned, proceeding from
Verulamium (which its form indicates to have
been originally a strong British station).   The
principal road, in a north-west direction, was
from the western angle or upper part, where the
entrance can yet be traced, flanked by large earth-
works, and is a confirmation that the original
trackways were considerably to the left of the
present turnpike road from St. Albans to Dunstaple : and although the ancient and modern
roads might occasionally converge, yet from the
village of Kensworth the separation is well defined,
and the ancient road crosses the higher Downs,
and where it is perfect is 25 feet broad, a mile
south-west of Dunstaple.   These Downs comprise

nearly 4,000 acres of indifferent pasture.* On this spot is the earliest British station, denoted by five large tumuli with several circular and oblong excavations, being the forms of the earlier British inhabitants.

Sir Richard Colt Hoare, who devoted his whole life to the examination of British antiquities, observes :—"The knolls generally contain not only the bones and the ashes of the dead, but various articles of utility and ornament, domestic utensils, weapons of war, decorations of the persons, perhaps insignia of honour, the things which contribute to comfort, to security, and the graces of life. Of these barrows, which the perseverance

---

* In summer a spot called the " Beeches " is a favourite resort of pic-nic parties, the old shepherd being generally at hand to render parties such assistance as they require ; if the season be at all fine this spot is one continued scene of festivity, but affords not the least shelter in a thunder shower. Mr. Nicholls in connection with the old shepherd, brings forward in his usual happy manner an interesting specimen of decorative art :

> " And here I've seen the youthful swain,
> Whom Love hath fettered with his chain,
> On sticks a carving Susan's name,
> The lass he loved so true."

and in a note adds :—"The shepherds on these hills frequently represent grotesque figures of animals, trees, birds, flowers, names, &c., on their walking sticks, with their pocket knives. One such stick has been shown to me, as the work of an old shepherd, and is divided into six compartments. The first portion is seven inches, and the last three, these are covered with hieroglyphics. The second is four inches long, having the sun, moon, stars, foliage, a pair of doves, a star, diamonds, chequred heart, reeds, and a rabbit. The next four inches contains a cottage, pond with fish, bridge, angler with hook and line, elm trees, and a lady and gentleman shaking hands. Then we have another five inches exhibiting farm-house with cottage, pale fencing, gate and fir tree. Eight inches and a-half more, and we see the dairy-maid feeding poultry, consisting of a hen with brood of eight chickens, and a large peacock. There is also a pig and a cow. His ingenuity finishes with a team at plough, consisting of plough, three horses, ploughman, boy, a fox, pack of hounds, with horse and huntsman, fencing and trees. The whole of which was purchased for the trifling sum of two shillings.

B

of the antiquary has explored, the contents indicate different stages of art. In some, there are spear heads of flint and bone; in others, brass and iron are employed for the same weapons. In some, earthen vessels are rudely fashioned, and appear to have been dried in the sun: in others, they are of a regular form, as if produced by the lathe; are baked and ornamented: but whatever be the difference in the comparative antiquity of the knolls, in different parts, it is a remarkable fact, that nothing whatever has been discovered in any exploration, which could at all indicate that this mode of sepulchre was practised after the Roman dominion had commenced in Britain. The coins of the conquerors of the world are not to be looked for here."

Close by the Five Knolls is Parscomb Pit, a great hollow, whose sides still exhibit many of the coombs or primeval dwellings. Tradition adds, that a church was intended to have been erected here, but that the materials were invisibly removed as fast as they were brought together. The earthen platform near the bottom is supposed to be a work of the Roman period thrown up for the purpose of exhibiting those feats of strength in which that people took so much pleasure; the neighbouring hills affording to thousands of spectators full views of the sports below. If the feats of gladiators were exhibited, they were usually between six and nine in the morning.

A learned antiquary speaking of the ancient habitations and places of sepulchre of the ancient Britons, says where they lived "is simple excavations formed in the earth," a group of which is seen near the base of a hill on the road to Luton, averaging generally eight feet in diameter, and three feet deep. When such positions are found, they are invariably in groups, shewing the gregarious and social habits of men in the rudest state. Here then, we have direct proof, that on this spot a colony existed long before the stations of Castle Hill or Maiden Bower, had any existence.

Beside this simple notice, we hear no more of this station, till the year 580. During that long interval, charity would have led us to hope that these people tended their flocks with care; cleared and cultivated their land; leading a calm seques-tered life, far from the busy world and party strife: but such an hypothesis would be contrary to the general custom of the Cassii. Ancient authors tell us, that the prowess of these people was used to little profit, for they were always quarrelling among themselves; and it was in consequence of these dissensions they were at last subdued by the Romans. If the Britons, as a nation, had made common cause, the Romans might not have prevailed against them. But the insular tribes (of which our friends at the bottom of the hill formed a part), were divided and disunited, en-vious of each other; and when one tribe was conquered, the others delighted in the misfortunes of their countrymen. The moral deduced from the fable of a bundle of sticks, may be applied with equal truth to families as to nations.

When the Cassii approximated to the pastoral state, they left the more exposed stations and formed pastoral camps. Strabo says, "The forests of the Britons are their cities, for when they have

made a very large circuit with felled trees, they
build within it houses for themselves, and sheds
for their cattle." These buildings were mere
wattled huts, such as still may be seen in large
numbers in the neighbooring parish of Eddlesboro
—minus chimney and window.

Cæsar also testifies that what the Britons call
a town, is a tract of woody country surrounded by
a vallum and a ditch, for the security of themselves and cattle against the incursions of their
enemies, which description exactly corresponds
with that circular earthwork about a mile and a-
half from Dunstaple, known as Maiden Bower; it
is about 2,500 feet in circumference, and lies at
the intersection of the trackways before mentioned.
It consists of a single vallum thrown up from the
external surface, at an angle of 45°, from 8 to 14
feet high, and it is not improbable that a stockade
was planted on its summit, composed of branches
of trees intertwined. Such precaution might have
been adopted, for the purpose of protecting the
inhabitants and their cattle within the enclosure
by night, from the attack of wolves, or other
predatory animals.   There is now no remains of
a fosse, although there can be no doubt there was
one originally, but obliterated by cultivation. On
the north-west side there is a gradual descent to
the meadows below, where are the remains of
mounds of earth, encircling the small streams
which issue from the base of the chalk Downs,
and may possibly been intended for fish-ponds,
or as reservoirs or dams, constructed for the
purpose of supplying the camp with that article
of prime necessity, water. It seems a natural

inference that such small springs would be thus embanked, to ensure an abundant supply of water for the Cassii and their cattle; and more especially, when the camp and Roman military colony occupied these stations contemporaneously, thence they carried the *Soa* (a vessel) to the *G-wella* (water). Hence we get the word Sewel, for the name of the village adjoining.

Maiden Bower is now a ploughed field, containing about nine acres of rich arable land; thus like many other interesting portions of Britain which it was the ambition of Cæsar to conquor, it has become entirely wasted. A corn-field covers the spot once teeming with human life: the edifices, whatever they may have been that adorned the spot, as well as the busy tribes who inhabited them, have sunk beneath the silent green sward; and the plough-share turns up the medals of the Cæsars so long dead and forgotten, who were once masters of the world.

But to return. The towns within woods were natural fortresses; and here the Druidical worship in the broad glades, surrounded by mighty oaks, which were their natural antiquities, and cultivated amidst knots of men held together by common wants as regards the present life, and common hopes with reference to the future.

There are many circumstances connected with Druidism which lead to the belief, that originally it was of Patriarchial origin, though perverted and depraved by the superstitions introduced in later days. The veneration for the oak, though a perversion, appears to have had some connection with that feeling, which led Abraham to erect his tent and his family altar, beneath the shade of an oak. The authority of the Druid was enforced by a singular custom. Just as winter begun, on a certain day, every family was compelled to extinguish their fire, and pass the night in cold and darkness. On the day following, an offering was carried to the nearest Druid, and fire procured for the sacred altar. No evasion was allowed. The mysterious beings, by whom the Cassii were taught to believe that every object of creation was tenanted, would, it was supposed give information of any act of disobedience to this idolatrous priesthood. Such was Maiden Bower, and such the condition of its inhabitants nineteen hundred years ago.

At a later period the descendants of the earlier tribes appear to have crossed their trackway Via Icenorum, and to have settled half-a-mile west of Maiden Bower, about two miles north-west from Dunstaple; formed one of those ramparted camps undoubtedly British known as Totternhoe Castle. It is situated on a projecting part of the hill: its distinctive appellation is derived from *Thot* a god of the ancient Britons, and *knoll* a hill. This idol was one whom the Druids delighted to honour, because they looked up to him as their protector in all their travels: no journey could be undertaken without first soliciting his aid, neither was their safety in any road not under the dominion of his priest. Thus, Thot the messenger of the gods became their leader and guide, and to his worship they erected altars on many a high hill, whenever such happened to be at or near their cross roads; thus giving the idolatrous priesthood, a distinct view for a considerable distance of the numerous roads leading to his shrine.

As we have said, these Cassii were a warlike people, and by no means deficient in skill. Not only did they fight in the field, but many strongholds similar to the one under consideration, were constructed by themselves on the top of lofty hills and surrounding them with ramparts of earthwork, so well designed and so well executed that they are easily recognised at the present day; which are standing proofs not only of their military skill, but that they were able to erect some more substantial buildings than mere wattled huts, before the invention of gunpowder. Totternhoe Castle if defended by resolute men, must have been impregnable. It consists of a lofty keep in the centre, with a slight vallum round its base, and a larger one of irregular form at some distance from it. On the summit of the hill, ridges are of solid masonry, placed in regular layers upon each other without mortar; thus, affording evidence that it is a production of the Cassii long before the arrival of the Romans, as it was very unusual for the latter people to construct any building requiring the use of stone without durable mortar.

The cemetries belonging to this station were two in number, situate between the station and the town of Dunstaple; the principal one being in the form of the long barrow, and which is of considerable extent, standing nearly east and west, latterly called Mill-bank, a windmill having been erected thereon. The other near it, was of a circular form, at the foot of the latter. Two small pieces of coin have been recently picked up, and being concave on the one side, and convex on the other, are supposed to belong to the Celtic era.

Screams round the Arch Druids brow the seamew—white
As Menai's foam ; and toward the mystic ring
Where Augurs stand the future questioning,
Slowly the cormorant aims her heavy flight,
Portending ruin to each baleful rite,
That in the lapse of Ages hath crept o'er
Diluvian truths, and patriarchal lore.
Haughty the Bard—can these meek doctrines blight
His transports ? whither his heroic strains ?
But all shall be fulfilled—the Julian spear
A way first opened ; and, with Roman chains,
The tidings come of Jesus crucified ;
They come, they spread ! the weak, the suffering, here
Receive the faith, and in the hope abide.

THE ROMAN PERIOD.

E are now entering upon a period when the forms of government, the religious ceremonial, names of persons and of places, modes of dress, manners and customs, are entirely changed by the all-conquering legions from Rome.

Passing by the visit of Julius Cæsar to the island, and his hasty retreat in the year 55 B.C., as well as the circumstances connected with the annexation of the island as a part of the Roman empire under Claudius, in the year 43, we reach the time of Vespasian, when Julius Agricola arrived in the year 78, and began those roads which afterwards extended across the country.

The Romans were undoubtedly the first road makers of which history has preserved any record. On vanquishing a barbarous country, their first efforts consisted in penetrating it with good roads, which they maintained with jealous care. They ran direct from one city to another, were divided accurately by milestones; mountains were perforated, and bold arches thrown over the broadest and most rapid streams. One important feature in the construction was, the bottoming of them with solid materials. Their first operation, seems to have been the removal of all loose earth and soft material, which might work upwards to the surface; then they laid their courses of small

c

stones, on broken tiles, &c., with a course of
cement above, and upon that heavy stones for
the causeway: thus a substantial and durable
pavement was formed, the expense being defrayed
by the public treasury.

One of the chief Roman thoroughfares, in an
oblique direction crosses the country from London
to the west of Scotland, was long known as the
Watling Street. It is carried through well-known
Roman towns, at regular distances, and whenever
it is left by the modern turnpike road, it still
shews an elevated crest. The original pavement
is also discovered in many places, though sometimes where it has passed over a mossy soil, such
pavement is beneath the surface. Watling Street
enters Bedfordshire about three miles south-east
from Dunstaple, in its way from St. Albans, then
called Verulamium to Fenny Stratford, known as
Magiovinium; and quits it a little beyond the
forty-second milestone, having passed through
Durocobrivae, or Maiden Bower.

In that amusing work known as "Dunno's
Originals," which is well worthy the attention
of the curious, Mr. Nicholls thus records his
observations on Watling Street: "Between Kensworth and Dunstable, near the top of Pitcharding
Lane, in the ditch are two large stones of a brown
sandy sort, and very hard and heavy. These
stones have been brought from some distant place,
as none of this kind are dug or found in this
neighbourhood. On examination, I discovered a
layer of these stones close to each other, along the
ditch by the side of the lane. These stones do
not appear as the foundations of buildings, not

being squared off, or worked in any way; but appear as paving stones placed in the ground as a foundation for other materials which covered them. The natural soil of this spot is a loose clay, with stratas of chalk intermixed; the worst material for making a road over in these parts. This method of paving the foundation must have formed a durable road, though attended with much difficulty in its formation; and perfectly agrees with the method by which the Romans formed their roads over loose ground, as already described."

The following lines on the Roman roads, are by Robert of Glocester :—

"Faire weyes many on ther ben in Englande;
But four most of all ther ben I understande,
That thurgh an old kynge were made ere this,
As men schal in this boke oftir here tell I wis.
From the south into the north takith Erminge strote,
From the east into the west goeth Ikeneld strete.
From southest to northwest that is sumdel grete
From Dover into Chester goth Watlyng-strete.
The ferth of thise is most of alle that tilleth from Tateneys,
From the south west to northest into Englande's ende.
Fosse men callith thilke wey that by many town doth wende,
This foure weyes on this londe Kinge Belin the wise,
Made and ordeined him with gret fraunchise."

In the itinerary of Richard, Dunstaple is called Forum Diannæ, which proves it to have been a considerable mart for trade, and being situated so near the intersection of two great roads, each extending over a large portion of the island, was convenient. This Forum Diannæ was situated in the third division of the province called Flavia Cæsarensis.

The other road connected with this town, is

Icening Street: it derives its name from the Iceni, a people who inhabited the present counties of Norfolk, Suffolk, and Cambridge. It enters the county of Beds., near Ickleford, a mile north of Hitchin, and crosses the turnpike road from Luton to Bedford, about the 16th mile-stone. Three miles north-west of this point, near Hexton, is a square Roman camp, called Ravensbury, double ditched, on a high point among the hills; from thence it passes through Great Bramington to Houghton; thence to the Roman camp or beacon at Totternhoe Castle. The camp here is in the form of a parralelogram, 500 feet in length, and 250 in breadth. Three sides are defended by a vallum and fosse, but on the south-west it extends to the edge of a precipice, forming a natural defence: on the north-west its boundary is formed by the vallum and fosse, and the fortified British camp Totternhoe Castle. The area is about four acres. This commanding spot in connection with the camp, previously occupied by the natives, was no doubt adopted by the Romans as a military post, which were always so near that if a beacon was lifted up at one station, it could be distinctly seen at the next, which would be the Ivinghoe beacon. Thus they were enabled to repeat the signal almost at the same instant, by which it was announced that some danger was impending; so that in a short time all the soldiers who guarded the line could be assembled.

The situation of this post having Durocobrivæ on the one side, and Forum Dianæ within a reasonable distance, did not require that it should be extensive. It was probably nothing more than the town guard, placed here because it was well suited for such a purpose, having a complete command of the surrounding country: a part of the hill is to this day called Tanguard-hill. This Roman road then crosses Watling Street at Duro-cobrivæ (Maiden Bower), and soon after enters Bucks., a little below Eddlesboro.

The town of Dunstaple and the fields adjoining seem exceedingly rich in the relics of this period, especially in coins and medals; and from these I select five, as being most interesting to the Christian reader. The earliest is that of Augustus Cæsar, who succeeded his uncle in the year 30 B.C., and reigned 14 years after the birth of our Lord. But probably none is more interesting than that of Tiberius (which is a thick brass coin), a man distinguished for the grossest vices, the most disgusting and debasing sensuality. He had been reigning about 16 years when the Herodians put the question to Jesus, "Is it lawful to give tribute to Cæsar?" "Shall we give, or shall we not give?" He asked for a penny, they produced one like the present, bearing the image of Cæsar; and though the pure and holy Jesus could not but look upon such an object with loathing, in remembrance of his crimes, He commanded them to render unto Cæsar all his due. Another, is that of Trajan; struck somewhere between the years 98 and 117. Then we have one of Vespasian, who distinguished himself in Britain: and here, Titus and his son were cradled up as it were in feats of arms, and thus acquired that knowledge necessary to punish God's ancient people. Vespasian and his son were recalled from Britain, in order that he might

take the command of the army sent into Judea,
the Jews having just risen in rebellion : thus the
prophecy of Moses in Duet. xxviii. 49v. received
a literal fulfilment ; Britain being as far as then
known, the end of the earth.   The last is that of
Constantine, who was a native of Britain, and the
first Christian emperor.   His name is associated
with the Imperial purple, from the year 274
to 337.

It does not always follow, that because the reverse of a coin exhibits the wolf and twins, that
therefore it must be Roman ; because Carausius
and others who became independent princes in
Britain, and had coins of their own, yet seemed
to think the Romulus, Remus and the Wolf were
necessary appendages to the currency.

The above and many others are still in possession of different individuals in the town, who
seemed to estimate them rightly as valuable relics
of the past.

A quantity of copper coins of Antoninus and
Constantine were discovered in digging for gravel,
near the Shepherd's Bush, in 1770.   The urn
which contained them was unfortunately broken.

The end of the fourth great empire prophesied
by Daniel, was now rapidly drawing to a close ;
the iron and the clay were for ever separating
from each other, and the feebleness of the empire
compelled the mistress of the world to emancipate
the Briton from her service, in the year 410.

THE SAXON PERIOD.

THE weak and defenceless condition of the islands of Britain, soon brought it under the power of the Saxons, who being busily engaged in war, neglected agriculture, architecture, &c. : thus, whatever knowledge the Britons had gained from the Romans was entirely lost. The buildings that had been erected were pulled down ; for it was their custom to destroy all towns and castles taken from their enemies. Thus they effected so entire a clearance of the Roman station, which stood upon the scite of the present town, that when Henry the First wished to rebuild it, he had to clear the ground by cutting down the forest trees which had covered it.

The battle in which the Romanized Briton lost his independence and his town, I consider was well contested on the western side of the present town, on the spot known as Leighton Gap, a word signifying overthrown by an enemy ; hence we have the derivative meaning, that which falls, or falls down. The term is used in its latter form by Spencer, " The gap'd forest" that is ruined. There was formerly a road through this gap, from Maiden Bower direct to Dunstable, passing between the long barrow and mill-bank : a number of human bones have been dug up at this point.

Once and only once does this part of Bedford-shire appear in the Saxon Chronicle; and that is, I believe, in connection with our old acquaint-ances whom we left at the foot of the hill, in the Luton road. Like their brethren on the west Downs, they had moved a little and formed a forti-fied camp a mile from Leagrave, on the margin of the river Lea, having the Icknield Street on the south-west. The fosse is very deep and broad, and in many places perfect; and as far as could be ascertained in 1854, described a circle of nearly 8,200 feet, including an area of about 30 acres. This, I presume to be the true scite of the Lygean-burgh, one of the four British towns which fell into the hands of the Saxons, after the battle of Bedford, in 580; for the following reasons. There is no town in the neighbourhood sufficiently near the river Lea having the termination "burgh," to justify the appellation Lygeanburgh being ap-plied to it. Secondly, the river Lea, or Lygea in the Saxon, rises near Houghton, flows through Luton into Herts., having this encampment in the road from Bedford to Aylesbury. And lastly, because in the immediate neighbourhood, at Chalgrave and Winfield, are traces of a hard-fought battle; from which circumstance, the latter place derives its name (*Win*, war, and field.) The entire valley, fields, and gravel pits abound with human skeletons; and pieces of armour are constantly turned up by the plough.*

---

* *Fig.* 1, is taken from the remaining part of an ancient iron or steel helmet, dug out with the gravel, from a field belonging to Mr. Hicks, of Toddington. *Fig.* 2, represents part of a spear-head, probably the pile or casting dart of the Romans. *Fig.* 3, is a piece of copper, over-laid with a thin plate of fine gold. *Fig.* 4, is a profile or side view of Fig. 3. *Fig.* 5, is a specimen of curious beads, appear to be made of agate. *Fig.* 6, an ollae or pot of redish clay. *Fig.* 7 and 8, re-present spear-heads of metal.

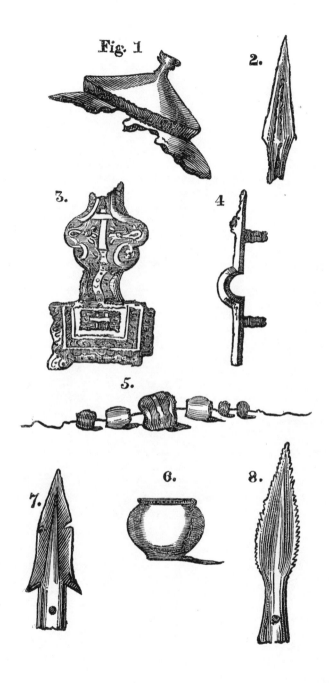

Fig. 1

2.

3.

4.

5.

6.

7.

8.

I must confess, I differ from Mr. Nicholls, as
to the date, neither do I think with him that the
presence of a single fragment of a Roman helmet
is sufficient to establish his position; simply because it is well known, that at the departure of
the Romans they left large quantities of arms and
armour behind them. I have carefully compared
his descriptions and drawings with the collection
of British antiquities deposited in the British
Museum, and believe them to belong to this rather
than an earlier era.

This town continued in a state of respectable
debility till the time of Offa, after which we hear
no more of it at all.

As far as I am aware, only one coin has been
discovered; it is of brass, and was ploughed out
the tract of Watling Street, and is thought to
have been a coin of the West Saxon kings. The
obverse represents a crucifix, surrounded with
trophies, swords, &c.

The history of the introduction of Christianity
among the West Saxons, in the year 627, is
peculiarly interesting.

During many centuries, that mysterious and
dreadful disease the leprosy, prevailed in our land
to an alarming extent; and in the days when
superstition as well as humanity prompted the
building of religious houses, its unfortunate victims
were not forgotten. In the ninth century there
were no less than 19,000 hospitals for this disease,
in the country, by far the greater part of them
dedicated to St. Bartholemew; and if the names
of lands tell anything of a place's history, then
we have good reason to suppose, that at Dunstable

D

the unhappy creatures found an asylum near
Perwinkle Lane, in those fields still called Spittle
Lands, Spittal Hall, Spittal Bottom.   A number
of old wells and other circumstances shews the
extent of the buildings.

During the reign of Edward the Confessor, the
scite of the modern town formed part of the earl-
dom of Harold, who ascended the throne, and was
killed at the battle of Hastings; and in this reign
the Roman roads are thus noticed, " not a stone
had been laid upon Watlinge Street since the
arrival of Hengist and Horsa, and the fosse way
was worse than the bottom of a ditch."

MODERN HISTORY.

DUNSTAPLE, a Market Town and parish in the Hundred of Manshead, union of Luton, county of Bedford; is 33 miles N.W. by N. of London, and about 20 S. by W. of Bedford; is situated east of the Chiltern hills, at the foot of the range in the centre of the Dunstable chalk Downs. The town is cruciform, the four principal streets taking the direction of the four cardinal points. The living is a rectory, formerly in the archdeaconry of Bedford and in the diocese of Lincoln, but now in the diocese of Ely. The estimated value of the living is £150 a-year. Tithe commuted in 1839: aggregate amount, £107 15s. 4d. Patron, the Lord Chancellor; the Queen being lady of the manor.

Those who prefer to have their own superstitions, will have it that Dunstaple is named after a brave defender of his country's liberty, a true Saxon soldier, who having survived the battle of Hastings, was joined by others of his countrymen and continued sorely to harass the Norman conquerors, by whom he is called a robber: and a cellar belonging to a public-house, in the last century known as the "Wheat Sheaf," at the corner of East Street, is spoken of as the cave which he used as a stable and into which he often retreated when pursued by his enemies. It is affirmed by some, that in this cellar, the post with ring and staple were seen as far down as the seventeenth century.

Those fond of " legendary lore" admit, that no author of this early period has mentioned that Dun, the robber, gave name to the town; at the same time, among the natives, it is a tradition handed down from father to son, throughout their generations.

The following account, though full of stirring interest to some readers, yet as a source of etymology, is not of the least value; nevertheless, in consideration of the former, I transcribe it entire from the national register of crime, remarking at the same time, that it is without date,—a very serious omission for the truthful historian.

"Thomas Dun was a person of mean extraction, born in Bedfordshire, and who, even in early childhood, was noted for his pilfering propensities and cruelty of disposition. He lived in the time of Henry the First, and so many were his atrocities, that we can only find limit for the recital of a few. The first exploit was on the highway of Bedford, where he met a waggon full of corn, going to market, drawn by a beautiful team of horses. He accosted the driver, and in the middle of the conversation, stabbed him to the heart with a dagger which he always carried about with him. He buried the body, and mounting the waggon proceeded to the town, where he sold off all, and decamped with the money. He continued to commit many petty thefts and assaults; but judging it safer to associate himself with others, he repaired to a gang of thieves which

infested the country leading from St. Albans to
Towcester, where they became such a terror, that
the king had to build a town to check his power
in the country, and which retains the name of
Dunstaple.

  " This precaution was however of little avail, for
he pursued his courses to a great extent. Among
his gang were many artists, who enabled him to
pick locks, wrench bolts, and use deaf files to
great effect. One day, having heard that some
lawyers were to dine at a certain inn in Bedford,
about an hour before the appointed time he came
running to the inn, and desires the landlord to
hurry the dinner and to have enough ready for
ten or twelve.

  " The company soon arrived, and the lawyers
thought Dun a servant of the house, whilst those
of the house supposed him to be an attendant
upon the lawyers. He bustled about, and the
bill being called for, he collected it, and having
some change to return to the company they waited
for his return ; but growing weary, they rang the
bell and inquired for their money, when they
discovered him to be an impostor.   With the
assistance of his associates, he made clear off with
a considerable booty of cloaks, hats, silver spoons,
and everything of value, upon which he could lay
his hand.

  " After this adventure, Dun and his associates
went and put up at another inn : they rose in
the night time, insulted the landlord, did violence
to the landlady, then murdered both and pillaged
the house of everything valuable.

  " Dun had an animosity to lawyers, and he

determined to play a rich one a trick. He waited upon him, and very abruptly demanded payment of a bond which he produced, and the gentleman found his name so admirably forged that he could not swear it was not his handwriting. He assured Dun, however, that he had never borrowed the money and would not pay the bond. He left him, assuring the lawyer that he would give him some employment. A law-suit was entered into, and several of his comrades came forward and swore as to the debt being just; and he was about getting a decision in his favour, when the lawyer produced a forged receipt for the debt, which some of his clerks likewise swore to, upon which Dun was cast. He was in a passion at being outwitted, and swore " he never heard of such rogues, as to swear they paid a sum which was never borrowed."

" This is one of the few instances in which he did not display that barbarity of disposition which is evinced in all his other adventures, and which makes us refrain from the enumeration of many of them. He became however, such a terror to everyone, that the Sheriff of Bedford sent a considerable force to attack him in his retreat. Finding, upon a reconnoitre however, that his force was equal if not superior to the sheriff's, he commenced the attack and completely routed them, taking eleven prisoners, whom he hung upon trees round the wood, to scare others by the example of their fate.

" The clothes of those they had hanged, served them to accomplish their next adventure, which was to rob the castle of a nobleman in the neighbourhood. They proceeded in the attire of the sheriff's men, and demanded entrance in the name of the king to search for Dun. After searching every corner, they asked for the keys of the trunks to examine them, which when they had received, they loaded themselves with booty and departed. The nobleman complained to parliament against the sheriff, when, upon investigation the trick was discovered.

"Nothing prevented Dun from accomplishing any object which he had in view, as he possessed the greatest share of temerity and cruelty that could fall to the lot of man. He would, under the disguise of a gentleman, wait upon rich people, and being shown into their rooms murder them and carry away their money.

"There was a rich knight in the neighbourhood from whom Dun wished a have a little money. Accordingly, he went and knocked at his door. The maid opened it; he inquired if her master was at home, and being answered in the affirmative, he instantly went upstairs and familiarly entered his room. Common compliments having passed, he sat down in a chair and began a humourous discourse, which attracted the attention of the knight. Dun then approached, and demanded a word or two in his ear. "Sir," said he, "my necessities come pretty thick upon me at present, and I am obliged to keep even with my creditors, for fear of cracking my fame and fortune too. Now, having been directed by some of the heads of this parish to you, as a very considerate and liberal person, I am come to petition you, in a modest manner, to lend me a thousand

marks* (about £666 13s. 4d.) which will answer
all demands upon me at present." A thousand
marks," answered the knight, "Why man, that
is a capital sum, and where is the inducement to
lend so much money to one who is a perfect stranger
to me; for to my eyes and knowledge, I never
saw you before in all the days of my life?" "Sir,
you must be mistaken; I'm the honest grocer at
Bedford, who has so often shared your favours!"
"Really, friend, I do'nt know you, nor shall I
part with my money, but on a good bottom: pray
what security have you?" "This dagger," says
Dun, pulling it out of his breast, "is my constant
security; and unless you let me have a thousand
marks instantly, it shall pierce your heart!"
This terrible menace produced the desired effect,
and the money was delivered.

"Dun had now continued his infamous course
above twenty years, the vicinity of the river
Ouse in Bedfordshire, being the scene of his exploits; and having fifty armed men on horseback,
at his command, he became formidable to both
rich and poor.

"The country, at last rising up against him,
he and his gang were so closely pursued, that they
were constrained to divide and to seek for shelter
in different directions. Dun concealed himself in
a small village, where he was discovered, and the
house he was in surrounded. Two of the strong-
est posted themselves at the door: with irresistable
courage Dun seized his dagger, laid them both
dead, bridled his horse, and in the midst of the

---

*The Saxon mark was in value 6s. In the year 1194, it was valued
at 13s. 4d. When the increase in value took place is not clear.

uproar forced his way through about one hundred and fifty armed with pitchforks, rakes, and whatever weapons they could find, pursued him and drove him off his horse; but to the astonishment of all, he again mounted, and with his sword cut his way through the crowd.

"Numbers flocking from all quarters, the pursuit was renewed. He was a second time dismounted, and now employing his feet, he ran for the space of two miles; but when he halted to breathe a little, three hundred men were ready to oppose him. His courage and strength still remaining unsubdued, he burst through them, fled over a valley, threw off his clothes, seized his sword in his teeth and plunged into a river, in order to gain the opposite bank.

"To his sad surprise, he perceived it covered with new opponents; he swam down the river, was pursued by several boats, until he took refuge on a small island. Determined to give him no time to recover his fatigue, they attacked him there. Thus closely pursued by boats, repeatedly struck with oars, and after having received several strokes on his head, he was at last vanquished.

"He was conducted to a surgeon to have his wounds dressed, then led before a magistrate who sent him to Bedford Gaol, under a strong guard. Remaining there two weeks, and being considerably recovered, a scaffold was erected in the Marketplace, and without a formal trial he was led forth to execution. When the two executioners approached him, he warned them of their danger if they should lay hands on him; he accordingly grasped both, and nine times overthrew them upon

E

the stage before his strength was exhausted, so that they could not perform their duty.

" His hands were first chopped off at the wrist, then his arms at the elbows, next about an inch from the shoulders, his feet below the ankles, his legs at the knee, and his thighs about five inches from the trunk. This horrible scene was closed by severing his head from the body, and consuming it to ashes : the other parts of his body were fixed up in different places in Bedfordshire, as a warning to his companions."

Having given the legend, now for the analysis. In the first place, a christian and surname is given to the man of mean extraction,—a circumstance most unlikely, at the time of his birth,—for surnames did not at all come into fashion for many years after, even among the nobility, letting alone the peasantry. We will give up the waggon-load of corn as a sort of may-be, but the next point we cannot so readily concede, viz. : that a nobleman should, in these troublesome times, admit eleven men into his castle, and without any objection allow them to remove his valuable property, simply because they choose to say, they came in the name of the king, without producing any official warrant. If he were a Norman, he must have detected easily the difference between the Norman-French and that of his intruders, and thus have suspected an imposition. Had he been one of the very few wealthy Saxons remaining, he would, by the same means have recognized them as countrymen of his own, and received their pretended mission with suspicion : for of all men, certainly Dun was not the man—a Saxon would be expected willingly to capture; add to this, Saxons were not usually found in places of trust and honour.

I think the last point is even more fatal to the story, than the preceding,—his death. Had it been in a popular tumult that he was executed, without a trial, then there had been some plausibility in the circumstance; but that he should have been officially committed to gaol and there remain fourteen days, and then executed without a trial, is I think, without a parallel. But I suspect the old monk knew too well that the report of a trial would have upset the whole story. Thus much for the internal evidence, now for the external. How unlikely that Henry, (who was surnamed Beauclerk, because of his superior learning), should place a market town in the centre of a band of robbers. Again, another author, equally deserving of credit, flatly contradicts the mode of his capture, and the manner of his death, by stating he

"Was hanged for the feates which he had done."

Again, it is contrary to all analogy, that the name of any particular family, in a town or neighbourhood, should supersede the original designation of such localities; on the contrary, wherever noble families have left their names associated with the spots in which they resided, or had property, they are always supplemental, as Eaton Bray, Drayton Beauchamp, Milton-Bryant, Newton-Longville, in each case the first is the name of the town or village, and the second a family name which has been added. On this point, my correspondence with the Keeper of Her

Majesty's Records fully bears out the position I have taken. The whole supposition therefore, is so much at variance with common sense, that I reject it altogether as a monkish fable.

Having thus cleared my way, I come to the true derivation of the word Dunstaple. It is a word in two parts. The first syllable Dun, is the Anglo-Saxon word for hill, as seen in the words Dun-dee, Dun-which, Dum-fries, Hunting-don, Snow-don, in all which cases, like our own, it has reference to the situation of the town, that of being on a hill. The word Downs is derived from the same source.

The second part, "staple." Henry the First re-erected the town, and in order to give the town a commercial importance, he established a staple there, which word signifies a market; and formerly, certain goods could not be exported without having first been brought to one of the Royal Staples, and there charged with a duty. The great commodity for exportation at this period, was wool, so that the formation of a market in the centre of that extensive Down district, must have been a matter of obvious necessity, as well for the purpose of sheep-farming, as to encourage the habits of pastoral life among the natives.

The word then simply means, a market on a hill, which exactly corresponds with its situation; and I venture to affirm, that any Anglo-Saxon scholar in any part of the world would give you the same answer, even though he never saw or heard of the place before.

The next point for consideration is, the means employed to bring the wool to the "staple;" and here I think, we meet with a very suggestive hint. At about the second mile from Dunstaple, towards London, we meet with a peculiar public-house sign, such an one as you will not meet with again I believe, within a circle of twenty miles, nor anywhere except on some of the great old thorough-fares of England, I mean the "Pack-Horse," and which at this time was the only means of conveyance. The animals were loaded with sacks or packs of wool thrown across the back, and if not too heavy, piled to a considerable height. The average weight for each horse was 400 lbs. A number together were generally conducted in a line; that which went before carrying a bell, by the tinkling sound of which the cavalcade were kept from straggling after night-fall.

The wool trade appears to have lingered for many centuries in the town. The last journeyman wool-sorter resident in the town, was a Quaker; he died at the beginning of the present century.

Whatever doubts may be entertained by others on the preceding points, it is admitted on all hands, that Henry I. rebuilt the borough of Dunstaple, and erected a royal seat near it for himself, and issued a proclamation inviting his subjects to settle near him at Dunstaple, offering them lands at a very small rent and making the burgesses free in everything as other burgesses in the king's realm; and in order to promote their spiritual welfare, he set up that noble church, of which the present structure is but a small part; which church being ready for the opening, the priests anxiously waited for St. Peter's Day (July 11th), that being the saint to whom the church was to be dedicated, for it was a custom in those times to consecrate the churches on the saint's day to whose honour it had been erected. The solemn eve arrives, and the faithful are called together by the consecrated bell, and prayer was said all that night within the Priory. According to the ancient custom in the Saxon church, at which time king Edgar enjoined "decent behaviour, and commanded the people to pray devoutly and not betake themselves to drinking and debauchery," the night was spent in prayer, following the example of our blessed Lord, before he consecrated his twelve apostles. The morrow is St. Peter's day; the church is opened with special service, wherein was celebrated the generosity of the founder and endower of the Priory.

The anniversary of watching and service was continued until the reign of Charles the First, when the Lord Chief Justice Sir Thomas Richardardson, who died in 1643, issued out an order against the ancient custom of wakes, and caused every minister to read it in his church; and St. Peter's day not always being found convenient to commemorate the opening, the services were by special authority, transferred to the following Sunday, which was ever after called the Feast Sunday, which Sunday is in fact nothing less than the anniversary of that consecration. Many of you remember how that day was spent in your youthful days. What a solemn reflection! Men met to commemorate a religious act, the consecration of a temple to the service of the Most High God, by swelling the synagogue of Satan. My friends and neighbours, let these words sink deep in your hearts! Henceforth, when invited to attend the Feast Sunday, remember it is the anniversary of consecrating a house to God, by constantly and prayerfully attending which, immortal souls may be brought to ask for the "good old paths," and walk therein. The object of the Feast Sunday is nothing less than the returning season for celebrating the consecration of your parish church.*

The king kept the town in his own hands until 1131, when he granted it, with all its rights and privileges, to the Priory of Black Canons, or Augustine Friars, placed at Dunstaple by permission of Pope Eugenius the Third. William of Carloil being Archbishop of Canterbury, was the first who fairly subjected the English church to the Papal dominion.

At the king's residence near the Priory, in 1123, Henry kept Christmas with great splendour, receiving at that time an embassy from the Earl of Anjou. This palace was not included in the grant to the convent, although the parish church of Chalgrave, an ancient structure of this period, was appropriated to the Priory. Its great antiquity has passed into a proverb, "As old as Chalgrave church."

---

* Easter Dues.—Easter Offerings are customary sums which have been paid from time immemorial in the Church, and are recoverable as small Tithe, before Two Justices of the Peace, by 7 & 8 Will. 3rd, c. 6, and subsequent Acts. Before the time of Edward VI., offerings, oblations, and obventions constituted the chief revenues of the Church, and were collected on Christmas, Easter, Whitsuntide, and the Feast of the Dedication of the particular Parish Church. By the 2 and 3 of Edward VI., c. 13. it was enacted, that such offerings should henceforth be paid at Easter;—a law or rule which is reinforced by the Rubric at the end of the Communion Service.

The king kept his Christmas here again in
1132, and so did his successor Stephen, in 1137.

In 1154, a friendly interview took place at the
palace in Kingsburie, between King Stephen and
Henry, Duke of Normandy, when it was agreed
that Stephen should enjoy the crown for life and
that Henry should succeed him, and that the
castles built by Stephen, amounting to 1,117,
should be destroyed. This arrangement soon
came into effect, for Stephen died the same year,
on the 20th of October.

Ten years after this, the burgesses of Dunstaple
received a summons from Henry II., to send
representatives to a parliament that met at
Clarendon, in Wiltshire, January 26th, 1164, in
order to compel Thomas a'Beckett, the archbishop
of Canterbury, first to degrade criminal ecclesiastics, and then to deliver them over to the usual
officers of justice in compliance with the ancient
customs of the land : the business ended in the
banishment of Beckett and the prohibition of
appeals to the Pope, and the payment of Peter's
pence. The burgesses of Dunstaple did not obey
the summons.

In the first year of Richard I., 1189, we meet
with a famous conspiracy of the monks, to impose
upon the credulity of the people, with a view to
strengthen their own authority over the minds of
the superstitious multitude. The following is a
translation from Hemingford, of a singular appearance in the heavens during that year. The
minuteness of the description and peculiarity of
the style must prove amusing.

" A stupendous prodigy, which about this time

was seen by many in England, must not be passed over in silence. Upon the high road which leads towards London, there is a street of no mean fame, named Dunestaple. There, while about noon they were looking up towards heaven, they saw in the height of a serene sky, the form of our Lord's banner, conspicuous by its milky brightness, and the form of a man crucified joined thereto, such as is painted in the church in memory of the Lord's Passion, and for the devotion of the faithful. Then, when this dreadful figure had appeared a short time, and closely attracted the eyes and hearts of the beholders, the form of the cross was seen to recede from him who seemed affixed thereto, so that an intermediate space of the sky might be observed, and soon after, this astonishing thing disappeared. Let every one explain as he thinks fit this wonderful sign, of which I am to be considered as a mere reporter, not as an expounder of omens ; for what it is the divine pleasure to signify I know not."

Whether he knew not, we have not now the power accurately to determine. Doubtless he was aware, that to reveal any secret of this sort to the common people would subject him, as it did Gallileo, to the loss of personal liberty, if not of his life.

Certain it is, that since the day that Constantine beheld a similar manifestation in the heavens, down to the last phenomena in nearly all respects similar to that seen at Poicters, in Dec. 1826,* the Church of Rome has shewn great aptitude in

---

* For the cause of this appearance, see the work on Light, pp. 76, 77, published by the Religious Tract Society.

F

using the wonderful phenomena of Nature to overawe the ignorant multitude; hence as the church degenerated from the simplicity of the gospel, and the cross of Christ began to lose its attractiveness, this cross of Constantine became the rallying point.

Richard de Morins was made prior of Dunstaple in the third year of the reign of King John, Herbert being archbishop of Canterbury. He held the office till the twenty-sixth year of the reign of Henry III., that is, from 1202 to 1242. He plunged as deep into brawls, breaches of the peace, and lawsuits, as any wicked worldling of his time; his life was a complete warfare with his neighbours, sometimes they cast him and sometimes he cast them at law. But nothing seems to have discouraged Richard, for he still went on and accumulated a vast estate to the Priory; and all that remains of the estate thus acquired, are the gate-way door and windows of the Porter's Lodge, and some rooms, one of which has been converted into a parlour.

In the midst of his reckless career, Richard had on one occasion been almost outwitted by a Jew, one Mossey, who forged a bond of his, for £70, and sued Richard upon the same. But the forgery, so says Richard, was so bunglingly performed, that the Jew was cast, and committed the prisoner to the tower of London; the rest of the Jews making the king, who was Henry III. a present of one mark of gold to defer his punishment; his majesty notwithstanding would certainly have hanged Mossey upon a gallows, had not the other Jews " says Richard, to save that disgrace to the law of Moses," given the king one hundred pounds more, and then Mossey took his oath to leave England never to return.

To do prior Richard justice, he well deserved what he was likely to have met with from Mossey; for in an ancient charter he appears to have authorised the Jews to settle under him, quietly, peaceably, and honourably, at Dunstaple, and there to profit by their trade, according to the custom of the Jews; for which they were to pay him, two silver spoons, every year of their lives.

But the most extraordinary transaction of all, was that the good fathers, used to borrow money of those Jews, who were now generally wealthy, having engrossed chiefly the commerce of the kingdom, on which account they were held in much detestation among the people.

The Jews even gave mortgages upon the livings of the monks for repayment, as appears was the case of one William Husseburn; and prior Richard was obliged to pay the mortgage, otherwise he could not have recovered the living out of the hands of the Jews. Perhaps one of the most curious particulars is, that it was a very common thing at that time in England for Priests to have wives, or concubines, and to leave their benefices from father to son, as was the case of the living of Bradburn, which descended from father to son for four generations.

During the primacy of Hubert, the palace built by Henry I. was granted by king John in 1204, to the prior and convent, who were to accommodate upon all future occasions of royal visits, the monarch and his suite within their own walls. No

part of this ancient palace now remains; but on
the spot where it once stood is a new farm-house,
and in the garden wall of this house is a curious
piece of carving, viz. the original Arms of the
Priory of Dunstaple. It was recovered, after
having been lost for centuries, by being used as
a building stone, in an old farm house opposite
the Priory. It seems to have been the centre of
a window or door-case, probably the centre of the
grand entrance, as Gothic mouldings were visible
on one of the quarterfoils surrounding the shield,
consisting of hollows, squares, &c., a certain proof
that it had been attached to other moulding used
in a building.

During the period Henry I. kept the town in
his own hands, it was a free borough; the burgesses were free throughout England, and possessed
the privilege of not answering before the justices
itinerant out of the town and liberty. Those
judges were to repair to Dunstable and there to
determine all suits without foreign assessors, by
the oath of twelve of the inhabitants.

The last step towards completing the settlement
of this place, was the foundation and endowment
of this priory; which Tanner says was done towards the latter end of the reign of Henry I. or
according to other writers, sometime after the
year 1131; it consisted of Black Canons, and
dedicated to the honour of St. Peter. To them
Henry granted the whole manor of Dunstaple,
with the lands pertaining to the town, viz., four
cultures of land round the town, the market, and
schools of the said town, with all its liberties and
free customs; sac, soc, tol, theam, infangenethef,

The Arms of the Priory of Dunstaple, is Argent, a Pile Sable charged with Ring and Staple, on a Bordure, Engrailed of the Third.

(See Page 44.

gūthbrith, hamsocne, clodwith, forstal, and fle-
menes ford, right of Cadenden, Kensworth, Totternhoe, and the four ways *(quadraria)* of the
said town, with safe passage to the market, under
pains of forfeiting ten pounds. He further granted
them leave to hold what they could purchase, and
exemption for themselves and servants from all
taxes due to the shire and hundred, county fines
for murder, tollage, pleas, geld and danegelds,
tydage, toil, passage, pontage, stallage, and all
customs and worldly services through the realm.
The king reserved to himself only his houses in
the town and the garden, where he used to lodge.
This charter bears the signatures of

Robert, Bishop of Hereford.	Humphrey de Bohun.
Simon, Bishop of Worcester.	G. Fitz Paine.
G. Chandler.	Robert Fitz John.
Robert de Sigillo.	Drago de Moncer.
N. Miles, of Gloucester, the	Maurice de Windsor ad Cumbra
Bishop's Nephew.	*(comb,* abbey.)

As attesting Witnesses.

The prior had also the power of life and death,
and sat with the king's justices itinerant, when
they came to Dunstaple on their circuits.

They had more than one gaol, for it appears by
the Chronicle of the priory that their principal
gaol was rebuilt in 1295. The site of this appears
to have been in the Middle Row, and the cellars
under the premises occupied by Mr. Weatherill,
seem to confirm this opinion, as they are very
deep, strongly arched, and from which there was
a subterraneous passage leading to the priory; it
was strongly arched and still open part of the
way. There is also another cellar extending
under the Back Street, connected with this; it
appears to have been a dark cell, having a curious

niche in the wall sufficient to form a seat for one
person; this though now thrown open to the
other cellars, was undoubtedly separate, as an
examination of the floor will testify. Doubtless
it was used as a solitary cell.

They had a gallows outside the town and liberty
of Dunstaple, at Edestrote, in the parish of Caddington; a field called Stret, or Stretch field is
supposed to be the site. There is also on the
western side towards Dagnall, a hill which still
retains the name of Gallow-hill, which on being
opened a short time ago, three skeletons were
found, probably they were criminals, who had
been there executed.

These extraordinary privileges, which were
confirmed by succeeding princes, caused many
disturbances between the townsmen and the priory
occupants; and some unequal assessments being
made in 1229, the people were so provoked, that,
out of resentment, they withdrew their tithe and
offering, scattered the prior's corn, and pounded
his horses; and though at the request of the prior,
the Bishop of Lincoln caused the offenders to be
excommunicated, they declared they would sooner
" go to the devil than be taxed," and had even
treated with William Cantilupe, for forty acres of
his field to build booths on, and quit the town.
This difference was at last adjusted by John, arch-
deacon of Bedford, the town paying sixty pounds
sterling for the remuneration of his rights to all
tollage, except the *misericordia* of four-pence, and
fines in case of violence.

During the insurrection, caused by unequal
taxations, in the reign of Richard II., in 1381,

the townsmen obtained from the prior a charter of liberties, but it was cancelled afterwards, as having been forcibly extorted.

In 1213, the town was destroyed by fire, and soon after rebuilt. After this fire, those bye-laws called the "Customs of Dunstaple," were introduced. I give the following as published by Mr. Hearne. "Shopkeepers may not brew for fear of fire, nor drive stakes without leave of the mayor. The townsmen and strangers must carry away the booths the same day they set them up in the market. No traders of this or other towns may buy victuals before one o'clock, nor go to meet the sellers out of the town. Bread made for sale at the price of a farthing, must be sold at the same price; and in like manner, ale when four gallons are worth one penny. When a widow loses her free-bench, she must deliver up to the heir, the fixtures fastened to the land, also the principal table with stools, the best wine cask, tub, basins, hatchet, best cup, coulter, and share, and the bucket of the well with the rope. Other chattels she may dispose of by will or gift, and she is not bound to answer for waste, unless such waste be done after the king's prohibition."

John being involved with the monks of Canterbury in a dispute about the election of an archbishop, Pope Innocent III. took upon himself to appoint Stephen Langton, an Englishman, then chancellor of Paris. The archbishop thus thrust upon the English church by the unwarrantable assumption of a foreign bishop, John refused to admit; whereupon the Pope placed the kingdom under an interdict, by virtue of which the churches were everywhere closed, all religious services were suspended, except the rite of Baptism. The dead were buried in common ground, which may account for so many bones yet being found in most unlikely spots; the statues and paintings of the saints were taken down, and the whole country was in the state of a land destitute of public religious worship. This state of things had continued six years, when the archbishop held a great synod at the Priory, by which the interdict was removed; the value of which, we can only estimate by remembering that the Papacy held the services and ceremonies thus forbidden, not only as a means of grace, but as the necessary passport to happiness in the world to come.

In 1215, John lay at Dunstable, on his journey to the north. The faithless king having set himself to recover the independence he had lost by the great charter just signed. He raised an army of foreign soldiers and committed such ravages, that the barons invited Prince Louis, of France, who was a relative of John's, having married his niece Blanche of Castile. John died in 1216, but Louis refused to return, and in 1217, he with the rebellious barons, halted for a night in Dunstaple, after the defeat at the battle of Lincoln.

Henry III. was so weak in character, that those about him were in effect the rulers of the land. It was a very unsettled time; many acts of lawless violence occurred, which required force to repress them. One well authenticated act of lawless violence is in connexion with Dunstaple, the record of which, will give a better idea of the little regard then paid to legal restraints unless supported by military power.

Anno Domini 1224, Fawkes de Brent a favourite of the late king, having been guilty of numerous depraved and villainous acts in the surrounding country, and presuming upon the impregnable strength of his castle at Bedford, which had been given him as a reward for his military services, set all law and authority at defiance ; and having been fined £3,000 by the king's justice itinerant at Dunstaple, for having made a forcible entry upon lands belonging to thirty-two freemen of Luton, to which he had no claim, sent a party of soldiers who seized Henry de Braybroke, one of the king's justices, and treating him with great barbarity, brought him prisoner to the castle. The king was at this time holding a parliament at Northampton, where the judges' wives by their tears and entreaties so moved the king and the whole assembly with their description of the outrage, that the king became highly indignant at these repeated atrocities, that he postponed the remaining business of parliament and marched to Bedford in person, attended by Stephen Langton, the archbishop, and the principal peers of the realm. On this occasion the archbishop and abbots granted a voluntary aid to the king, and two labourers from every hide of their land.

Before the arrival of the king, Fawkes had fled into Wales, and left his brother to defend the castle, with provision and ammunition sufficient for twelve months.

The following account of the seige, written by an eye witness, is extracted from the Chronicle of Dunstaple. " On the east side was one petraria,

G

and two mangonellas, which daily battered the
tower ; on the west side two mangonellas ruined
the old tower ; and one mangonella on the south,
and one on the north, made two breaches in the
walls opposed to them. Besides these, there were
two wooden machines, raised above the height
of the tower and castle, for cross-bowmen and
scouts. Also many others in which the cross-
bowmen and slingers lay in ambush. There was
also a machine called a cat, under which, the
miners had free passage to sap the walls of the
tower and castle. The castle was taken by
four assaults. In the first was taken the bar-
bican ; in the second, the outer bail ; in the third,
the wall near the old tower was overthrown by
the miners, through the breach of which, they
were in great danger, made themselves masters
of the inner bail. On the fourth assault, the
miners set fire to the tower, and when the smoke
burst out and great cracks appeared in the tower,
the beseiged surrendered. The sheriff was ordered
to demolish the tower and outer bail. The inner,
after it was dismantled, and the ditches filled up,
was left for William de Beaucamp to live in. The
stones were given to the canons of Newnham
priory, near Bedford, and the church of St. Paul's,
at Bedford, and appropriated by them to building
a long wall round the priory, and the erection of
a stone bridge over the river Ouse.

The men of Dunstaple made the second assault,
in which, the outer bail was taken, for which
service they had a considerable share of the
plunder. Many lives were lost by the fall of the
tower. The judge was released, and the fortress

taken by the king, after a seige of nine weeks,
during which, the beseiged disputed the ground
by inches. Fawkes' brother was taken, and he
and twenty-four of his officers were executed.
Culmo, another brother, received the king's
pardon. Fawkes himself hastened to Bedford to
crave that mercy he had neglected to show to
others. He was brought thither under the protection of the bishop of Coventry, and was
pardoned on condition that his estates should be
confiscated, and he should leave the kingdom.
And he who had exceeded all the nobles in
England, in wealth and splendour, was obliged to
beg his bread in France, without any certain
dwelling-place."

While the king and his nobles were thus engaged, the monks, who had peculiar facilities for
accumulation of livings, had not been idle. Their
influence with some neighbouring lord of the
manor, would often win him to make over the
church on his estate, and the tithe with which it
might be endowed, to their own abbey; the
meanwhile they undertaking to provide for the
fulfilment of the ecclesiastical duties belonging to
it. The following instance connected with the
priory, will serve as an illustration. We must
omit the Latin, because it would be too lengthy
and not interesting to general readers, but the
following is a correct translation thereof.

In 1240, Lord Alan de Hyde and his wife
Alicia, were admitted into the priory of Dunstaple, and gave to the priory one virgate of land in
Chalton, one virgate in Leegrave, and four shillings
rent, and half a mark rent in Stopsley, and twenty

marks and three shillings rent in Dunstaple, for
the maintenance of those who celebrate the anniversary in Dunstaple church to commemorate his
soul therein. " Richard de Morins, prior of Dunstaple, to all the faithful in Christ, health; Be
it known to them, that by unanimous consent,
we have received Lord Alan, of Hyde, and Alice
his wife, into the fraternity of our house, and
moreover have obtained for them a canonical or
secular priest, as long as either of them shall live
to minister in their own chapel at Hyde, at the
expense of the said Alan and Alice, and after
their death we will assign to them a priest by
turns for a week to pray for them, and the souls
of their ancestors, and successors, and relatives,
and our benefactors and all the faithful dead;
and they have commended and given their bodies
to God, St. Peter, and our church, and we have
written down their names to be noted and carried
round to religious houses with the names of our
priests and converts, and it is to be known also,
that the prayers aforesaid are to be celebrated
after their death in our church of Dunstaple."

The following year prior Richard let the before-
named rents to one Walter Hyde, Knt., on a lease
for ever, at forty-four shillings a-year. The
Cartulary of Dunstaple also speaks of other places
in the immediate neighbourhood, as

Pulloxhill, the rectory and advowson of the
vicarage was given by John Pyrot to the priory
of Dunstaple.

The great tithe and rectorial manor of Studham
also belonged to it.

The impropriate rectory and advowson of the

vicarage of Husborn Crawley, which was endorsed in 1220, was also theirs.

So also the great tithe of Flitwick.

The site of Rokesac was granted by William, Earl of Albemarle, and Hawise his wife, to the canons of Dunstaple and the canons of Rokesac. It is probable the monks were removed before the Reformation.

In 1244, a considerable number of discontented barons and knights assembled at Dunstaple and Luton, for the avowed purpose of holding a tournament, but in reality to prosecute their political designs. The tournament was prohibited by royal mandate, but they did not separate before they had given a convincing proof of their formidable power, by sending Sir Fulk Fitzwarren to the Pope's nuncio, Peter de Roches, whose proceedings had given great offence to the English, with peremptory order in the names of the barons and knights, assembled at Dunstaple and Luton, that he should quit the kingdom. An order which the nuncio, finding the royal authority insufficient to protect him, was obliged to obey; but the pope being aware of his military talents, made him general of his army. What must be thought of a church where such characters bear rule? It is always an unfavourable symptom as to the state of piety, when the ministers of religion are found needlesly active in secular affairs, especially in matters of warfare.

Nine years before the circumstance narrated, a remarkable character was raised up in the providence of God, connected with this diocese; in every respect well fitted for such a period, and one of such importance as to demand particular notice. This was Robert Grosseteste, who became bishop of Lincoln, in 1235. He was energetic in his resistance of the encroachments of Rome upon the English church, and protested against the extortions of the pope. The turn of affairs so recent at Dunstaple, could not fail to attract the notice of the good bishop, and the manner in which he describes the humble man, forms a pleasing contrast with the character of Peter de Roche. "The humble man not only sees that he has nothing in himself, but he is also stripped of all desire to possess in himself the springs of self-exaltation. Condemned in himself and corrupt before God, he despairs of help from his own powers, and in seeking, he finds him who is the true life, wisdom, and health, who is all in all, who is the incarnate Son of God, who descended into our vale of sin and misery that he might raise us from its depths. By leaning upon him alone, every true christian rises into true life, and peace, and joy. He lives in his life, he sees light in his light, he is invigorated with his warmth and he grows in his strength, and leaning upon the beloved, his soul ascends upward; the lower he sinks in humility, the higher he rises toward God. Thus he is induced to place his whole dependence on the Lord; to abhor himself, and always to prefer others; and to take the lowest seat as his proper place. Let the humble soul beware, lest even if he do find some evidence of this temper in his soul, he be inflated with the discovery, because he ought to know, that it is from the Lord alone that he is what he is. It behoves him, who would be found unfeignedly humble, to see whether he has the genuine marks of humility in practice ; whether he can bear to be rebuked by an inferior ; whether he is not inflated by praise ; whether among equals, he is the first to labour, and the last to exalt himself ; whether he can render blessings for curses, and good for evil." Such was the kind of teaching the inhabitants of Dunstaple received, whenever their superior minister came among them ; and what was better calculated at this time to allay the ruffled feelings caused by the exciting circumstances through which they had just passed? We need not wonder that such teaching was so unsavoury to the church of Rome, as to cause the good bishop to be favoured on one occasion with a bull of excommunication from his holiness the pope.

Anno Domini 1247, king Henry III. his queen, Eleanor of Provence, and his family visited the priory, when the monks presented the king with a gilt cup, the queen with another, and their son and daughter, prince Edward, and the princess Margaret, each with a gold clasp. In return, their majesties bestowed on the church eight pieces of silk, and the king gave an hundred shillings for the making a thurible and a pix. On his majesty being informed that the waste lands had proved a temptation to squatters to make encroachments thereon, a suit was entered into before the itinerant justice of the assize to effect their dislodgement, which took place the same year.

The year 1265 furnishes a striking instance of the effect produced by evil example. The soldiery having been trained to robbery and violence for the good of their employers, had no very nice distinctions between mine and thine, and could see no harm in doing a little for themselves in the same way when the tempting opportunity offered.

Whilst therefore Henry and his barons were engaged in fierce dispute, a party of men set off for Flampstead, and having accomplished the object of their predatory expedition were endeavouring to return, but this, a retributive providence did not permit. Without dwelling on the painful details of this unhappy visit, I will give two or three sentences as they are worded in the ancient manuscript, omiting such parts as refer to the humiliating scenes the unhappy women were called to pass through at the hands of a licentious soldiery.

"In the yeare 1265, and in the tyme of the barons warre against Henry III. fifty soldiers entered the nonrye of Flamsteade and spoiled it of all that ever there was, and * * * * * * * * before they came to Dunestaple, the crye of the countreymen overtook theim and they were all taken and slaine.

This nonrye was valued at £30 yearly."

The priory church of Dunstaple was originally in the form of a cross, as cathedrals generally are, with a bell tower in the centre, supported by four lofty arches, parts of which belonging to the eastern pillars still remain. Three massive pillars or shafts are composed of clustered columns with hexagonal capitals. The whole structure appears to have been built upon a very expensive and magnificent plan.

From the insertion of squares of flints there can be no doubt but that the present bell tower is not near so ancient as the other parts of the west front, whose angles terminated with similar buttresses and turrets.

It is said, that Henry VIII. intended to have made it a cathedral, and to erect it into a see, of which, Dr. Day was to have been the first bishop.

Upon the design being abandoned, a considerable part of the priory Church was pulled down, as all that remains at present is the nave and two side aisles, or that part extending from the west door to the cross aisle or choir entrance, a space extending about 120 feet.

The combination of various styles of ancient architecture is exhibited in these remains. The inside is chiefly Norman, and undoubtedly part of the original structure. On each side of the nave are six circular arches, of considerable height: they consist of four mouldings, with a pilaster in the middle between each arch. The arches of the upper windows are also circular, as well as the ground arches of the east end.

The windows are of a later date than the building itself, which has been repaired with brick in various places. The east end is crossed by a flat wall, and the two nearest arches on each side, form the present choir. A beautiful stone rood loft of four pointed arches, with clustered columns ranging over the west door : beneath it is a rich oak screen.

The roof is oak, with finely carved knobs of flowers and cherubims, and the ends of the beams

H

are supported by strong posts, sculptured to represent the twelve apostles, each standing on the
back of a large bird.

The west front is singular and grotesque, and
has been considered "as one of our great national
curiosities," from its extraordinary mixture of
pointed and circular arches, and by the singular
arrangement of the ornaments. The great door
is under a semi-oval arch, with four pillars on
each side, which have Saxon capitals supporting
five mouldings, the outermost of which, is ornamented with zigzag work; the second has angels
and foliage in alternate ovals; the third, beasts'
heads, fissant foliage; the fourth, a spread eagle
and the signs of the zodiac, of which, Pisces and
Capricorn are still remaining; the fifth, flowers.

There appears to have been on the capitals two
busts of the founder and endower, Henry I.
wearing his crown, David playing upon the harp,
and a figure prostrate before him: a bishop in
his robes with a mitre and crosier, and a bearded
man in a cap: two more bearded men hold a scroll
perpendicularly, on whose top is a headless body.

The lesser door has seven mouldings on five
pillars, exclusive of the inner, composed of roses
and laced work, nail headed quarterfoils. The
arch between the two doors is half a zigzag and
half a straight moulding; and the interlaced arches
within rest on capitals charged with grotesque
flowers. The columns consist of very singular
greater and lesser joints, placed alternate, not
unlike one species of the fossils called *Entrochi*.
The space over the small door is ornamented by
various compartments of carved work, representing

flowers. Above the doors are two rows of arches; the first row consists of seven flat arches with pedestals for statues; the second, of six small and two large, opening to a gallery leading to the bell tower with a seventh arch between the latter, placed over the door, all on treble clustered pillars. One of the uses, and perhaps the primary use of this gallery was for the priest to ring the Sanctus bell, whenever the Trisagium, or Holy Lord God of Sabbaoth, was said, so that all persons within and without the church, on hearing it might fall down on their knees in reverence of the elevated host.

Over the west door are three ornamented niches, and under the west window of the lower tower are four roses in square. The present tower is at the north-west angle of the building, and has two rows of niches, which were formerly filled with statues. In one of the niches are the remains of the lower part of a statue, which, by the drapery, was intended to represent an apostle, no doubt St. Peter, as the church was dedicated to that saint. There was formerly another tower at the opposite side corresponding with this. The turret of the remaining tower, inclosing a staircase, projects a little beyond the west end face. Mr. Pennant thinks that this and the corresponding tower were those mentioned to have fallen down in 1221, when they destroyed the prior's stall and part of the church.

Mr. Nicholls considers those curiously ornamented oak pillars or shafts on which the emblems of Christ's Passion are portrayed, with other devices of which there are not two alike, each varying from its fellow in form or design, " were some part of the prior's stall, then beat down by the falling of these towers: they long formed part of the front of a pew in the south side of the chancel near the vestry-room, before the commencement of the restoration; they were a curious specimen of ancient workmanship, and appear to have been wrought with the knives of the friars."

For the following observations, together with others on monumental brasses, I am indebted to an esteemed friend.

" As you enter the church by the belfry door, against the pillar, is the ancient stoup surmounted with the head of the ever blessed Virgin; and in the north aisle at the bases of some of the pillars are a few specimens of the ancient pavement. They consist of two or three glazed earthenware tiles, the back ground of the tile is red, and the inlaid figure is white: other examples may be found, but the figures are entirely obliterated. The size is about four inches by six; judging from the most perfect example, four tiles appear to have formed a geometrical figure called a quarterfoil. Owing to the fragile nature of the material, and the wear of ages, but few perfect specimens are found; so that it is difficult to form an adequate conception of the beauty of the design or workmanship. The employment of this effective kind of decoration, was doubtless, suggested by the discovery of the Roman tesselated pavements, which probably were more frequently discovered some centuries since than at the present time.

The pavements of the houses of our forefathers, seven or eight centuries since, were performed by simply beating the earth into a compact mass: in buildings of a better description, stone pavements were introduced of a massive and costly character; but this was thought not sufficiently ornate for the church, so the encaustic or burnt tiles were introduced, which like all other branches of ecclesiastical art, gradually deteriorated till even the mode of manufacture was forgotten. It has been lately revived by Minton, of Staffordshire, whose tiles are extensively employed in the decoration of churches.

The figures usually employed in the Decorated period, were monograms, arms of benefactors, prelates, orders and sacred symbols. In the Perpendicular period (about the fifteenth century,) the designs were for the most part copied from the surrounding tracery and geometrical figures, as in the case under consideration.

As a general rule, these tiles increased in beauty and complexity of design as they approached the altar; so that the floor of the chancel, both for profusion of colour and beauty of figure, rivalled the most costly woven fabrics of the present day; the general effect being heightened by the subdued and mellow tints which fell from the richly stained windows. Many other tiles of the same size and workmanship as those previously mentioned are to be found in the north aisle, but all traces of ornament have long since been obliterated from their surface.

Over the south-western arch are distinct traces of the distemper painting, with which the walls of the church were formerly covered. The figure of an angel can be traced, seeming in the act of adoration; the countenance is peculiarly express-

ive. On the arch beneath, are the remains of the
zigzag painting, which can be traced under the
chevron. The date of the whole is probably about
the middle of the fourteenth century."

The Chronicles say, "that the body of the
church was repaired in 1273, by the parishioners,
but chiefly at the expense of Henry Chadde;"
this is supposed to be that part at the chancel end,
where a number of bricks have been worked in;
it does not mention that any tower was rebuilt.

Besides the priory, there was a convent of friar's
preachers or black friars, established at Dunstaple,
by permission of Bonifiace, archbishop of Canterbury, in 1259, sorely against the will of the prior
and canons. The friars being patronized by the
court, it was in vain to oppose them. Upon the
suppression of this house, the yearly revenue of
these friars amounted to no more than £4 18s. 4d.
This priory was in a field near Sattle square, in
the South street of Dunstable. There was a
church or chapel belonging to it, with a burial
ground : human bones and skeletons have been
discovered in removing the roots of large walnut
trees, which grew in that field or orchard. The
site was granted to Sir William Herbert ; and is
now the property of G. Fossey, Esq. In the year
1835, the site of the building was dug up and
examined ; it appears to have been very extensive.
Part of the wall about two feet and a-half high,
and nearly forty feet was standing. The interior
appeared to have been lower than the surface outside, and filled by and levelled with the rubbish
that was left at its demolition. There were steps
remaining which seem to have led from one part

of the convent to another, and stairs which appeared likely to have descended to a vault for interment. In one part there was standing the base of a pillar, about a foot in diameter, and two feet high,—which, from its situation, it is probable was one of the supporters of a a groined roof, and stones were dug up which when placed together formed a circular arch; others, that had been the tracery of windows, painted tiles, stained glass, and some French coins of the reigns of Charles VIII. and Louis XI. A leaden coffin, and another of stone were discovered, both of which contained skeletons; they did not appear to have been disturbed since their interment, as their bones lay in the most perfect order. The skeleton in the leaden coffin seemed to have been a man about six feet high; that in the stone coffin apparently a youth, as none of the teeth were wanting or decayed, but no trace was found to tell in what age they lived or what name they bore.

THE UNKNOWN GRAVE.

No name to bid us know
    Who rests below;
No word of death or birth,
    Only the grasses wave
Over a mound of earth,
    Over a nameless grave.

Did this poor wandering heart
    In pain depart?
Longing, but all too late
    For the calm home again,
Where patient watchers wait,
    And still will wait in vain.

Did mourners come in scorn,
    And thus forlorn
Leave him with grief and shame,
    To silence and decay,
And hide the tarnish'd name
    Of the unconscious clay ?

It may be, from his side
    His lov'd ones died;
And last of some bright band,
    (Together now once more),
He sought his home and land,
    Where they were gone before;

No matter, limes have made
    As cool a shade,
And lingering breezes pass
    As tenderly and slow
As if beneath the grass
    A monarch slept below.

No grief, though loud and deep,
    Could stir that sleep;
And earth and heaven tell
    Of rest that shall not cease,
Where the cold world's farewell
    Fades into endless peace.

                      MISS PROCTER.

There was also a hospital for lepers belonging to the prior and canons of Dunstaple, who appointed the warden; it was founded in the 13th century, and is said to have been on the west side of the town. About the year 1817, three of the old wells fell in, as the earth sunk to the depth of two or more feet, opposite the Tythe barn belonging to the rectory, on the south side of the road, at the west end of the town. Likewise part of a stone foundation, built with yellow or gravel mortar and Totternhoe stone, was discovered in the bank of this field by the road-side at the time they used to dig hurlock from the bank, before that piece of waste land was enclosed. This was probably the site of this leper's house.

In 1265, Henry III. and his queen again visited Dunstaple, attended by cardinal Attaboni, the pope's legate, Boniface being archbishop, and Simon de Mortfort, earl of Leicester, his brother-in-law; the latter remaining there some time, choosing rather to court public favour than royal friendship, and was now in effect the ruler of the kingdom. An extraordinary altercation took place between the king and Montfort. Leicester reproached the king for a breach of promise re-specting the reward his services merited. Henry sharply replied, "that he did not think himself bound to keep his word with a traitor." Leicester retorted, "Were you not a king you would find it an evil hour in which you uttered such language," adding "that it was difficult to believe such a prince was a christian and had been at confession." "I am a christian and have been at confession," answered the king. "What sig-nifies confession without repentance?" rejoined the earl; "I never said the monarch repented anything so much as the bestowal of so many favours upon one that had so little gratitude and so much ill manners."

In the fourth year of Edward I. 1276, the king's falconers having had an affray with the servants of William de Breton, who had been confirmed as prior October 8th, 1274, and the chaplains with whom they lodged: the king

I

attended in person, to try the matter, and summoned a jury of thirty-six out of two hundred
unconnected with the town or convent, to inquire
into the affair. Upon the inquisition, it appeared
that the affray began by the falconers, who had
killed one of the chaplains in a riot.

In 1283, we find the men of Dunstaple and
the prior involved again in angry disputation,
when the former built sheepcots at Limbury,
and drove their sheep and cows there, in order to
avoid paying the latter his tithe of lamb's milk
and wool.

In 1290, the corpse of queen Eleanor was deposited one night, at the priory. Upon this
occasion, two bawdekyns of precious cloths were
given to the convent, and one hundred and twenty
pounds of wax. As the procession moved through
the town, the bier stopped in the middle of the
Market-place, until the clergy of the priory had
assembled in solemn procession and conducted the
corpse to its place in front of the high altar. A
proper spot was then marked out by the chancellor and nobility attending, for the erection of a
cross, or rather column, which was adorned with
statues and the arms of Castile and Leon quarterly,
and those of Ponthieu hanging on vines and oak
trees. When the chancellor marked the spot, the
prior of the convent William de Wederrus (who
had been nominated to the dignity 8 Cal. Feb.
1280, then vacant by the resignation of the last
prior), assisted at the ceremony and sprinkled the
ground with holy water. The cross was erected
by that eminent builder, John de Bello, a native
of Battle; it stood by the road-side, near the

entrance of the public-house known by the sign
of the "Rose and Crown," south of the house
called the Cross-house.* It continued an ornament to the town for upwards of 370 years. Prior
de Wederrus resigned in 1303.

The women of Spain were remarkable for the
richness of their tresses; and Eleanor appears
to have possessed the beauty of her country-
women. The statues generally represent her
ringlets flowing down each side her face, and
falling on her neck, from under the royal diadem.

> Here in the centre once was seen
> The monument of Edward's Queen :
> Love's sacred tribute, raised to tell
> His grief for her he lov'd so well.
> Methinks I see the long array,
> Move slowly o'er the blackening way,
> And hear the awful words resound,
> Which told that spot was holy ground.
> Then, mighty king, that eye of thine
> That flash'd through conquer'd Palestine,
> Droop'd fireless o'er thy consort's bier
> Wet with affection's softest tear;
> That form which laid so cold and low,
> The kindest thou couldst ever know,
> Watch'd o'er thee through the lands afar,
> And soften'd all the toils of war ;
> More keenly felt than thou couldst feel
> The wild assassin's venom'd steel,
> And sav'd (when weeping hope had flown)
> Thy life, regardless of her own.
> Those sacred stones were wrench'd away
> In mad rebellion's gloomy day,
> When Cromwell's wild fanatic band
> Spread guilt and horror through the land.
>   G. DERBYSHIRE.

---

*This house stood opposite the Red Lion, the front of the house
toward London.

John, of Cheddington, was elected prior 8th December, 1303, and died 1351, and was succeeded by John Marshall.

One small coin of this ambitious and warlike king has been found near the priory, bearing his effigy, crowned on the one side, while the reverse has cross molines, charged quarterly, with three pellets and a superscription LONDON, IACIVI, perfect.

As we have before intimated, by the charter of Henry I. there were two markets granted to the town, and a fair at the festival of St. Peter : the markets were then held on Sundays and Wednesdays. To these another fair was added on the feast of St. Fermund, by king John. At the request of the prior, who observing the crowds of people assembled to celebrate the festivals of the patron saints, and applied to the crown to hold fairs at these times for the accommodation of strangers, and with a view to increase his own revenue by the tolls which the charters authorized him to levy at these fairs; hence the multitude of attendants increased, some of whom were actuated by religious, others by commercial views. There is now only one market, which is held on Wednesday; and four fairs, Ash-Wednesday, May 22nd, August 12th, and November 12th.

Profit and loss are a pair of terms which seem generally associated together. Whatever advantage the town may have gained from the visits of Edward, they more than lost through the messengers and servants of his son four years after this last mournful visit.

The Chronicles record that during prince Edward's long stay at Langley, in 1294, the priory sustained great loss by the market; his kitchen consuming more than two hundred messes a day, and his servants taking up all the butter, cheese, eggs, and other commodities brought to the market and even from the tradesmen's houses, and paying for nothing.

A grand tournament was held here in 1341, in commemoration of the great victory in which two hundred vessels were taken from the French, and thirty thousand men destroyed. King Edward III. and his queen were present, when Edward knelt down and thanked God for his success, and directed a national thanksgiving.

A false lustre has been thrown over the character of Henry V.; while every unprejudiced mind will find it stained with persecution and carnage, as shown in connexion with our town, which by-the bye is the first insight we get into the trading population. In the year 1414, Dunstaple was famous for its breweries, by which many of its inhabitants were raised to affluence. Among them was one William Murlie, who sallied out to join the so-called insurrection of the Lollards in the Ficket field, behind St. Giles's, London. He took with him a pair of gilt spurs in his bosom, and was followed by two led horses, with rich trappings. This probably gave rise to the report of his expecting to receive knighthood from Lord Cobham; but instead of which he had the hard fortune to be taken at Haranguay Park, and was condemned under the statue "*De heretico comburendo*," which Arundel had obtained, and hung with the gilt spurs about his neck.

THE MARTYR; OR THE DEATH OF WILLIAM MURLIE, OF DUNSTAPLE, A LOLLARD,* IN 1414.

Of hope and joy was the martyr's song,
As he passed the Arena's space along:
As he raised his fettered hands on high,
And came in his Master's cause to die.

There was no fear in the Christian's mein,
In his cloudless brow, or his eye serene;
No trace in that calm and stedfast air
Of a groundless hope or a wild despair.

For how could he fear who still relied,
With steadfast faith on the Crucified;
And knew that the blood on Calvary spilt,
From his soul had wash'd away its guilt.

Oh! it fires with joy the Martyr's eye,
To be counted worthy thus to die;
He prays with the prayer of faith to heav'n,
And strength to endure the hour is giv'n.

And is not the crown of glory worth
A few short hours of pain on earth?
O God, upon us thy grace bestow,
That we may endure and win the race.

T. A. W.

It is remarkable, though here said by their enemies to be in insurrection, scarcely any of this

---

*Note.—Psalm singing at this period, was considered such a grievous innovation, that those who took delight therein were called, by the way of reproach, a Lollard; a word derived from the Flemish *"lollen,"* to sing.

people were put to death for political offences, but
almost invariably suffered as heretics; and the
following will give some idea how far the views
entertained by this persecuted people were in
accordance with Scripture, and how widely it
differed from the fashionable notions of the day.
During the trial the following question was
proposed :—

QUERIST.—" Do you believe there remains any material bread after
the words of Consecration spoken over it?"

RESPONDENT.—" The Scripture makes no mention of material bread.
In the Sacrament there is both Christ's body and bread; the bread is
the thing that we see with our eyes, but the body of Christ is hid, and
only to be seen by the eye of faith."

Notwithstanding the persecutions above referred
to, England as a nation, was at this period justly
styled "Merry England," for the love her sons
had for melody and song. Dr. Burney says "that
there existed a wide-spread taste for melody in
England, at a very early period, especially in
counter-point, or music in parts; which

" The ploughman whistled o'er the furrow'd land."

Landini, an Italian writer of the 15th century,
says, " that many excellent musicians came from
England, crossing seas, Alps and Appenines, to
hear the performance of a celebrated organist
called Antonis degli Organi:" and another author,
who was leader of music in the chapel royal of
Ferdinand, king of Naples, not only mentions the
excellence of English vocal music in parts, but
attributes the entire invention of the counter-
point, to John, of Dunstaple, so called from his
being born in this town. " A person," says an
old author, " if a reader hitherto, it is high time

that he now take notice of a being of such perfection, since meeting with this man my pen before
famishing now surfeits.　For this John, of Dunstaple, was John of all arts, as appeareth by his
double epitaph,—one inscribed on his monument,
the other on his memory.　But be it premised of
both, that we will not avouch for the truth of the
Latin, or quantity of these verses, but present
them here as we find them, with all their faults
and his virtues on whom they were made."

On his Tomb, in St. Stephen's, Walbrook, London.

Clauditur hoc tumulo qui cælum pectore clausit
Dunstable I Juris Astrorum conseinsille...novit abscondita
　　　pondere cæli
Hic vir erat tua Laus tua Lux tua Musica princeps
Quinque tuas dulces per Mundum sparserat Arles
Suscipiant proprium Civem sibi Cives.

which literally translated is :

" John Dunstaple lies buried in this tomb ;　a man who held reason
in his breast, who knew the laws of the stars, and the hidden sweets of
the vast heaven ; this great man was thy glory, thy light, thy chief
musician, who hath dispersed abroad throughout the world thine own
sweet Arts.　Thine let the heavenly citizens receive, fit fellow-citizens
with themselves."

The Second made by John Wheathamstead, Abbot of St. Albans.

Musicus hic Michalus alter novus & Ptolomœns
Junior ac Atlas supportans sobore cælos
Pausat sub cincere melior vir de mutiere
Nunquam natus erat vit ii quia labe carebat
Et virtutis opes celebretur fama Johannis
Dunstable in pace requiescat & hic sine fine
　This Dunstable died in 1445.

which translated is :

"Here rests beneath the soil, a musician, a seer, a Michael, a modern
Ptolomy, and a younger Atlas, bearing heaven's weight upon his
shoulder ; a better man was never born of woman, because he was
free　from　all stain of sin, and was singularly possessed of every
virtue.　Let John of Dunstaple's renown be celebrated in every age,
and here let him rest in perpetual peace."

The following is a translation from the original

Latin, in the ancient parish register, still in the
church, but which is usually considered spurious;
it purports to be an account of the charter of the
foundation and privileges of the town of Dunstaple,
and is supposed to have been written during the
time of John Roxton, who was confirmed prior,
Dec. 18th, 1413: for a sight of which, together
with certain other interesting matter, I am indebted to the kindness of the present rector :—

"Lord Henry, king of England, son of king
William, held and possessed in his domain the
towns of Houghton and Kensworth. But there
was a spot near Houghton, where the two royal
roads Watlinge and Ickneld meet, was everywhere
woody and so full of robbers, insomuch that a
loyal subject or even courier could not pass
through without being killed, or at least losing a
limb, or some of their goods. He the said king,
with a view to the restraining such evil practices,
commanded that place to be grubbed up; and
built hard by, for himself, a royal palace, which
they called Kingsburie, and that court contains
nine acres.

"Wishing moreover to establish a town there,
he (the king) caused proclamation to be made
through all parts of his kingdom, that all who
came to take up their abode there, should for
every acre pay twelve-pence per annum, and shall
have and all singly hereditaments, privileges,
and acquittances all over his kingdom, the same
as the city of London or any other English borough
had had in ancient times.

"And thus the said place was built by such
people. And because a certain robber named

K

Dun used to practice his depredations there, that town was called Dunningstaple. But the king detained in his own hands the town of Dunstaple, as a free borough of his own, for seventeen and a-half years. The burgesses of the said town were free and quit throughout all England, in the manner aforesaid, during the whole reign of the said king. They were never required to answer before any of his itinerant justices, or any other of the king's ministers, without the town or liberty of Dunstaple; but the judges and deputies of the sovereign came down to Dunstaple, and all pleas were determined by twelve jurors, sworn in from among the burgesses, without the union of any stranger. The same king also established and held a market in the said borough, twice a week, and a fair at the feast of St. Peter *ad vincular* (St. Peter's chairs), lasting three days. And they had a free gallows for hanging thieves, outside the liberty of Dunstaple, in a place called Westcote. At length the said king Henry I. within the liberty of the said borough built a church in honour of St. Peter, as he had long intended and placed a prior and regular canons of the order of Augustine, named black canons there. He gave likewise to them and their successors, free unrestricted, in pure and perpetual alms, the aforesaid church, the said borough, with the burgesses, markets, fairs, liberties and all privileges, whatever he (the king) had been used to enjoy from the profit and all other sources, when he held the said borough in his own hands. He also granted and assigned to them, whatever liberty he could by his royal power bestow on them: to have and to hold for ever, just as he himself had held the said borough from God.

"But the king aforesaid kept in his own hands his royal mansion, because as yet, they had no fit habitation within the enclosure of the canons or priory.

"The said prior and canons have moreover, the confirmation of the charter by king Henry II. and king Richard, with an addition or grant of several privileges; likewise the confirmation by king John, and by his gift, his own palace and estate of Kingsburie aforesaid. Likewise by the gift of the same king John, a holiday at the feast of St. Fermund, which lasted three days. Likewise they have a confirmation of king Henry III., of the charter of king Richard, and another confirmation of the charter of Henry I., the founder of the aforesaid church. And in consequence of these bequests and confirmations, the said canons had all pleas and amerciaments of their own men, and the justiciaries and ministers of the lord king (the prior always sitting with them) determined all causes within the liberty of Dunstaple. Likewise the prior had his own clerk, as well as the justices their clerks, and kept the roll of every verdict. And during the reigns of all the aforesaid kings, the prior, and canons, and burgesses always for the time being, peaceably enjoyed the same privilege.

"Now also, in the said borough of Dunstable, there are many tenants in capite of the prior; and many tenants, who for their tenements pay the prior the service due to their tenements, and they are all free men, as they were in the time of

king Henry, under whom the borough was founded.
And during all this time, the church of Dunstaple, the subsidies of the borough and the profits
of the markets were severally taxed to the amount
of one hundred shillings. And the said taxation
still exists. Three-fourths of the site of the
borough are in the fee of Houghton Regis, for
which the said lord king Henry I. gave to the
tenants of the town of Houghton, out of his own
forest of Buckwode, in exchange, (now called
Buckwood Stubbs); and one fourth of the town
on the western side is reputed to be in the fee of
Kensworth."

In the year 1457, queen Margaret brought
Henry VI. on a visit to Dunstable, but nothing
of importance is recorded ; and the reign of his
successor might have been passed over in silence
had it not given rise to a custom, a corruption of
which has been embodied in a lively form, occupying a very prominent place in the embellish-
ments of our public buildings :—Swans were
anciently considered as the " king's game." Edward the Fourth ordained, that no one whose
income was less than five marks should possess a
swan, and imprisonment to any one who should
dare to touch their eggs : the marks of the several
owners were on their beaks, and the sign of the
royal swan, or swan-with-two-nicks becoming
unintelligible to the sign painter, was perverted
into the ' swan-with-two-necks ;' hence the origin
of that sculptured figure in the Middle-row.
Closely allied to this, is swan-upping or the taking
up of the cygnets to mark them, on the authorized
day. The Monday following Midsummer-day is

now changed into the ridiculous phrase "swan-hopping."

In the church of Dunstaple, but situated on the west side of the town, before the dissolution, there was a house of fraternite friars of the brotherhood of St. John the Baptist. John Cotton, the last prior of this friary subscribed to the king's supremacy, May 6th, 1534.

The following interesting circumstances, in an old antiquarian book in the British Museum, is thus given respecting them. "At this town is kept a funeral pall, now used to cover the corpse at the interment of some of this parish, for which is paid six-pence, that is always given to the poor by its keeper, at present, Mr. Miller.

"It is still, notwithstanding its age, as fresh and beautiful as at first making, and was the gift of Henry Fayrey and Agnes his wife, unto a fraternity or brotherhood dedicated to St. John the Baptist, in this town of Dunstaple. It is made of the richest crimson and gold brocade imaginable, and so exquisitely and curiously wrought, that it puzzles the greatest artists of weaving now living to so much as guess at the manner of its performance. It is 6ft. 4ins. long, by 2ft. 2ins. broad, from whence hangs down a border of purple velvet 13ins. deep, whereon is lively and most richly worked with a needle, St. John the Baptist between fourteen men and thirteen women, all kneeling: under the foremost is written Henry Fayrey and Agnes Fayrey: between the arms of the Mercers, viz. : G. a denui virgin with her hair dishevelled, crowned, issuing out (and within an oole) of clouds, all proper, A on a fess compone, B & G, 3 amulets, O between six crosses, battone S. The Haberdasher's arms, barry nebule of six A, and B on a bend, G a lion passant guardant O, and on a shield party per pale O and B, a chevron between three eagles displayed counterchanged, as many lozenges A, on a chief G. Thus are the sides; but at the ends is only St. John, between a gentleman and his wife; under them is written John and Mary Fayrey. It appears from a monumental stone of black marble in the middle aisle of the church, containing the effigies in brass, of Henry and Agnes Fayrey in their grave-clothes, that Henry died in 1516. The following is the inscription:

"Off yo charite yy for the soul of Fayrey and Agnes his wife which lyeth buried under this stone; and the said Henry decessid the xxbiii dai of December A no Dni mcccccxbi."

An engraving of the stone and brass is to be seen in "Fisher's Genealogical Collections of Bedfordshire."

After this, I have no doubt but that the tradition of the town, as given by Mr. Nicholls is true: that it was not an altar-cloth, but a funeral pall given to the church; and whoever appropriated it as private property, was guilty of sacrilege.

The descendants of this John Fayrey appear to have coined tokens for themselves, having a shield with bearings on it, and the words "John Fayrey, Dunstaple," legibly round it. The house occupied by the fraternite friars is supposed to have been opposite to the church of St. Mary Overs, which was on the south side of Butt's-lane, as there appears to have been considerable buildings on the north side. Hollow places that have been wells may be traced in this field. The second house of friars was valued at the great spoilation at £9 8s. 7d., and was of the order of fraternite friars of the brotherhood of St. John, the Baptist. The house thus occupied belonged to the Wingate family in 1642.

Part of the land belonging to this fraternity was set apart as a public recreation ground, and the outdoor sports formed a distinguished feature of this period, and were not confined to the middle and lower classes; even the rich and noble were glad to fly to active and boisterous sports. The very lowest order of the female sex of the present day would shrink from games which even ladies then resorted to. Cudgel-playing, wrestling, and bear-baiting were almost every-day amusements. And that neglected piece of ground so long the eyesore of Dunstaple, was at this time enjoying its high tide of popularity, and it is much to be regretted that ever it was appropriated to any other purpose than that of a public pleasure ground, being so conveniently situated, I mean the "Butts," which is only a corruption of the word "bolt-ground," in allusion to those feats of archery, so often performed within its area, and which was thought so important as to be the subject of several statutes in the reign of Henry VIII.

Fathers were to provide bows for their children when seven years' old, and masters were to provide bows for their apprentices. Latimer speaks of archery "as a wholesome and manly exercise, requiring constant practice from childhood." An archer's dress added much to the grotesque

character of the May-day games and other rural
sports, as they wore scarlet boots and yellow caps.
The use of the bow was considered important, not
only to keep up the use of a weapon famous in
English warfare, but as a manly sport, strengthen-
ing to the body : in this latter respect, it has been
succeeded by cricket.   But the modern cricketer
can no longer enjoy his favourite sports without a
tiresome march to some more elevated spot on the
Downs.

The following were the favourite sports at this
period :

> " And they dare chalenge, for to throw the sledge,
> To jumpe, or leape over ditch or hedge ;
> To wrestle, play at foote-ball, or to runne,
> To pitch the barre, or to shote of a gunne ;
> To play at loggets, nine holes, or ten pinnes,
> To try it out at foote-ball by the shinnes,
> At tick, tacke, seize noddy, mau and ruffe ;
> At hot cockles, leap frogge, or blindman's buffe :
> To drink the halper pottes, or deal at the whole cann,
> To play at cheese, or pue and inke horne ;
> To dance the morris, play at barley broke,
> At all exploits a man can think or speak ;
> At shove groate, venterpoynte, or cross and pile,
> At beshrew him that's last at any style ;
> At leaping o'er a Christmas bonfire,
> Or at the drawing dame out of the myer ;
> At shoote cocke, gregory, stoole-ball, and what not ;
> Picke poynte, toppe, and scourge, to make him hotte."

There is a custom still kept up by the Free
boys (though fast dying out in the neighbouring
towns,) which while it carries with it the appearance of much childish simplicity, was not always
an unimportant and unmeaning affair, viz.:—that
of erecting oyster grottoes at the corner of the
streets.   I believe the custom is fast dying out

in the neighbouring towns; although it is one of great antiquity. Mr. Thomas, an excellent anti-quarian, considers "that in the grottos formed of oyster-shells, and lighted with candles, to which on St. James's Day (August 5th), we are invited to contribute by cries of "Pray remember the grotto!" we have a record of the celebrated shrine of St. James, of Compostella."

Such grottos may have been formerly erected on the anniversary of St. James, by persons, as an invitation to those who could not visit Com-postella to show their reverence for the saint, by almsgiving to their poorer brethren. There is a popular notion, that whoever eats oysters on St. James's Day will never want money for the rest of the year.

Mr. Steele noticed some curious ornaments about various parts of the church. The east part of the chancel, says this gentleman, is raised by two steps, and was formerly the choir of the church. The ancient stalls still remaining, where under each seat (visible upon turning them up for prayers), is carved some extravagant fancy one in particular, under seat is neatly cut a woman spinning with rock and spindle, and on the ground a sneering friar preacher, while his busy hand is searching her petticoats.

Another represents one of those frequent con-flicts Dunstan is said to have had with the devil, when he pinched the devil's nose with a pair of tongs, for interrupting him at prayers: all which shows, the deep-rooted jealousy of the ancient clergy towards the regulars, who had supplanted them, and heart-burnings between the parties,

L

which were injurious alike to religion itself and the
Establishment which should have been its support.

Nor was Dunstaple alone in this grievous schism.
The architecture and ornaments of the churches
everywhere bespoke it. Many of the grotesque
figures which are to this day seen decorating the
spouts of the roofs, or the labels of the windows,
were probably meant as a fling at the monks;
and satirical caricatures may still occasionally be
seen on the painted glass of our cathedrals.

Meanwhile, neither of these ecclesiastical parties
seem to have been aware, that by their mutual
criminations, they were preparing the nation to
demand a reformation in the manners of all; and
that each were throwing stones at the other, when
the houses of both were made of glass.

At the south-east corner was formerly the fragments of a stone, whereon was carved a figure as
large as life, with apparently a hand holding a
crowned head, which some have supposed represented Ethelbert, king of the West Saxons, who
thought he was beheaded by Offa; yet it was
through jealousy, not having anything to do with
religion. I am therefore inclined to think it was
intended for king Edmund, who with great firm-
ness, died a martyr in 871, boldly, as a king de-
claring the christian principles by which he was
actuated. Nothing of this kind attended the
death of Ethelbert. Of the death of Edmund,
Father Cressy informs us, " That his head was
struck off by his enemies, and after they had used
all manner of contemptuous scorn upon it, they
cast it into a thicket of the wood adjoining, where
it remained a whole year's space. But the chris-

tians assembling, they reverently took the body out of the unclean place where it had been cast, and then with all diligence sought for the head, and whilst every one of them with equal affection searched each corner of the wood, there happened a wonder not heard of in any age before. For whilst they dispersed themselves in all parts, and each demanded of his companions, " Where's the head ?" the same head answered them aloud, in their own tongue, "Here ! Here ! Here ! Neither did it cease to cry out in these words, till it had brought them to the place. And to add to the wonder, there they found a mighty and fierce wolf, which with its fore foot held the head, as if appointed to watch and defend it from other beasts. When they were come, the wolf quietly resigned it to them, so with joyful hymns to God they carried it and joined it to the body. The wolf in the mean time followed them to the place where they buried it, after which, the wolf returned to the wood : in all which time neither did the wolf hurt any one, neither did any one show any disposition to hurt the wolf. Nor was this all; for about fifty years after his death, the sanctity of the king was testified by miracles."

In all probability, what appeared to be a hand, was the paw of the wolf. The church of Rome enumerate Edmund, amongst her saints, and certainly he was more deserving of that honour than many whom that church has canonized for acts of treason and rebellion.

Belonging to the priory of Dunstaple, at Roke-sac, a hamlet of Flitwick, three miles from Ampthill, was a small monastery, which appears to have been a cell to Dunstaple.

At the dissolution of religious houses, the revenues of the priory of Dunstaple were estimated, according to Dugdale, at £334 13s. 3d. clear yearly value. On October 17th, 1534, twenty-sixth Henry VIII, the last prior, Gervase Markham with Thomas Cleybrooke and eleven others, subscribed to the king's supremacy, and continuing till the dissolution in 1539, had on the giving up of his monastery, a pension of £60, assigned him for life. He lived till the month of September, 1561, and was buried at Dunstaple, as appears by the parish register. The following monks also were granted pensions:—Thomas Cleybrooke, £9; Richard Kerte, £8; Augustine Curtes, £8; George Edwards, £7; John Stallisworth, £7; Richard Bowstood, £7; Edward Green, £6; Richard Somer, £6; John Nyxe, £5 6s. 8d.; Nich. Cleybrooke, £2; John Percival, £2.

Gervase Markham had taken an active part in the proceedings relative to the divorce between Henry VIII. and Catherine of Arragon, who had been for a few months the wife of prince Arthur, his brother. Her father Ferdinand, of Spain, had consented to the marriage, and pope Julius III. authorized it by a bull, in which, he assumed the power to dispense with both the laws of God and man. This bull produced the difficulty,—for the church of Rome is incapable of error. It was the horns of this accommodating bull that tossed the papal supremacy out of England.

The only way out of the difficulty which pope Clement VII. could suggest, and it was one worthy of the man,—was that he might allow Henry to

MESS^{RS.} MUNT & BROWN'S MANUFACTORY.

have two wives. To the simple reader of Holy Scripture, no such difficulty would present itself, though it took the doctors seven years to settle it.

The commissioners sat at Dunstaple to receive the replies from the universities, in answer to the question, "Can a man marry his brother's widow?" It resulted unfavourably to Catherine, who was then residing at Ampthill park, and had been summoned by the commissioners to appear before them in the priory church, which she refused to do. The sentence of divorce was publicly pronounced by archbishop Cranmer, on the 23rd of May, 1553, in the Virgin's chapel, within the priory church, commanding her at the same time to assume the title of the dowager of prince Arthur. The women of England were naturally opposed to these proceedings, which tended to shake the security of the marriage state.

After the dissolution of this convent, prior Markham had a pension of £60 per annum. He died in the month of September, 1561, and was buried at Dunstaple, as appears by the parish register. The site of the priory was granted by Mary I. to Dr. Leonard, chamberlain in 1554. It is now a large straw bonnet manufactory belonging to Messrs. Munt and Brown, of London, and finds employment for three hundred hands. At the dissolution of the monastery, the manor and priory lands had reverted to the crown.

The following verses are taken from the ancient records, kept at the priory:

"*Verses concerninge the Name and Armes of Dunstaple*, 1558."

"By Houghton Regis, there, where Watlinge Streete
Is cross'd by Icknell way, once grew a wood

With bushes thick orespred; a coverte meete
To harbour such as lay in waite for blood,
There lurkte of ruffians bolde an hideous route
Whose captaine was one Dunne, of courage stoute.

" No travailer almost coulde passe that way
But either he was wounded, rob'd, or kil'd
By that leude crewe, which there in secreete lay :
With murthers, theftes, and rapes, their hands were fil'd,
What booties ere they tooke, ech had his share ;
Thus yeere by yeere they liv'd without all care.

" At last king Henrie, first king of that name,
Towards the northern partes in progresse rode ;
And hearinge of those greate abuses, came
Unto the thicket where the theues abode ;
Who on the comminge of the kinge did flie
Each to his house, or to his freinde did hie.

" Wherefore the kinge, such mischiefes to prevent,
The wood cut down ; the way all open layde
That all trew men, which that way rode or wente,
Of sodaine sallyes might be lesse affrayde ;
And might descrie theire danger ere it came,
And so by wise foresighte escape the same.

" This done, he rear'd a poull both houge and longe
In that roade-highway, where so manie passe ;
And in the poul let drive a staple stronge,
Whereto the kinge's owne ringe appendant was ;
And caus'd it to be publisht that this thinge
Was done to see what thiefe durst steale the ringe.

" Yet for all that, the ringe was stol'n away,
Which, when it came to learned Beauclerke's eare,
By skylfull arte to finde, he did assay
Who was the theife, and first, within what shyre
His dwellinge was, which this bould act had done,
And found it to be Bedffordshire, anon.

" Next in what hundred off that shyre might dwell
This vent'rous wighte, kinge Henrie caste to find ;
And upon Mansfield Hundred, straight it fell,

Which being founde, he after bent his minde
To learn the parish, and by like skyll tride
That he in Houghton Regis did abide.

" Lastlie, the parish knowne, he further soughte
To find the verie house where he remaynde ;
And by the precepts of his arte he toughte,
That by one Widow Dun he was retayned ;
The widowe's hoase was searched, so wil'd the kinge,
And with her sonne was founde, staple and ringe.

" Thus Beauclerke by his arte, found out the thiefe,
A lustie tall younge man of courage goode,
Which of the other ruffians was the Chiefe ;
That closlie lurked in that waylesse wood.
Then Dunne, this captain thiefe, the widowe's sonne,
Was hanged for the factes which he had donne.

" And where the thicket stoode, the kinge did build
A market towne for saulfetie of all those
Which travail'd that way, that it might them yielde
A sure refuge from all thievishe foes ;
And there king Henrie, of his great bountie,
Founded a church, a schole, and priorie.

" And for that Dunne, before the wood was downe,
Had there his haunte, and thence did steal away
The staple and the ring, thereof the towne
Is called Dunstaple untill this day ;
Also in armes, that corporation,
The staple and the ringe give thereupon."

The monasteries having been suppressed, travellers had no place of resort, except inns ; of
these, the larger ones usually retained the form of
an open court-yard, with galleries communicating
with the various ranges of apartments. In process of time the open court being cleaned, formed
convenient places for theatrical display ; the per-
formers occupying the area, whilst the spectators

filled the galleries. Of this period, the only
remaining monument of this kind in the town is
the gateway to the "Anchor" yard, adjoining
the Town Hall, with its antique window over it.
The usual way of ingress and egress was by side
entrances under the gateway. The innkeeper
now became a person of note : not unfrequently
the incumbent of the parish was the tavern-keeper
and entertained the travellers.

Music was very much esteemed at this period,
for we read that John Coput, in the middle rents,
kept a number of keyed and stringed instruments,
that his customers might amuse themselves while
waiting their turn to be shaved. In the middle
classes, every one was supposed to be more or less
acquainted with music. Not only did the good-
natured John dress their hair, but also relieved
the mouth of troublesome companions, and was
one of the five classes admitted to practice Sur-
gery : hence, that long pole so often seen at the
barber's shop, representing blood and bondages,
by the alternate stripes of red and white.

During the reign of queen Elizabeth, theatrical
amusements began to assume a more regular form.
Punch and Judy is a relic of one of these ancient
mysteries,—in Latin called 'Pontus cum Judacis,'
in English, 'Pontius Pilate with the Jews.'

After the Reformation, the profane Scripture
mysteries were discontinued ; and it is deserving
of remark, that Dunstaple is generally allowed to
have been the first place in the kingdom where a
theatrical representation of any kind was at-
tempted ; and was a play exhibiting one of the
miracles of St. Catherine, which was performed

within the priory, probably in the cloister, or else the guest hall, but I think the former. It was conducted by a secular priest named Geoffrey, in the year 1560, being four years before the immortal Shakespeare was born. The plays of the former, were however destined to give way to the comedies and tragedies of the latter. Geoffrey subsequently became abbot of St. Albans.

Elizabeth being fond of display, was accustomed to make progresses in all parts of her dominions, which served greatly to preserve her popularity : on these journies she visited the stately mansions of her nobles, so many of which are still the ornaments of our sylvan scenes. During one of the progresses in 1572, she visited Dunstaple; on which occasion she was entertained with pageants, in which the quaintness of the prevailing taste was sadly blended with the chivalrous feeling which still cast a lingering lustre on the habits of society.

A shilling of this queen's reign, in most excellent preservation, exhibiting a most perfect likeness of Elizabeth, habited in the customary dress of those times, has recently been turned up by the plough, in a field belonging to Mr. Joseph Gutteridge.

Perhaps this is the most convenient place to introduce the subject of counterfeit coins, and the reason why they were so common up to this period of our town's history ; but which went out of use during the successor of Elizabeth.

The weight of the earlier Saxon penny was 24 grains, hence the term "penny-weight;" but it was soon reduced, and under the Norman kings

M

it became still less. In succeeding reigns it
gradually dwindled, until the reign of Elizabeth,
when it became a mere spangle,—she being obsti-
nately averse to a copper coinage for England.

The parliamentary rolls furnish us with abundant evidence of the inconvenience experienced by
persons in humble ranks, through the want of
small change. Many of the complaints state,
"that for want of small money, the poor man
lost his penny;" an expression implying great
inconvenience, whatever its precise signification
might have been.

The penny was wont to have a double cross
with a crest, in such sort, that the same might be
broken in the midst, or into four quarters; and
there can be no reasonable doubt that the custom
of breaking love-money as a pledge of fidelity,
originated in the public practice.

> "The halfe of silver six-pence broken,
> 'Twixt youths and maids a true love-token."

The small change seems to have been managed
chiefly by means of counterfeit coins, as abbey
pieces, blackmail, Nuremburgh counters, and
similar base currency, introduced by Jews and
other foreigners, and of which our townsmen
availed themselves, as is evident from the considerable number found in and about the town; a
good collection of which are in the possession of
Mr. Gostelow, to whom, for a sight of which I
am much indebted. They are now of no value,
either as works of art, or weight of metal,—they
are usually of brass.

Obv.—A female figure, holding a Conucopia, &c.
Inscription.—EX PAVBERTAS.   At the foot of the
figure, WOLFLAVE.

Two abbey pieces,
Obv.—The most blessed Virgin, under a Canopy.
Abe Maria.

The second are,
Obv.—Triple Crown.
Abe Maria Gracia, P. C.
Rev.—Cross and Fleur-de-lis, (highly ornamented).

One small coin, in silver,
Obv.—A Priest bearing a lighted Taper.
Rev.—Not legible.

In the year 1557, Richard Mantell gave and bequeathed unto the use of the poor of the parish of Dunstaple, two closes of sward, opposite the Park lodge, in the town of Luton; that nearest the road abutting the house, and measuring 1a. 2r. 18p.; the other west but adjoining, containing 1a. 2r. 22p.

COMMERCE, SOCIAL INSTITUTIONS, &c.

WE have now arrived at that dark period of English history, the time of the Great Rebellion, which overthrew both the altar and the throne, but ostensibly directed against Charles I.; and Bedfordshire was one of those counties in which he had no party that openly espoused his cause. In the second year of that rebellion, we find, six hundred Royalists hastening on to Bedford, closely pursued by the Round-heads, under command of the Earl of Essex, who it appears, quartered in Dunstaple, in 1643. According to Dr. Bates, "notwithstanding the eagerness of pursuit, they appointed a time for fasting and public prayer, and then with great solemnity burnt the pictures of our Saviour, the Virgin, and the saints, and so renewed their martyrdom, and with no ordinary devotion did they pull down the cross of good queen Eleanor, although it was not only useful, but one of the chief ornaments in the town."

The site and part of the foundation were discovered enclosed, or set round with oak posts, in the form of a circle, at equal distances, when the roads were improved and the houses removed from the middle of the street, in 1803. These houses are noticed in the Parliamentary survey of all lands belonging to the royal family at the death of Charles I., and are those called

"middle rents:" they together with other parts
of the manor were taken possession of by the
State. The same commissioners also mention,
that a number of persons had made encroachments
upon the Lord's waste.

Notwithstanding the gloominess of the picture
and the general apathy of the country, it is
gratifying to find that at least in the royal manor
of Dunstaple, some were found who continued
faithful to the church, and most devoted in
attachment to their king. Among the prominent
was Frank Marshe: for though his rank and
position would not allow of his being a club-man,
yet no doubt they had his encouragement and
support; for whilst they were engaged in the
protection of their own, and their neighbours'
goods, he was struggling for the welfare of his
church and king, as we gather from his monumental stone :—

FRANCUS MARSHE,
De Dunstaple Generosus
Exodema Sepulchro,
cum Rebecca conjunge pia
Hic sepultus jacet,
Cujus
Assidua in Deum pietas,
Inviolata (dum vixisset usq ad aras)
In Anglicanum Apostolicam Eclesiam Constatia
Nec nom inconcusea in principem fidelitas
Temporibus (heu) nefandissimis
Carolum &c., Martyrum Sanctissimum
Carolum Mortalium Clementissimum
Jacobum Imperatorum Augustissimum
Paternalis in Liberos Amor;
Exima in pauperes Charitas
Exemplum presentibus documentuino posteris Praebuit.
Ille { Obijt } 29° May Anno 1685 } Ætat 61°
Alla { Obijt } 28° Junij Anno 1682 } Ætat 65°

which in English reads :—

" Frank Marshe, of Dunstaple, gentleman, and in the same
tomb with Rebecca, his wife.　Here lies buried; whose
constant piety towards God, inviolable attachment through life
to God's altar and worship, constancy towards the English
Apostolic Church ; also, his unfailing fidelity in alas, most
depraved times! towards his king, the most holy Martyr, that
most beneficent of all men, king Charles, and the most illustrious commander James.　His fatherly affection for his
children ; the wonderous charity toward the poor, gave an
example to his contemporaries, and a pattern to posterity,

He $\Big\}$ died $\Big\{$ 29th May, in the Year 1685, $\Big\{$ aged $\Big\}$ 61 years.
She $\quad\quad\quad$ 28th June, in the Year 1682, $\quad\quad\quad$ 65 years."

After the restoration, the same property came
back to the Crown.

One unsightly block now remains containing
about twenty houses, some four or five paying a
quit-rent.

During last summer, Mr. Robinson picked up
in the garden, a small silver two-penny piece of
the Commonwealth.

Obv.—A Shield bearing St. George's Cross.
*Rev.*Two Eseutcheons, side by side ; the first charged with
St. George's Cross, the other with the Irish Harp, between a branch of palm and laurel.　Over the Shields,
.i i.

These coins are distinguished from all others
in the English series.　The types furnished the
Cavaliers with a subject for much joke and
ribaldry.　The double shield on the reverse was
called "The breeches for the Rump" (parliament).
A wag added the following epigram :—

" May their success like to their coin appear ;
Send double crosses for their single cheer."

The immediate effect of the death of Charles I.,
was to loosen everywhere throughout the kingdom

the bonds of order and good government. The usurper prevailing, the wildest fanatics both in civil and religious matters, took the lead; and the fabric of society was for a space shaken to its very basis.

The great object of the Barebones parliament was, according to their own statements, to pave the way for the reign of the Redeemer, and that there might be nothing left which could by possibility impede its arrival. They proposed to a-bolish the clerical function, and to confiscate the property of the church. Marriage they pronounced to be a mere civil ceremony, and ordered it to be contracted in the presence of a magistrate, the bands being proclaimed in any public place. Therefore, under the date 1654, we find several such entries as these in the old register:—

" The intention of Marriage betwixt Thomas Wats and Jane Long, both of Dunstable, was published in the Market, according to ye Act in that behalfe, on Sept. 27th., Oct. 4th. Oct. 11th. They were Married Nov. 2nd., 1654."

The date of the entries at this period, are very irregular, and the entries themselves sadly inter-mixed. On the page following the one from which I have just made an extract, bearing the date 1654, the following note is written :—

" Some Births of Children, not before registered, born before the coming forth of the late Act, are registered since (by the Parish Registrar,) at the issue and upon the testimonie of the parents of the said children."

Here follow two pages of births, extending from 1643,—the first entry of births to 1665.

It is evident that the "parish registrar" was not the clergyman, but some official created under the late act; who was authorized to make these entries into the parish book, as in a totally different hand, with different ink, and perhaps subsequently.

There are inserted among these births, divers entries of baptisms, which as I take it, were by the rector or minister for the time being.

It is curious also, that although baptisms appear to have been eschewed by "the late act," and births recorded instead, yet the burials were not; as the deaths are not inserted, but the burials.

The book is signed in 1655, 1656, by the two churchwardens, and by Thos. Hawkins, registrar. Then the confusion in the registries becomes distressing. Thomas and Ellen Robets give their son the name of "Honesty;" another is called "John Mavel." Then we meet with one Clerk, whose three daughters on the 16th of December, are named "Faith, Hope, and Charity;" and on the 19th of the same month, the burial of "Faith and Charity" are recorded. On the 7th of April, 1654, we read that "Ann Sprat, a little maid, was slain by the fall of a stone."

In looking back to the time we are now about to take leave, every thoughtful man will be ready to exclaim in the language of our beautiful Litany, "From all sedition, privy conspiracy and rebellion, Good Lord, deliver us!"

History next presents to our notice Elkanah Settle, a native of Dunstaple. He was well known as a dramatist and political writer; was contemporary with Dryden, and during the sway of party, many preferred his compositions to those of his rivals: he lived in the time of Charles II.,

being born at Dunstaple, Feb. 1st., in the year
1647—8. Butler has severely satirized him as a
contemptible author, but it is probable that
party prejudice in some measure pointed his lines;
wherein after calling him a zany, and giving a
description of his qualifications and employments,
enters upon his skill in poetry :—page 187, line
358.

> " Beside all this he ser'vd his master
> In quality of poetaster ;
> And rhymes appropriate could make
> To ev'ry month i'th almanack.
> When terms begin and end could tell,
> With their returns in doggerel ;
> When the Exchequer opes and shuts,
> And a sow-gelder with safety cuts :
> When men may eat and drink their fill,
> And when be temp'rate if they will ;
> When use and abstain from vice,
> Figs, grapes, phlebotomy, and spice.
> And as in prison mean rogues beat
> Hemp for the service of the great,
> So Whackum* beat his dirty brains
> T' advance his master's fame and gains.
> And like the devil's oracles,
> Puts into dogg'rell rhymes his spells,
> Which over ev'ry month's blank page
> I' th' almanacks, strange bilks presage.
> He would an elegy compose
> On maggots squeezed out of his nose :
> In lyric numbers write an ode on
> His mistress eating a black pudden ;
> *   *   *   *   *   *
>
> *   *   *   *   *   *
>
> His sonnet charmed th' attentive crow'd,
> By wide-mouth'd mortal troll'd aloud,
> That circl'd with the long-ear'd guest,
> Like Orpheu's lock'd among the beasts.

* Settle.

N

A carman's horse could not pass by,
But stood tied up to poetry :
No porter's burden passed along,
But serv'd for burden to his song.
Each window like a pill'ry appears,
With heads thrust through, nailed by the ears :
All trades run in as to the sight
Of monsters, on their dear delight
The gallow-tree, when cutting purse
Breeds business for heroic verse,
Which none does hear but would have hung
T' have been the theme of such a song.

Doubtless the man possessed some merit; for one thing is certain, that from the year 1691 to 1708, he was employed by the city of London to invent pageants for Lord Mayor's day. The pageant of 1708 was not exhibited, in consequence of the death of prince George of Denmark, the husband of queen Anne, who died on the 21st of October. After this year, poor Elkanah's talents were no longer required, he being the last of the poet laureates of the city of London.

The singularity in the date of Elkanah's birth requires a little explanation. It was not until a comparatively recent period, that the beginning of the year was subject to any general rule. Christmas-day, the first of January, day of the Conception, the 25th of March, and Easter-day have all been used, at various times. Pope Gregory XIII. on reforming the calendar in 1582, ordered it to begin henceforth on the first of January. In France and England the same practice commenced about the same time; but in the latter country, it was not until 1752, that legal writs and instruments ceased to consider the 25th of March as the beginning of the year. This plan was found exceedingly inconvenient; for when it was necessary to express a date between the first of January, which was the commencement of the historical year, and the 25th of March which opened the legal year, error and confusion was sure to occur, unless given in the awkward fashion seen in the date of his birth, meaning 1647 historical, or 1648 legal year*

Dunstaple at an early period was famous in the annals of Puritanism, this will partly account for the peculiar opinions of Elkanah Settle, noticed in another place. This fact may be accounted for in various ways; but principally it may be traced to the prophesyings in the reign of Elizabeth, and the active part taken by the people of Bedfordshire, Huntingdonshire and Cambridgeshire against Charles in the civil war; they were united by a league, known in history as the "Eastern Association," and rendered important service to the parliamentarians. The prophesyings were meetings of clergymen, held in various parishes at stated intervals, under the sanction of certain of the bishops, for the purpose of prayer and expounding of the Scriptures; they did not always confine themselves to these subjects, but frequently attacked the discipline of the church: such synods were held in the Dunstaple church for a long period, till the peremptory mandate of Elizabeth to archbishop Grindal commanded that they should cease throughout his diocese. Al-

---

* For a list of his pageants, the reader is referred to the works of the Percy Society.

though Elkanah received his education in Dunstaple at an early period of his life, he removed to London, and there passed his days in penury, writing those poems which have gained for him no enviable notoriety, and have long since been consigned to oblivion. It is well known that in his time the system of writing dedications to some great man, abounding with the most fulsome flattery, was the universal practice amongst authors.

Each dedication was understood to have its price, varying from five guineas to a hundred and upwards, according as it was a poem, play, or history : that is, the man to whom it was dedicated rewarded the author with a present, in return for the honour of receiving a dedication. Some of the most needy authors received more for their dedications than they did by the sale of their works. Elkanah turned this system to a singular and not very scrupulous use. It was his custom to write an epithalmium, poem, ode or play, &c., and to affix a most sickening dedication, with *blanks* for the name of the person to whom it was dedicated, when in want of money, he carefully inserted with his pen the name of some nobleman, and sent him a copy ; the bait took, and the dishonest poetry frequently received large sums for an imaginary dedication, the dupe not detecting the fraud, and supposing the whole edition was dedicated to him. The above fact is recorded in " Disraeli's Curiosities of Literature, Vol. 1." The name Elkanah is suggestive. The following remarks with reference to this, occur in "Wilke's Boswell's Life of Johnson." He said, " The last city poet was Elkanah Settle. There is something in names which one cannot help feeling. Now Elkanah Settle sounds so queer, who can expect much from that name? We should have no hesitation to give it for John Dryden in preference to Elkanah Settle, from the names only, without knowing their different merits."

Another curious fact connected with the reign of Charles II., was, that tradesmen were allowed to coin money for the accommodation of their business: and the tradesmen of Dunstaple, unwilling to lose any of the advantages possessed by their neighbours, availed themselves of the privilege by issuing copper and brass money.

One bearing the inscription, "William Chew's half-penny," was struck in the year 1667, so we learn on the one side, while the reverse has "Dunstaple halfpenny." Here we have a direct proof that a currency was actually struck for his own accommodation, and that of his customers. But the next taken is far more interesting: the legend is "Daniel Fossey, at Dunstable, 1638, his half-penny, D. F." Daniel does not feel disposed to tell us the situation of his residence, or the nature of his occupation, at least not in so many words; but if we turn the token we learn it, quite as intelligibly, by his placing on the reverse of the coin, a greyhound courrent carrying a hare in its mouth, and two tobacco pipes crossing above with a roll of pig-tail below,—thus indicating to those whom it might concern, where an evening might be convivially spent, and a quiet pipe of the best tobacco enjoyed.

The third is one of brass, with a figure in

armour : in the centre is the name William
Element : *rev.*—in Dunstaple, E. W. E.

Admiral Smith, who had an opportunity of
examining a large number of tradesmen's tokens,
says, " It is a curious fact, that there is no instance of a double christian name on any of the
Bedfordshire tokens."

Obv.—WILLIAM FOSSEY, in the Field, a Swan.
Rev.—IN DUNSTAPLE, 1667, a Bunch of Flowers, W. F.
Obv.—DANIEL FINCH, with his Coat of Arms in centre.
Rev.—IN DUNSTAPLE, 1668. F. D. S.

Among the poems which the author of Hudi-
bras is said to have left in the possession of Mr.
Longueville, and which were published in 1759,
though many of them are considered spurious,
reference is made to certain parts of the legend
of Dun, with which doubtless he became acquainted
during his residence with Sir William Luke, a
well-known covenanteer and Puritan, who was
colonel in the parliamentary army, and scout-
master general in the county of Bedford. Though
Buller himself was most orthodox, both in his
religion and loyalty. The whole neighbourhood
from Hockley-i-th-hole to St. Albans, was well
known to the great poet. The following is the
quotation referred to :—

> " Near Dunstaple, upon the Down,
> There stands an ale-house, and but one ;
> Not far from hence, if we may credit
> Some ancient authors that have said it,
> Erst dwelt, to make the story brief,
> Old Dun, that memorable thief :
> Within a hollow, under-ground,
> Apartments still are to be found, ·
> Where both himself and horse retreated,
> And still all hues and cries defeated."

I am aware that the above lines have been used as an evidence on one side, in proof that the name Dunstaple is derived from Dun, the robber; and Butler is supposed to have been in possession of information we cannot now obtain. I think both suppositions wrong, after having carefully read Butler.

Among the lesser antiquities of the town, that which was erected in West street, and remained for many years a terror to evil-doers, is thus graphically described by Butler :—

Part 1. *Canto* 2, *Line* 1130.

" An ancient castle that commands
Th' adjacent parts; in all the fabric
You shall not see one stone nor brick
But all of wood by powerful spell
Of magic made impregnable.
There's neither iron-bar nor gate,
Portcullis, chain, nor bolt, nor grate,
And yet men durance there abide,
In dungeon scarce three inches wide;
With roof so low, that under it
They never stand, but lie or sit;
And yet so foul, that whoso's in,
Is to the middle-leg in prison;
In circle magical confin'd,
With walls of subtle air and wind,
Which none are able to break thorough,
Until they're freed by head of borough.

The last representative of a degenerated race, which seemed to have a prescriptive right to occupy this stronghold, was Thomas Roberts, who sat in the stocks for hours, through committing misdemeanors by getting drunk and using abusive language. It is asserted he was excited through some oppression, as it was generally for attacks

upon the same person.   Subsequently they went
into disuse, and in the same year the new cage
was built, they were entirely taken down.

Then we have his description of the whipping
post, which generally was near neighbour to the
former.

> " At th' outward wall, near which there stands
> A bastile, built to imprison hands ;
> By strange enchantment made to fetter
> The lesser parts, and free the greater ;
> For though the body may creep through,
> The hands in grate are fast enough :
> And when a circle 'bout the wrist
> Is made by beadle exorcist,
> The body feels the spur and switch,
> As if 'twere ridden post by witch
> At twenty miles an hour pace."

Then we have the following lines in praise of
the practice of whipping :

> " Whipping, that's virtues governess,
> Tut'ress of arts and sciences ;
> That mends the gross mistakes of nature,
> And puts new life into dull matter ;
> That lays foundation for renown,
> And all the honours of the gown.
> This suffered, they are set at large
> And freed with hon'rable discharge.
> Then in their robes and penetentials,
> Are straight presented with credentials ;
> And in their way attended on
> By magistrates of every town :
> And all respects and charges paid,
> There to their ancient seats conveyed."

Whether William Placeham found the advantages thus described, I am unable to say, but one
is certain, he was the last boy that was flogged
at the old stocks, in front of the Alms-houses in

Pub.d by J. Tibbett,   High Str. Dunstable.

N. TODD. Sc.

OLD   BAPTIST   CHAPEL.

West-street, his offence being that of stealing apples: and Thomas Richardson on being affixed to the Red Lion sign-post, was made to smart under the lictor's rod for deserting his family. Subsequently the public infliction of such summary punishments went into disuse, and the posts and stocks were removed.

The thread of our narrative must now take a different turn, by which we shall cease to wonder at the intolerant measures of Charles II., when we find it so little understood in private life. As a proof of this, I give the following, copied from the tablet in the church. It is a remarkable bequest of one Strange by name, but stranger still by nature. It is as follows:—" William Strange, by will, dated 7th of June, 1664, gave a messuage and lands in Houghton, yearly rent of £10, for the use of the poor of this parish (Dunstaple), aged, impotent, weak, sickly, poor housekeepers and others, who frequent God's ordinances and Divine worship, and not Quakers or common beggars; to be paid on St. Thomas's-day." The same is duly observed; for the town crier to this day goes round the town at the time appointed, and publicly announces with a stentorian voice and the ringing of his bell, that the gift is for church people only.

Little did the short-sighted man suppose that the poor despised Quaker would one day become the principal banker in the town, and the only one to stand his ground under severe pressure.

Dunstable appears to have been the place to which the Society of Friends repaired from the neighbouring towns, for worship, until the year

o

1799. Their meeting-house was in West-street;
it with the burial ground attached has now become
the property of Mr. Darby, butcher. No vestige
of the old building remains, and the grave-yard
is desecrated by the tramp of cattle, and the blood
of slaughtered animals destined to become the
food of man.

In the year 1673, some of the followers of John
Bunyan removed from Bedford into the neighbouring village of Kensworth, and open-air meetings were held in the "Dell-hole," under the
pastorate of Mr. Hayward. In 1708, a piece of
ground was purchased, and a building erected
at a cost of £40 in a part of the field called St. Mary
Overs. The first minister settled amongst them
in Dunstaple, was a hedge-cutter, of the name of
Brittain, whose income averaged eight shillings
per week. He appears to have continued with
them, till the 11th of February, 1754, and was
buried in the ground adjoining. This meeting
was considered the central point of all the Baptists
in the neighbourhood; here they assembled from
Tring, St. Albans, and Kensworth once a month,
to break bread, and the minister preached in each
of the foregoing towns in succession on the Sabbath day, and the fourth at home.

The building was enlarged in 1807, while Mr.
Hughes was pastor, and became as large again as
it was before; it had now a double roof.

Three times has the church divided, and the
offshoot, like a will-o-th'-wisp, having given a
short bewildering light, spent itself out, one only
has come down to the present time. Thus the
church which began in a dispute between two

brothers, has discovered the truth, that schism is her sin, and schism is her punishment.

During a violent storm on a Sunday afternoon, in 1849, part of the roof fell in, endangering the lives of the worshippers. It thus became necessary to pull down the entire structure, when the present building was completed during the same year, at a cost of £500.

There are monumental stones erected to several of the pastors, in the burial ground, and a neat marble tablet to another, under the west gallery. There is one altar tomb: the oldest stone bears the date of 1740, and one stone is remarkable for bearing inscriptions on both sides, which are now scarcely legible.

There is a small Sabbath-school in connexion; its present pastor is Mr. Carpenter; the building is calculated to hold 400 people.

Butler's lines aptly describes the state of things we have been describing :—

Part 1, *Canto* 1, *Line* 503.

Whate'er men speak by this new light,
Still they are sure to be i-th' right.
'Tis a dark lantern of the sprit,
Which none see but those who bear it;
A light that fell down from on high,
For spiritual trades to cozen by :
An ignis fatius that bewitches,
And leads men into pools and ditches.

Within the year 1713, Mrs. Blandianna, daughter of John Marshe, Esq., founded and endowed within the parish, a lodge for harbouring therein six poor maiden gentlewomen, descended from reputable parents, and members of the church of

England; they must be above forty years of age, and possess a private income of £30 a-year, independent of the sum they receive from the foundation. This lodge is in Kingsburie, and in the benefaction of which, she received the assistance of another lady, so that the annual income is nearly £180 per annum.

Blandianna died unmarried on the 21st of December, 1741, having left several charities for the benefit of the minister, and poor of this and several other towns and parishes in the county of Bedford.

About this time stage coaches began to run, and then revived the " deeds of olden time." A numerous gang of desperate robbers infested the town and its vicinity, and committed the most daring robberies and shocking murders. Private carriages could not pass through the town without having an armed servant to ride before, and on each side a horseman well supplied with arms and ammunition, as well as a formidable weapon in the sword case. Numbers of human skeletons have of late years been discovered by workmen while digging in the earth, and the manner in which they appear to have been crushed into holes, clearly shows the violence and gloominess of their end. Many stories of this horde are still repeated by old people that have heard them from persons then living. The following are literal facts :—

A reward was offered for the apprehension of one of them who had made himself notorious by his depredations; and it was rumoured that he was at a public house in the neighbourhood, to which, at night they frequently resorted. Influenced by the reward, two of the inhabitants entered the house for the purpose of securing him, when the servant girl blew out the light to favour his escape, but at the same moment, one of the men seized and held him with a strong grasp. The attempt was fatal, the robber plunged a dagger to his heart, he uttered a scream of terror and agony, staggered a few paces, and fell dead. Lights were speedily procured, and numbers rushed in to behold the scene of murder. While they were still gazing on the pale and bloody corpse, they were struck with fear and horror on beholding the murderer at the door; with a stern voice he exclaimed, "Who have I stabbed?" on being told who it was, he replied, "I am sorry for it, he was not the man." He immediately disappeared, no one being hardy enough to take him.

A young man who called himself a horse dealer, took up his abode at Dunstaple, and possessing a genteel appearance, he soon engaged the affections of a female of respectability, the attachment was mutual, and they were soon married; but his profession continually rendered it necessary for him to be absent during the greater part of the night, which at length excited her fears and suspicions. For a long time, tears and entreaties were ineffectual to extract from him the real cause of his absenting himself at such unseasonable hours, but at length he disclosed to her the melancholy truth, that her apprehensions were too well founded, he was what she dreaded to hear, a robber. In vain did he strive to soothe her fears, tenderness served but to wound her more, and a reward being set upon his head, her life was sealed with anguish and misery. Still he braved the death that threatened him, and his nightly visits were marked with all the agony and affection which fear and danger always so much increase. The weight on her heart was intolerable, and she endeavoured to obtain some relief by disclosing the secret to a female friend; that friend, with cruel duplicity, abused the confidence reposed in her. At midnight, he was torn from her arms, and shortly after, tried, condemned, and executed. The chords were broken, reason never returned, for many years she wandered about the neighbourhood sad and melancholy, the expression of her pale and wasted countenance excited pity and regret in all that beheld her; at midnight she never slept, but with watchful and anxious expectation looked for her husband till she died.

The last case occurred just at the outside of the town near where the railway station now is. The small inn referred to, is generally believed to be the one formerly standing opposite the Bull close. The tale is no fiction; the circumstances of the ring and ducats, for which twenty guineas were asked, actually took place; the silversmith subsequently became one of the leading men in London, and his name was mentioned to the writer, but prudence still forbids it being made public.

The desolate range of chalk hills, just beyond Dunstaple, seems, from a very early period, to have been a kind of " land-debateable," of honest men and rogues. From those days, when the toiling monk, seated in his desk, in the sunny oriel, set about inditing every particular which his wonder-loving contemporaries detailed to him, to those matter-of-fact times, when the "penny-per-liner," in his Grub-street attic, manufactured "horrid murders," and "highway robberies," for the delectation of the readers of the Flying Post and Daily Courant, was this warfare, in which, as generally happens, the rogues had the best of it, there carried on. But as might well be expected, the tales of the monkish chronicler far exceed, in picturesque interest, those of the Grub-street wonder-maker. The picture of the bold band of outlaws, issuing from their leafy coverts among the Buckinghamshire woods, and attacking the rear guard of the king's household, as, with their heavily laden wains, they journied along at the rate of three miles an hour, towards the palace of Dunstaple, possesses far more of the romantic, than the account of "the fair complexioned young man, with brown Ramilies wig and suit of light chocolate, who, attended by six men, did, on the night of the 17th instant, set upon the York Dispatch, and did take from thence all the trunks, mails, and baggage, shooting the coachman dead upon the spot, and grievously wounded two gentlemen, whose names we forbear at the present to mention."

Rather more than one hundred years ago, a singular occurrence on this "land debateable" took place, the particulars of which we will now proceed to relate to our readers.

It was autumn, and evening was just setting

in, when a horseman stopped at the small inn
that stood at the extreme margin of this celebrated
part of the Northern Road ; and, ere the landlord
was aware of the presence of a guest, he had dismounted, and entered the bar.

" A cold and bad night, coming on your
honour," said Boniface, with one of his lowest
bows ; for, partly by the fading light, and partly
by the cheerful blaze of the large fire, he had
already discovered that the cloak in which the
stranger was wrapt was of the finest scarlet cloth,
and that the narrow gold lace that edged the
three-cornered hat was no counterfeit, but the
genuine manufacture of Little Britain. Satisfied
therefore, that the stranger must have " money
in his purse," he proceeded to suggest the propriety of preparing a warm posset for the master,
and a feed of corn for the horse.

" No, no, master landlord," said the stranger,
" a draught of your best ale will do ; I've some
miles to ride to night."

"Surely your honour can never think of crossing
the hill," cried Boniface ; " 'tis perilous, indeed,
and night coming on."

" Alack, sir, interposed the hostess, " 'tis indeed a sad night—it will rain, your honour, and
perhaps snow. Farmer Gubbins' lad this time
last year, went out to seek some sheep, on just
such a night, and he was found next morning,
your honour, stiff, quite stiff."

" But, good dame," replied the stranger, laugh-
ing ; he had but two legs to help him, and I
have four."

" Ay, sir, but the road is desperately bad ;"

persisted the landlady, determined to make a bold stroke for a guest.

"And truly, your honour," responded the landlord, taking up the cue, "a gentleman's coach and six broke down, near the top of the hill, though three boys were scotching the wheels; there is a great pit-fall, too, out yonder."

"But, good man, you forget the moon that is to rise in half an hour;" said the stranger, and he drew from his pocket a huge, gold repeater, of almost the size and shape of a turnip.

"Your honour had better be cautious;" whispered the landlady, pointing to the adjoining kitchen, where several rustics were sitting.

The stranger laughed at her praiseworthy caution. "Nay, good woman, I have no fear of highwaymen."

"Heaven grant your honour may meet none! —but your honour had better stay."

"I cannot, my good woman,—I leave England to morrow; so be quick."

"Then your honour will go on?" said the landlord, bringing the pewter tankard, and the long stemmed glass. "But I trust," he continued, lowering his voice, and looking oracular —"you carry but little about you."

"Naught but what I can well afford to lose," replied the traveller, with a careless laugh, and a slap on his waistcoat pocket.

A deep, but suppressed sigh seemed to form an echo to these words; and the traveller looked toward the kitchen from whence it appeared to proceed; the rustics, however, who were discussing their ale, were in too merry a mood to allow

P

a sigh to escape them; but in the farther corner,
he perceived a well dressed young man sitting
thoughtfully, with his arms folded on his breast.

"Please your honour, gie us summut to drink
your honour's health;" said one of the rustics,
coming forward, and making his very lowest bow.

"Well, my lad," replied the good-humoured
stranger, "I don't care if I give you a Queen
Anne's half-crown, to drink confusion to all Pre-
tenders and Jacobite plots; for they do sore
damage to our London trade—so here it is, and
much good may it do you."

Not stopping to receive the vociferous thanks
of the delighted rustics, the traveller threw down
his reckoning, wrapt his scarlet rocquelaure closely
round him, and proceeded to remount his good
steed. "Farewell, master landlord:" said he,
"I have never yet met a highwayman, and 'twill
be strange if I do to night."

Onward rode our cavalier, not heeding the
coming darkness—perchance he was bent on some
expedition of high emprize—perchance wrapt in
sweet musings on his lady. Alas! romance-
loving reader—the age of chivalry had long passed
away: it was the era of Dutch taste, and of French
poetry—the prosing, matter-of fact, earlier half
of the 18th century—the year 1720. And well
fitted for the age was our hero. He was no
knight, pricking forth in search of adventures,
but Mr. James Clementson, the 'substantial'
Hamburgh merchant of Mincing lane: his
thoughts most probably engaged upon his bales
of merchandize, or, if a female name arose to his
tender recollections, amid the softening influences

of ' the twilight hour,' it was that of ' De vrow Johanna' the gallant barque which, on the morrow, was to convey him far beyond the pleasant chime of Bow-bells. Well, onward rode Mr. Clementson, looking and steering due southward. But what was that light echo, which followed each almost noiseless tread of Strawberry's hoofs on the soft chalky road? He looked back, and perceived a well-mounted horseman making directly towards him. Flight was vain, for the middle of that road had scarced been reached, and his pursuer was gaining fast upon him. A "highwayman, truly!" said he; "it is well I have pistols for him."

The well mounted pursuer soon drew up close behind him. "I have a request, sir, which you must not refuse;" said he, in a low and hurried tone.

Mr. Clementson recognised in his pursuer the young man whom he had just before seen seated in the inn kitchen; and struck with his bewildered air, and the irresolute tone in which he addressed him, his curiosity now almost superseded anger. "What is this the new method of saying "stand and deliver?" said he.

" I have a ring, sir," replied the other, endeavouring by a violent effort to suppress his agitation, and extending a ring with the left hand, while the other grasped a pistol; " and for this ring I must have twenty guineas."

" This is a bad trade," said Mr. Clementson, sternly; at the same time eyeing the highwayman with a feeling of interest he could not resist;

"here's my purse: off with you, and seek a more
honest livelihood."

The young man put back the proffered purse:
"No, take the ring, pray you, and give me
twenty guineas; lend, lend it me, I pray—only
twenty guineas."

"A strange highwayman!" muttered Mr.
Clementson, again surveying the supposed robber
with a degree of interest for which he could not
account. "Well then," said he, counting out
the twenty guineas, "mayhap trouble may have
brought you to this; but be warned by me, and
seek out a honest calling: so, give me the ring,
and away."

The stranger eagerly snatched the gold, faintly
articulating, "Heaven bless you!" and Mr.
Clementson, not sorry to escape so easily from
his first encounter with a highwayman, spurred
Strawberry onward, first casting a look behind.
There sat the young man, motionless on his horse,
the hand which had been so eagerly stretched
forth to secure the golden treasure still half held
out, and his eyes, with a wild and sorrowful expression, fixed vacantly on the lowering sky.
"Poor fellow!" ejaculated the kind-hearted
merchant, "I should like to know what hath
brought him to this." He now examined the
ring for which he paid so high a price: it was of
plain gold, with a good sized mocha stone, evidently not worth much above a pound; but with
no inscription, or crest, or initials, or anything
that might lead to a discovery of its late owner.
Although baffled and disappointed in this, he
determined to keep the ring as a memorial of his

first encounter with a highwayman ; and no other event befalling him on his journey, the next day saw Mr. Clementson set sail from the shores of England.

We must now request the kind reader to exert that plastic faculty which enables him to " put a girdle round the earth in full ten minutes," and to review the changeful events of a long and busy life in an hour ; for we must overleap ten years, and take our standing on Ludgate hill, on a fine October morning, where we shall again meet our worthy friend Mr. Clementson. Just returned from his sojourn abroad, he is taking a quiet stroll through London streets, marking the various changes that have taken place during his ten years' absence. And many, as may be well supposed, were the changes he noted—many an old name removed from beneath the well-remembered sign, and many a young tradesman, sprucely dressed with laced cravat and ruffles, occupying that post of honour, in the shop or in the counting-house, where the old gentleman, in his flowered morning gown and velvet cap, erewhile stood, placidly summing up his gains, and keeping a sharp look-out over his sons and apprentices. The ten o'clock bell, at length, warned Mr. Clementson of the time for his accustomed lunch, and he turned into the London coffee-house. One minute, however, he stopped at the door, regardless of the bowing waiters, for the splendid show of plate that graced the windows of the opposite silversmith's shop absolutely dazzled him : he looked up to the sign :—a mermaiden freshly gilt, upon whose bright mirror, which, according to old established belief, she held in her left hand, appeared the name of "Ellersby." "Ah! so it is:" ejaculated the merchant, musingly; "poor Master Hayward gone to his long home! But who is this Ellersby?"

"What, my old friend Clementson! cried a voice at his ear." He turned quickly round, and recognised one of "the old familiar faces" with which he had been long intimate before his sojourn abroad,—Mr. Cooper, the silkmercer of the Black-amoor's Head, in Cheapside. Friendly greetings passed between the pair, and they proceeded to the little private parlour to discuss their pint of Madeira.

"And so poor Hayward is gone" said the merchant, "and yet he could not have been so very old."

"Master Hayward is alive and well: he has retired from business to his house at Shacklewell, for he leaves it in excellent hands. Ah! 'tis nine or ten years since you left England, else you would have heard of Henry Ellersby. A lucky young fellow is he, for the day after to-morrow he is to marry his master's daughter."

"Lucky indeed!" responded Mr. Clementson, "for Hayward hath doubtless made many a thousand, and there are only, I remember, his two daughters, Chloe and Betty, to share his fortune: then this Ellersby was his apprentice?"

"He was," replied the mercer, "and such an apprentice! 'Tis said he is come of a good family though he never took upon him about it. It is Mistress Chloe that he is to marry—I sold her twelve yards of white ducape but last week for the wedding dress."

Two or three other neighbouring tradesmen now came in, each, like the mercer, brim-ful of the praises of the fortunate apprentice. Indeed, eulogies upon Henry Ellersby, and anticipations of his happiness, seemed to supersede every other topic. The never-failing subject of Jacobite plots, abuse or commendation of the Walpole administration, the menacing aspect of affairs in the Spanish Main,—even city politics, and city news, were forced to give place to details of the handsome furniture purchased for the young couple, to a bill of fare of the wedding dinner, and a sharp dispute between the mercer and his neighbour, a draper, whether Mistress Chloe would wear with her bridal attire of white ducape, her Valenciennes lappets and ruffles, or her suit of Brussels lace.

"Well, I'll even go and take a peep at this lucky young fellow," said Mr. Clementson, resuming his three-cornered hat and gold-headed cane: "there must be somewhat very taking, methinks, about this Master Ellersby, since everybody speaks so highly of him."

Mr. Clementson crossed the way, and placed himself before one of the windows, poring admirably, as it seemed, on the tempting display of salvers, tankards, and chocolate pots, but keeping a close watch on the shop-door. His curiosity was not fated to remain long unsatisfied; for an interesting young man, extremely well-dressed, came to the door, and having beckoned a carriage that stood a short distance off, handed two ladies

into it, and then, with a gentlemanly bow, retired. "Is *that* Mr. Ellersby?" cried the merchant, scarcely conscious to whom he addressed
the question.

"Ay, that it is,—Heaven's blessings on him!
said an old woman who stood just beside, with a
basket of ground ivy: "Yes, 'tis good Mr. Ellersby, the charitablest, worthiest, and most
religiousest gentleman in London.

"The rascal!" muttered Mr. Clementson, with
a tremendous thump of his gold-headed stick,
"the very rascal who cheated me out of twenty
guineas, and gave me that paltry ring! Here's
a world for you! The poor rogue gets hanged,
and the rich one laughs at him. Well, my fair
sir, you shall have good cause to remember, ere
long, the Dunstaple road!" Thus saying, he
paced onward, scarce knowing which way he
went, turning over in his mind twenty different
plans by which he proposed to drag successful
villany to light, and uttering splendid tirades
against wealthy knaves, which might have thrown
a political union into paroxysms of delight. The
more violent the grief, it is said, the sooner it
will come to an end; and the same may be said
of anger. In a short time, wonder, and curiosity,
and doubt succeeded. This young man must
even at that very time have been an apprentice
to Master Hayward;—what therefore more unlikely than that he should have been permitted
to absent himself from his master's house for so
long? and what, too, more unlikely than that a
sober young man of good family should either
have stood in need of comparatively so small a

sum, or taken that course to obtain it? Many stories, well-authenticated ones, had been told of personal resemblance being so strong, than even intimate friends had been, for a moment deceived. Might not this be the case here? Still, while allowing, and even willing to allow, the full weight of these doubts, the conviction that Henry Ellersby, the silversmith of Ludgate-hill, was the highwayman in the encounter on the Dunstaple road, returned with overmastering force to Mr. Clementson's mind. But this conviction was now associated with many mitigating circumstances. Although proffered the full purse, the young man resolutely refused to take more than the twenty guineas, while even that he would not receive without the exchange of his ring; and then arose vividly to his recollection, the motionless attitude, the half-extended arm of the young man, when he last saw him on the darkening road, and that look of wild and fixed despair which he cast on the lowering sky.

Hours passed away ere Mr. Clementson could satisfy himself as to what course he should adopt, and the bells had now chimed four. The hitherto crowded streets were beginning to be deserted, both by belles in brocade, and thrifty housewives in calimanco, all homeward bound to refresh themselves with their early cup of bohea, when Mr. Clementson again found himself before the door of the Mermaid. He looked into the shop, now empty, and took a close view of its master, who was standing apparently looking over the ledger. "It must be he," said the merchant, and entering he asked for Mr. Ellersby.

Q

The genteel, interesting young man came forward, and respectfully inquired the wishes of his new customer.

"I have been many years abroad, Mr. Ellersby," said the merchant, "and I have some foreign money which I would wish to sell for old gold and silver." The young man bowed assent, and requested his customer to walk farther in. Mr. Clementson drew a Dutch ducat from his purse, and threw it on the counter. "I must have *twenty guineas* for this," said he.

"Twenty guineas!" cried the silversmith, in uncontrolable surprise.

"Yes, twenty guineas," said Mr. Clementson, firmly.

"Good sir, what can you mean? it is scarcely worth ten shillings!"

"Very likely, Mr. Ellersby, very likely; very likely; but what say you to *this?*" and he removed the glove from his hand; "Ten years since I paid twenty guineas for this very ring."

The young man clasped his hands in agony.—"You did sir, you did? and principal and interest both are at your service. But O, sir, spare me—no, not me, but the worthy family that know not of this my only crime!"

"This seems a strange affair;" said Mr. Clementson, much moved at the extreme agitation of the young man: "yet do not distress yourself, but tell me how it came to pass that on that *one* evening, you came to lay aside an honest and respectable calling to enact the highwayman on the Dunstaple road?"

"I will tell you sir, for you have a right to

know all," returned the young man, glancing a hurried look around him ; "but,—but—Mr. Hayward is now in the counting house: might I ask so great a favour, as that you would call on me any time in the evening? The money I have at hand, and I will instantly count it out to you."

" I will call on you an hour or two hence," replied Mr. Clementson. " In the meantime be not cast down ; your secret will be safe with me ; and loath indeed should I be to disturb Master Hayward's good opinion of you ; so farewell !"

The kind-hearted merchant returned to the opposite coffee-house, and sought to beguile the time by turning over a file of newspapers, when the following advertisement struck his eye. " If the gentleman drest in a scarlet roquelaure, and mounted on a strawberry horse, who, on the night of the 14th of October, 1720, met a young man near Dunstaple, and received from him a gold ring with a mocha stone, will call upon Dr. Calamy, in Charterhouse-square,* his loan, with the interest thereon, will be repaid with many thanks." Surprised and delighted at this additional proof that the good opinion which he could not help forming of the young silversmith, was well founded, Mr. Clementson turned over the other papers, and found the same advertisement iterated, and re-iterated. " Poor fellow, poor fellow ! ejaculated he, " it must have been some strange thing indeed that forced him to this. Well, I know not how it is, but I feel greatly interested in him."

Punctual to his appointment, Mr. Clementson

---

* Minister of St. Mary's, Aldermanbury.

soon after knocked at the now closely-barred door
of the Mermaid, and was ushered into the counting-house; Mr. Ellersby soon after appeared, and
casting a suspicious look around, as though he
really believed the old proverb, 'walls have ears,'
counted out the money, which he placed before
his guest; while, in a low and agitated tone, he
said, "It appears, sir, that you have heard of my
good fortune. Alas! had any of my kind neighbours known half the sorrow I have suffered on
account of this my great crime, they would soon
have retracted their opinion of my happiness."

"Do not distress yourself any longer on this
account," said our merchant, kindly; "I have
seen your advertisements, and reference to a
worthy minister who, I am sure, would never
give his countenance to any one undeserving of
it; so proceed, I pray you: tell me what led to
it, and then let it be dismissed for ever from
your mind."

"I will, sir.—Through the great kindness of a
friend,—indeed, the only friend of my late
mother,—when my apprenticeship was half completed, I was transferred from a very incompetent
master, to the care of good Mr. Hayward. I had
been with him not more than a year, when I
received intelligence of the dangerous illness of
my mother, and I requested permission to go and
see her. Although he was on the eve of a
journey, he kindly consented, and, as he was
going by the Dispatch, he granted me the use of
his horse. Would that that kindness had never
been granted, for then I could not have followed
you! I soon arrived at Dunstaple, but it was

only to see my mother reduced so low as to be unable to leave her poor cottage, from whence the landlord daily threatened to eject her, on account of arrears of rent. Almost beside myself, with barely more money than would serve to carry me back again, I went to the landlord, a proud and a wealthy man ; but the only answer I received was, that she must remove on the morrow. Scarcely knowing what I did, I entered the inn kitchen, where I first saw you, and sat down to think,—but no, I could not think,—to lament over,—O, to curse this hard fate. Twelve pounds were owing for rent alone ; and where was I to raise them ? My mother's friend was dead—Mr. Hayward was on a long journey. To whom could I look, and look for aid by the *morrow ?* And then, when I revolved in my mind the scanty wardrobe, the wretched income of my poor mother, compared with her former condition, your merry laugh rung on my ear, and your well-filled purse glittered to my frenzied imagination like the delusive well-spring that mocks the thirst of the eastern traveller ; and then more maddening than all, when I heard you boast, proud and heartless as it seemed to be, that all that glittering treasure you could well afford to lose, the temptation overcame me—I rushed to the stable, saddled my swift-footed grey, and gallopped after you."

" And truly you were greatly tempted," said the kind-hearted merchant, " but proceed."

" Truly I was, sir ; and yet let no man say that he is *forced* to evil. Better thoughts arose in my mind, even while I was pursuing you ;

and once I had almost turned my horse's head and gone back!—but distrust prevailed: "Twenty guineas," said I, "will pay all, and leave my mother sufficient to carry her to London, yet how is it to be raised? I will not *be* the highwayman though I act his part, for I will give my ring as an acknowledgment that the money shall some day be paid." Miserable subterfuge! it could not disguise from my conscience even then, that I was a robber. But O! how bitterly did I feel that truth when the forbidden gold actually touched my hand, and this remembrance has haunted me through many an anxious day, and many a restless night. At length, after nearly three years of anxiety, I opened my mind to Dr. Calamy, on whose ministry we attended, and told him my fatal secret; but still, although from that time to this, I have caused advertisements to be inserted in the papers, I never received any intelligence. O! sir, I thank Heaven that I have at last seen you, for you know not the load of trouble that is now removed from my mind."

"Think no more of it from henceforth, Mr. Ellersby," cried Mr. Clementson; "I only regret that you did not make me acquainted with your circumstances, for the purse and all its contents should have been at your service. So your mother was of a good family you say? What, did she marry contrary to their wishes? Alas! I have great reason to lament that such things are sometimes scarcely forgiven."

"It was so, sir; my mother so greatly offended my grandfather by her marriage, that even after my father's death, and when she was reduced to very great distress, he absolutely forbade her even to cross the threshold of Mickleham Hall."

" Of Mickleham Hall ! her name then was—"

" Mary Clementson," returned the young man with a sigh.

" O, my nephew !—my only nephew !" cried the merchant overjoyed ; only three days since I returned to Old England, wealthy indeed ! but sad at heart, for methought I had no relation in the wide world wherewith to share it. Thank Heaven ! to-day I have found a relation a son of my dear sister, Mary Clementson. This is the happiest day of my life, ay, the happiest, my own nephew ; for old James Clementson has found a staff for his age, and an heir to his fortune, in his dear sister's son, Henry Ellersby."

As early as 1712, the subject of public education seems to have occupied the minds of Mrs. Frances Ashton, Mrs. Jane Cart, and Mr. Thomas Aynscomb. By two indentures, bearing the dates of 1724 and 1727, the Free School is endowed with lands in Caddington, Luton, Houghton Regis, Flamstead, Totternhoe, and Whipsnade.

Frances Ashton was sister to Jane Cart. Her gift is dated 1727, and consisted of a farm and malthouse, containing about 116 acres, lying within and about the township of Luton: some of these lands have been sold, and portions exchanged.

Jane Cart, in the same year, gave upon trust for the use of the same school, for teaching and clothing forty boys of the parish, and other charitable purposes of the same place. A farm lying at Cowridge, and containing 52A. 0R. 5P.; also

64A. OR. 39P.; part is situated in the township of Luton, and part in the hamlet of Limbury.

In 1701, the manors of Cawdwells, in Eddlesborough, was sold, together with the manors of Fitzhugh and Bowells to William Chew, of Dunstaple, who bequeathed them to trustees, for the support of the Free School in the town, and other charitable purposes: one of these farms contain 112 acres.

William Chew gave a third part of the endowment for the school, which according to the tablet in the church, consisted of £150 per annum.

The candidates to be eligible for admission must be seven years of age, capable of reading the New Testament, must have been born in wedlock, and his parents have been regular attendants at the parish church at least two years before admission on Whitsun Thursdays. Connected with this last requirement, I observed a candidate, son of a dissenter, placed regularly for the required period, on the end of a seat near the vestry, so as to form a conspicuous object to the view of the rector, in his movement to and from the robing-room. But one day, the brother all at once exclaimed, "Sir, we aint going to church any more: John got his clothes yesterday!" I need add no more—the fact speaks for itself. The present income of this charity is £330 per annum, £37 of which is expended in clothing of the boys, £60 as a salary given to the master, who also enjoys the privilege of increasing that amount, by taking boarders. This institution long held an honourable position among scholastic institutions, enjoyed the patronage of the wealthy

Endowed School, Dunstable.

all around, until the year 1837, when a change of master's took place.

Among the celebrated masters of this school we meet with William Gresham, whose hymns were used for a number of years in the church, and his musical compositions, especially the services, are yet the favourite music of several neighbouring choirs.

Mr. John Corfield, who has just left, was a diligent student in botany, and possessed some rare specimens in that science: and on resigning his charge, a handsome writing desk with the following inscription, on a silver plate, was presented to him:—

"Presented to Mr. John Corfield, by his late Pupils, in testimony of their gratitude and esteem, for his earnest and zealous labours, as Master of the Free School in this Town, during the last 19 years."
Dunstable, May 27th, 1856.

Seven trustees have the management of this charity; and in former times, when they visited the town officially, they were met by the town governors and populace at the "Half-Moon," when the horses being removed, and ropes attached to the carriage they were drawn into the town with every sign of rejoicing.

If a sufficient number of boys for the object of this, should not be found in the parish of Dunstaple, they may be taken from the parish of Kensworth, Eddlesborough, Houghton Regis and Luton.

Mrs. Ashton and Mrs. Cart each likewise left £16 a-year, for apprenticing a boy of the said school, and for setting him up in trade alternately.

R

The boys wear caps with red tassels, but if he loses a relative by death, he is furnished with a cap having a black tassel, for a certain period.

From the monuments in the church, we learn that Mrs. Jane Cart died in 1736, after having given a set of plate for the Holy Communion, and other elegant decorations to the church, and instituted the Lord's-day afternoon lecture, and left a distribution of bread weekly, and other benefactions to the town.

Frances Ashton, her sister, in addition to the almshouses and school, left £5 a year to be given away in two shillingworth's of bread every Sunday for ever.

The following extract is from the " Times."— Judgment by the Master of the Rolls, March 26th, 1859 :—

" In the year 1727, and before the passing of the Mortmain Acts, Mrs. Frances Ashton left certain property for the institution of two distinct charities,—the one being as far as material to the present issue, the establishment of almshouses for six poor women ; and the other the creation of a fund for thirty poor curates, and thirty widows of poor curates, to be approved by the trustees of the testator's bounty. The property left to each of these charities was distinct,—the almswomen, and the curates and their wives being endowed out of different estates. The Ashton trust had been settled in 1848, and since that time a sum of £6,000 had accrued under the estate left to the almshouses. The contention—friendly on all sides—before the court was, for whose benefit this sum should be applied, whether to increase the incomes of the six almswomen, or to swell the funds of the curates' charity; or in default of either of such appropriation, whether it might not be advantageously employed in the establishment of a school. The court has diligently considered all these suggestions, and looked upon the accretion of the £6,000, as a charitable fund unanticipated and undisposed of by the institutress of the charities specially created; and such being the case, the court would follow the salutary precedents bearing upon such a case, and decree the establishment of the school, as suggested. As the testatrix belonged to the Church of England, the school would be a Church of England school, to which however, the children of Dissenters would be admissible, on such terms as the court might hereafter approve."

Over the altar is a large and handsome picture of the last supper, painted by Sir James Thornhill, father-in-law to the celebrated Hogarth: it is similar to that in St. George's chapel, Windsor, painted by West,—exhibits Judas turned from the group toward the spectator, and possesses terrible malignity of expression. It was presented to the parish by the two sisters Cart and Ashton, in 1723, and intended to represent the circumstances recorded in the 13th chapter of St. John's Gospel.

Near the altar steps, lie the remains of two young ladies, whose names have been embalmed in poetry and prose, Mary and Elizabeth, daughters of the late Solomon Piggott, the rector.

Of the former, who died on the 29th of May, 1822, whether we look at her as the little girl with black silk spencer and white frock, climbing

the hills in Greenwich park, and anon diving into
the thickest woods, sitting under the umbrage of
venerable trees in the green room of Nature, as
Mary called it, and partaking of the rural repast
on the velvet sod; or as she advanced towards
maturity, in the study, among her favourite authors; or sat with her in the social circle, where
her sober wit was always ready at hand for use,
and put forth without hesitation : but it was wit
which never had a sting in it, it was wit that
pleased ; it was the sparkling of benevolence, the
expression of kindness and satisfaction. Or if
we visit the closing scene, and view her surrounded by weeping friends, in every case we
see exhibited the beauties of practical religion, as
the words drop from her lips, " Father, I wish I
was not so attached to the world, and my connection with it, but how can I help it ? I hope
the Lord will make me willing to leave it, when
it shall be his pleasure to call me." How beautiful the expression, for one so young ! Besides
the funeral sermon, a poem containing 57 eight-
line verses, was written in commemoration of
Mary, bearing the title "The Loves of Guardian
Angels."

Elizabeth died July 28th, 1827, aged 17 years,
and the commemoration sermon was from Job v.
26th; and a poem composed to her memory, containing upwards of 400 lines, supposed to be
written by her father, and may be read at length
in a work entitled " A Father's Recollections,"
published in 1831, by Longman.

I give the following extract as a specimen of
the whole :—

"Our Lizzy's sweet and heavenly mind
Was formed for that blest world of love :
She never spoke but what was kind,
She ever acted Noah's dove :*
The olive-branch of peace she bore,
To quell domestic strife or jar :
She peace proclaimed, and ever wore
The face of love, — she hated war.
A mind so peaceful and serene,
Was form'd not long for this rude earth,
Born for a milder, heavenly scene,
She to that place of second birth
Was early called by heavenly love,
To mingle with the blest above.
Methinks I see on Sabbath morn,
Our Lizzy in the Sunday School,
Teaching young beauties to adorn
Their minds with wisdom's brighter rules.
Methinks I see her lightsome feet
Tripping to neighbouring cot to greet,
With charity's sweet smile, the poor,
And bringing medicines to their door."

This young lady fell a victim to her affections·
It was her affectionate attention in nursing a
beloved brother, which brought on the fever, and
carried her off : she braved every danger for his
sake, she caught his fever, and ere she took to
her bed, presented her garments to her sister, as
if she knew she should never need them again.

---

* The expression contained in the fourth line has reference to the
following circumstance, thus recorded by the Rector, in his Diary :—
"Before my parsonage was finished, they removed me to a large house
on the margin of a sweeping river. For nearly a week after our removal, we were surrounded with a high swelling flood, which literally
insulated us from the neighbouring market town, and with which, all
the communication we had was by boats. I shall never forget the
pleasing calm I enjoyed, in the bosom of my family, with whom, I
seemed delightfully separated from a frowning world, by the rolling
billows. Dear Mary enjoyed it ; she said it was like Noah in the ark
with his family ; and regularly in our wave-encircled dwelling, the
morning and evening notes of prayer and praise ascended to Him whom
the winds and seas obeyed."

The relics of a third person also claims a passing notice, as being associated in every good word and work, with the above family,—I mean Miss Brown, the daughter of Frederick William Brown, Esq., of Dunstaple park. The death of this amiable and prudent young lady, at the age of 26 years, produced great sensation at the time amongst the young people of Dunstaple. She had grown up much beloved and respected by all who knew her, for her good sense, amiable manners, retired virtues, and correct taste, she was ever ready to give a helping hand to every good institution, and to send relief to the poor.

In an age of frivolity, thoughtlesness and vanity, when so many of the fair sex are hastening to scenes of dissipation, or wasting their days in reading worthless books, that vitiate the taste, weaken the judgment, pervert the imagination, unfit the mind for the sober duties of domestic life, and above all weaken religious principle, if not undermine the Christian system ; it is a high gratification to find that this young lady found her chief happiness in domestic scenes, in meditation, and in books of sterling sense, devotion and piety. Her example in this respect, should be inculcated upon the young; and may you, my beloved young friends, acquire her taste, and follow a similar path of thought and reflection. Be moderate in your lawful enjoyments,—be cautious what you read,—that they may be works of good sense and sterling piety,—and give some of your hours every day to devotion, and all your days to heaven—that if you are cut down like a flower, you may bloom in the paradise of God.

Many wept when they heard of the departure of a lady, whose sympathy and bounty they had so often felt; and the crowd that attended her funeral and listened with solemn attention to the sermon which followed, from Isaiah xl. 8, proved the respect which they bore toward her when living, and their affectionate remembrance of her; all which things cause the natives of this town to have strong feelings of interest in their own parish church. Venerable from extreme antiquity, and firm as the hills around it, it stands as a part of their native land, and to endure with the country to all ages.

It appeals moreover, to all their affections, by motives which penetrate the inmost heart; bring before the worshipper his birth, his domestic happiness and duty, the memory of departed friends and his own death. Within he sees that ancient font (which once was fixed to another part of the building), at which he was baptized; and the altar where he knelt at his marriage. Around it he contemplates the graves of his friends, and the spot that may one day be his own; and loves to talk of the time when the church-yard was much better wooded than it is now, and though unable to tell by whom those stately trees were planted, yet no such difficulty remains about their removal, for he tells with sorrow, that in 1783, a tree, forming one of a long row of beech was cut down in consequence of a large arm splitting off, and damaging the timber; and says, with a sigh, that this was only the forerunner of an entire clearance, which took place in 1811.

Various stone coffins, one with chalsee and

pattery, have been found by different persons
digging for stone, on the site of the ancient eastern part of the church.

In 1745, Mr. Willis informed the society of
Antiquarians, that at the east end of Dunstaple
church, about two feet under-ground and about
three feet from a side wall, with the feet close to
a cross-wall, was found a stone coffin; the. lid
was composed of four stones, the piece at the foot
was a separate one, the head, sides and bottom of
stone; under the head an eminence instead of a
pillow, in a hollow or niche, corresponding with
the head. The skeleton was entire, except the
ribs, which had fallen in. The head inclined to
the left; between the upper bone of the left arm
and the back-bone, was a glass urn, fallen down,
and the lid off, stained with deep brown on the
inner side of that part which lay over the stone.
About the feet were pieces of leather, very rotten,
which by holes pierced, appear to have been
sewed together.

Among the few objects of interest which now
adorn the church-yard, is a semi-Gothic tomb
erected to the memory of Kitty Crawley; a
wooden cross over the ashes of Philip Higgs;
and a subscription monument erected to the
memory of John Underwood, who was killed by
some means, not satisfactorily explained, on the
night of the 4th of November, 1855. The inscription is as follows:—

In Memory of John Underwood,
who Died November 4, 1855,
Aged 59 Years.

Struck by the shafts of death from hands unknown,

At length poor John is laid in hallowed ground:
The mind mysterious, which Almighty God,
In wisdom infinite did circumscribe;
And made him what the world an idiot calls,
Hath fled for ever to its heavenly home.
The rugged frame which veiled the immortal spirit
Hath paid its debt, and crumbles into dust:
But when that form uncooth, which fools despised
Shall rise again, all bright and glorious,
The image of its wise and great Redeemer;—
How many proud and learned of the earth
Shall wish poor John to take their place by thee.

The meadow adjoining, was bequeathed by Mr. Thomas Whitehead, in 1654, for the endowment of a school at Houghton, and producing in 1820, the sum of £50 per annum.

In the year 1723, we again meet with another instance of active benevolence, and Mrs. Cart is busily engaged in founding the Green Almshouses, for six poor widows, who are allowed 2s. 6d. weekly, with gown, petticoat, 3 pairs of stockings and shoes yearly, and a gift at Whitsuntide of £2 2s. 6d., and at Christmas £1 10s.

Those founded by Mrs. Ashton are called the "Blue." The inmates are six poor women, who receive 8s. per week. She also bequeathed land for the purpose of raising annually the sum of £6, to be paid to each of the poor women in her almshouses, to buy her a gown, firing and other necessaries: the residue, after deducting the expenses for repairs, to be divided in equal portions between the inmates. They now receive the same amount of clothing as the Green Almshouses.

As far as I have been able to ascertain, the earliest stage coach passed through Dunstaple to

s

Birmingham, a distance of 116 miles, and took three days, as is shewn by the following advertisement :—

" The Litchfield and Birmingham stage coach set out this morning (Monday, April 12th, 1742), from the Rose Inn, Holborn Bridge, London, and will be at the Angel, and Hen and Chickens, in the High Town, Birmingham, on Wednesday next, to dinner ; and goes the same afternoon to Litchfield. It returns to Birmingham on Thursday morning, to breakfast, and gets to London on Saturday night, and so will continue every week regularly, with good coach and able horses." Thus a whole week was occupied in a journey from London to Litchfield, by Birmingham. This appears to have been the only stage coach for a considerable period passing through Dunstaple ; and one Thomas Laurence, who died at the age of 100 years, said, that when it passed through the town, after dark, men walked in front carrying lanterns : the utmost speed allowed even for mails to travel, for the next forty years was not more than $6\frac{1}{2}$ miles per hour.

The difficulty of drawing coaches over Chalk-hill, even with the assistance of four additional horses, at three miles an-hour, afforded great facilities to numerous robbers, who after committing the depredations retreated to Eaton hassocks. This state of uncertainty, induced the commissioners to lay out £16,000 in purchasing and completing a new road round the base of the hill.

A man of Sewell, having been found guilty at the Bedford Assizes, of robbing the mail-coach upon the highway between Dunstaple and Chalk-hill, was hung in chains in the corner of that close, called "Gib close." After the flesh and skin had wasted off and nothing remained but the bones, a pair of starlings built their nest in the skull, and hatched their young; the brood became the property of a Mr. Peters, (a family well-known to Mr. Holmes, sen., still living in the town). Some of Peters' family migrated to Spittal-field, London, carrying a portion of the brood with them; and death subsequently carrying off those friendly birds, their skins were preserved and stuffed, and in that manner, are still to be seen. The post was destroyed by a party of wild Irish recruits, in 1803.

At one period, eighty stage coaches passed through the town daily; and the magnificent stud of greys (not a horse worth less than £40 each), kept at the Sugar Loaf, were the admiration of all the nobility, especially the royal dukes of York, Gloucester, and Clarence. Lord Byron was a visitor here, as well as Henry Braham, who led all England captive by his musical talents. Nor must we omit Daniel O'Connell, who assembled his political partizans and addressed them on his ideas how to remedy existing evils, finishing with his favourite couplet, which occurs in Lord Byron's magnificent poem, "Childe Harold:"

" Hereditary bondsmen know yet not
Who would be free himself must strike the blow."

Then the marquis of Waterford, under some disguise or another, would startle the fair damsels with his spring-heeled boots. So great was the prosperity at this time, that the waiter and chambermaid's perquisites at the "Sugar Loaf," were not less than £100 a-year each. This inn, together with the "Crown" nearly opposite, were not stage houses, but inns, for the use of the nobility and private families, paying an annual postage duty to government, varying from £500 to £600 a year.

During the American war, as many as one hundred soldiers have been billeted at these two inns at a time. Guests were obliged to retire, to make room for military men, who paid nothing for their beds, thus causing a loss of £300 a-year. At this period, that low building was erected, known as the "Sugar Loaf Tap," then called the "Soldier's House;" but the most grievous inconvenience felt in the town was during the erection of Weedon barracks, when the proprietor of the "Bull and Mouth" contracted for the removal of a large amount of military stores, to accomplish which, he hired all the rabble of London, who were billeted in the houses in the same manner as soldiers. Their dishonest and disorderly habits, obtained for them the name of "Newgate Blues."

During the coaching prosperity, the town of Dunstaple maintained its character with the epicure for its larks, which for size and richness of flavour are not equalled in the world. Multitudes of these delightful warblers were caught by labourers, with trammeling nets, and yearly sacrificed to pamper his unpitying appetite. The favourite morsel was deliciously cooked in fifteen minutes, by a peculiar and secret method, known only to Mr. Johnson, senr., and sent ready dressed in two-dozen tins, to all parts of England, Ireland, and Scotland. A regular book, known as the "lark book," contained the names of various noblemen, to whom supplies were regularly sent. The Queen Dowager was accustomed to receive them to the last. The store-room has been increased by twenty dozen in a single night. They are now dressed in perfection, only by the cook of the "Red Lion," to whom Mr. Johnson communicated the secret, in 1840.

Bingley in his "Animal Biology," says, "that as many as 4,000 dozen of larks, (*Aluda Arvensis,*) have been caught in the neighbourhood of Dunstaple, between September and February. It is pretended that these are all British birds, but our home-bred flocks are greatly augmented by arrivals from Northern Europe; hence that thin and emaciated condition in which at the early part of the season so many are found. After having recovered the effects of their migration, they fatten in a surprising manner, and if they escape the net, make their way back again to the continent, in the spring."

This state of things continued till 1836. In that year, the number of coaches had declined to 32, paying at Puddle-hill Gate, the week ending June 4th, 1836, £35 14s. The corresponding week, the following year, June 3rd, 1837, four coaches less were running, and the amount of tolls had sunk to £29 17s.; while on June 2nd, 1838, only twelve coaches remained, paying the sum of £12 1s. 6d. toll. Two days after that date, the last coach stopped.

Table of coaches and tolls at Puddle-hill Gate, for the week ending June 4th, 1836 :—

		£.	s.	d.
1	Estafetta - -	1	4	0
2	Rd Rover, Manchester	1	4	0
3	Defiance - -	1	4	0
4	Telegraph - -	1	4	0
5	Royal Bruce -	1	4	0
6	Bee Hive - -	1	4	0
7	Tartar - -	1	4	0
8	Umpire - - -	0	19	6
9	Red Rover Liverpool	1	1	0
10	Express Leeds -	1	4	0
11	Courier Leeds -	1	4	0
12	Wonder -	1	4	0
13	Independent Tallyho	1	4	0
14	Emerald - -	1	4	0
15	Real Tallyho -	1	4	0
16	Patent Tallyho -	1	4	0
		£18	**16**	**6**

		£.	s.	d.
	Brought forward...18	18	16	6
17	Crown Prince -	0	18	0
18	Rein Deer - -	1	4	0
19	Greyhound - -	1	4	0
20	Swallow - -	1	4	0
21	Defiance Birmingham	1	1	0
22	Hope - -	1	4	0
23	Times - -	1	4	0
24	Commercial - -	1	4	0
25	Northampton -	1	4	0
26	Leicester - -	1	4	0
27	Leighton and Woburn	0	9	0
28	Wellingborough -	0	9	0
29	Daventry and Rugby	0	9	0
30	Pickfords Vans -	2	2	0
31	Antelope - -	0	18	0
32	Chapman & Co's. Vans	0	19	6
		£35	**14**	**0**

Week ending June 3rd., 1837.

		£.	s.	d.
1	Estafetta - -	1	4	0
2	Rd Rover Manchester	1	4	0
3	Defiance - -	1	4	0
4	Telegraph - -	1	4	0
5	Royal Bruce -	1	4	0
6	Times - -	1	1	0
7	Rein Deer - -	1	4	0
8	Star - - -	1	4	0
9	Umpire - -	0	19	6
10	Red Rover Liverpool	1	1	0
11	Express Leeds -	0	19	6
12	Courier - -	0	19	6
13	Wonder - -	1	4	0
14	Independent Tallyho	1	4	0
		£15	**16**	**6**

		£.	s.	d.
	Brought forward...15	15	16	6
15	Emerald - -	1	4	0
16	Real Tallyho -	1	4	0
17	Ruby - -	1	4	0
18	Victoria - -	0	18	0
19	Greyhound - -	1	4	0
20	Hope - -	0	19	6
21	Hope - -	0	19	6
22	Commercial -	0	19	6
23	Northampton -	0	18	0
24	Leicester - -	0	18	0
25	Leighton and Woburn	0	9	0
26	Wellingborough -	0	9	0
27	Warwickshire Hunt	0	18	0
28	Pickfords Vans	1	16	0
		£29	**17**	**0**

Week ending June 3rd., 1838.

		£.	s.	d.
1	Rd Rover, Manchester	1	4	0
2	Defiance - -	1	4	0
3	Star Liverpool -	1	4	0
4	Express Leeds -	0	19	6
5	Courier - -	0	19	6
6	Wonder Shrewsbury	1	4	0
		£6	**15**	**0**

		£.	s.	d.
	Brought forward...6	6	15	0
7	Real Tally Ho -	1	4	0
8	Swallow, Shrewsbury	0	19	6
9	Northampton -	0	18	0
10	Leicester Union -	0	18	0
11	Wellingborough -	0	9	0
12	Warwickshire Hunt	0	18	0
		£12	**1**	**6**

The last coach stopped on June 4th, 1838.

The following observations are in the handwriting of Mr. James Tongue, being certain remarks on the decline of traffic, occasioned by the London and Birmingham railway opening to Denbigh Hall, it is as follows :—" Of the 12 coaches now running, I am told that there is not one getting a living. I do not expect half of them to remain on the road three months, although summer time. The prospect for us, is truly alarming; there is not more at present, I believe, than one-fourth of the posting, about half the gigs and horses, and about one-half the oxen and sheep, and every week we are threatened with fresh reductions of the little trade left."

The town however, did not give up its trade without a struggle ; hence, the road up Chalk-hill was considered a loss of time, and the commissioners resolved in 1837, to lower the hill, which they accomplished at a cost of £10,000, under the vain hope, that the increased accommodation would enable the coaches to compete with the new railway, then in progress.

An old proverb, mentioned by Fuller, deserves notice, viz. :—" As plain as Dunstaple road." It is applied to things plain and simple, without either welt or guard to adorn them ; as also to matters easy and obvious to be found, without difficulty or direction; such this road, being broad and beaten, as the confluence of so many roads leading to London from the north and north-western parts of the land.

The court rolls commenced in 1743, the first entry being dated in the month of January in

that year, when the jewry complained of timber
having been laid in the streets of the town, parcels of the lord's wastes : the rolls shew that a
great number of presentments had been made of
nuisances and encroachments on open spaces in
the streets, parcels of the lord's wastes, and
sundry fines imposed.

The township of Dunstaple covers an area of
520 acres, is situated on the side of the Chiltern
hills ; contained in 1801, 243 houses, inhabited,
2 uninhabited, and 296 families, giving a population of 1,296. The number of houses had
increased in 1841, to 386, while in 1857, they
were found to number 938, chiefly of brick, the
assessment being £7,000. The appearance of
numerous traces of old foundations of buildings,
and the great number of old wells having been
filled in, which frequently sink in after very wet
and frosty weather, and these being discovered
from time to time in fields far removed from the
present range of houses, leads the attentive
observer to conclude, that before the dissolution
of the priory, the town must have been much
larger and more extensive than at present.

Dunstaple was for a long time supplied with
water, for culinary purposes, by four large ponds;
that in West street where the sheep-fair is now
held, another before the "Saracen's Head," a-
nother near the "Crown," and the last facing
the "Sugar Loaf;" these received the rain water
from the neighbouring hills : but at present many
wells are used, averaging about 70 feet in depth,
which afford an excellent supply of water.

According to the returns made under the

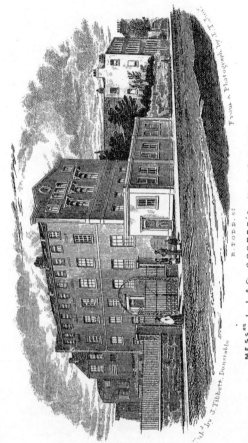

Engd. by T. Todd.

From a Photograph.

Pub.d by J. Tibbett, Dunstable.

R. TODD. S.

MESS.RS I. J. & C. COOPER'S MANUFACTORY.

Population Act, the town has steadily increased in the number of its inhabitants, as shewn in the following Table :—

Census of 1801, No. of Inhabitants, 1296
,, 1831, ,, ,, 2117
,, 1841, ,, ,, 2582
,, 1851, ,, ,, 3587*

Of late years Dunstaple has undergone much alteration in its appearance : the ponds which formerly supplied the town with water, have been filled up, being no longer necessary, and old groups of houses have been removed which once proved a great inconvenience to travellers. There are now but few houses remaining, which have the appearance of antiquity ; this is a source of regret to the antiquary, but although he may lament to see the works of other times obliterated, yet even he must acknowledge, that the hoary dwellings of antiquity are seldom the seats of trade and opulence, and that whenever the inhabitants of a town become industrious and flourishing, the mouldering walls of distant ages are gradually swept away.

Formerly Dunstaple was governed by a mayor, but lately by four constables, a churchwarden and two overseers. The poor rates in 1837, was £602; and other charities besides those already mentioned, amount to about £200 per annum.

The original trade of Dunstaple consisted in ornamental straw work, which formed a very pleasing branch of art, and is especially interesting to the natives of this town, since its cultivation

---

* Of whom 1290 were Males.

T

led to several improvements in the tools used, and in straw hat making.

The tedious process of splitting, opening, flattening and polishing straws by hand, was superseded by an ingenuous little machine, which performs the work more quickly, equally and effectually.

In ornamental straw work the straw is dyed, of various colours. The process of dyeing being complete, the straws must be sorted, not only for distinct colours, but for shades of the same colour; because it generally happens that a number of straws dyed in the same solution, do not all take the same shade. The rough edges are then cut smooth, for which purpose they ought to be placed upon a hard even board, and so covered with a thin flat iron ruler, that the ragged portion only may project; this is cut off by means of a lancet-shaped knife.

It is recommended to paste the under surface of the straws thus prepared to large sheets of thin paper; each sheet to contain one distinct colour or tint, and when the pasting is completed, to subject the whole to a strong pressure in a press, taking care to interpose between each sheet of straws a few folds of blotting paper, and a stout board the size of the sheet. After remaining in the press for about twenty-four hours, the sheets may be removed and preserved for use in a large portfolio.

Ornamental straw work is of two kinds; one presenting a flat surface, and the other raised. The first preparatory processes are the same for both kinds of work, the raised specimens being the result of a strong pressure in a mould.

The most simple description of work is in imitation of the ancient tapestries, called Bergamots; it is accomplished by means of narrow length of straws, of different colours, cut from the sheets prepared as already described These lengths are first pasted on paper side by side, the order of which must be determined by the taste of the operator.

For example. In order to produce a figure of bergamot, the following process must be adopted: A number of lengths of straws of different colours must be passed, side by side, upon a sheet of paper thus:—One of blue, one-tenth of an inch in width; then one of white, one of blue, one of yellow, one of black, and four of azure, all three-tenths of an inch in width; one of green, one-tenth of an inch; one of azure, one of green, one of yellow, one of red, and four of azure, all three-tenths of an inch in width; one of black, one-tenth of an inch in width; one of azure, one of black, one of yellow, one of blue, four of azure, all three-tenths of an inch in width.

In this arrangement, there are three series, each seperated by a narrow length, which commences the series. If the paper is not full, a new series can be added, and varied according to taste; but it is necessary always to finish with a complete series.

This arrangement must now be subjected to a tolerably strong pressure, until dry; it is then cut into strips, at right angles, to the direction of the length, and each strip is to be one-tenth of an inch in thickness. Each of these strips of course contains all the colours employed in the first arrangement; they are to be pasted one by one, upon another sheet of paper, and by varying the heights of the extremities of the strips, according to a determinate order, a variety of pleasing patterns can be produced.

By varying the above process and employing moulds, a variety of beautiful figures are produced. Several specimens submitted to my inspection, were of most elaborate design.

When laid work was made use of in the manufacture of hats and bonnets, it was cut into strips of different widths, for the front and head-piece, out of pasteboard, so that but little sewing was required. This kind of work constituted the principal trade of the town till the end of the last century. While the number of coaches passing through the town found a ready means for the manufacturer to dispose of his goods, which were sold to passengers and private families, in the porch of the " Sugar Loaf," which then occupied that part where the pillars now are in front of the hall door, which when first built by Jane Cart, in 1717, ran through the centre of the building; thus accounting for the sinking of the line of brick-work and windows over that entrance.

In the beginning of September, 1724, we meet with Dunstaple in the following curious manner, connected with Geo. I.:—"His Majesty's fatherly love to his people appeared upon all occasions, and about this particularly. About the beginning of September, one Heaton was soliciting for a patent to make hats of bent or straw, which would have been extremely prejudicial to thou-

sands of poor people about Hempstead, in Hertfordshire, Dunstaple, Luton, &c., in Bedfordshire.
Heaton's project alarmed the masters, and Mr.
John Miller, of Dunstaple, and Mr. Thomas Birch,
of Hempstead, introduced by His Grace the Duke
of Bridgewater, presented a petition to the king,
setting forth the danger they were in of losing
their trade and livelihood, if Heaton's patent took
effect. His Majesty received their petition very
graciously, and gave positive orders to the Lord
Viscount Townsend, that a speedy stop should be
put to the said patent. which gladdened the
hearts of those thousands of manufacturers of
straw, who thought their bread and their being
in so much peril."

Gipsy straw hats were worn in this country
about the year 1745 or 1746; and when Arthur
Young visited Dunstaple in 1768, the straw plait
manufacture appears to have been established, for
he says, " At that place is a manufacture of
basket work, which they have carried to a great
perfection of neatness and ingenuity, and make
thereof hats, boxes, baskets, &c., a large quantity
annually, but not a great number of hands employed by it. These various fancy articles are of
different coloured straws." The remains of this
once flourishing and highly-interesting trade still
lingers in the town, although shorn of its pristine
ingenuity and loveliness. A few simple table
mats and pipe-light cases now constitute the sole
object of the artistes' employment, and they are
only of the old school; so that every year they
decrease in number, causing the probability that
in a very few years it will cease altogether.

Though Heaton did not succeed in obtaining his patent, yet the value and importance of his invention was not lost sight of by the Society of Arts, who for a long series of years offered encouragement to attempts for the improvement of British straw manufacture, which called forth many interesting communications and led to great improvements. As early as 1805, the society presented a gold medal to Mr. Wm. Corstin, of Ludgate-hill, for a substitute of his invention for Leghorn plait. His plait was formed of rye straw, and was so good that some specimens had been examined by London tradesmen who confessed their inability to discover the difference between them and real Italian Leghorn.

Mr. Corstin states that 781,605 straw hats had been imported from 1794 to 1803, and that in the 1st four years of that period, 5,281 lbs. of straw plait, (which was equal to 25,405 hats,) had been brought to this country. In addition to the difference of quality between the Leghorn and British plait, it is stated that the cheapness of labour on the continent gave a great advantage to foreign competitors; so much so indeed, that the best Hertfordshire straw might be, and actually was, sent to Switzerland, plaited there, and thence returned to England, paying the import duty of 17s. per lb., and yet sold 25 per cent. cheaper than that plaited in this country.

The exclusion of foreign hats during the war with Napoleon, led to many improvements in splitting, finishing, and bleaching the straw; indeed so far was this successful, that some of the women employed upon straw plaiting earned a guinea a-week. But the cessation of the war permitted the importation of foreign hats : their superiority in fineness, colour and durability soon regained for them their preference over our home-produce, so that the domestic manufacture declined. Still the wages continued good; for wearing the Dunstaple straw hat had become fashionable in many parts of the country, and an inducement was thus held out to numbers to learn the trade. This was the case with many of the lace makers, who, on the decline of the pillow lace in 1820, betook themselves to straw plaiting as a desirable resource.

The qualities of the plait is materially influenced by the season of the year when the straw is plaited. Spring is the most favourable season for plaiting, bleaching and finishing; the dust and heat of summer, the benumbed fingers of the workpeople in winter, when compelled to keep within their smoky huts, plaiting the cold and wet straws, is injurious to the colour of the hats, which no bleaching can entirely remove.

Dunstaple hats are made of whole straw, plaited in long narrow slips or ribbons, which are afterwards sewed together in the form of a hat or bonnet. The weight and clumsy appearance of these bonnets, first suggested the idea of splitting straws into strips, but it was a considerable time before method was invented of performing this in a perfect manner. According to the evidence of Agnes Ashwell, now widow Siret, living in an adjoining village, the first splitters were made by the French prisoners, about the year 1804—5, and were of bone, one inch and a-half in length, with the cutting knives at the end; the straw being put on the point was thrust over the splitter, something in the same manner as oziers are now split by basket makers. Norman, a blacksmith, living upon the spot now occupied by Mr. Joseph Gutteridge's farm, made an improvement by working the machine in iron, but still retained the upright position; subsequently Janes, another blacksmith, turned the end at right angles and formed an elbow about half-an-inch in length, and brought it to a point, placing the fangs or cutting knives at the lower end in the form of spokes, by which the straw is divided into as many portions as desired. His machines were still made of iron, and very similar to those now in use, differing only in the metal used, brass being much cheaper, though far less durable. The enormous price of these machines prevented them from getting into general use; as much as two guineas having been paid for a single instrument.

Auother improvement was made in 1815. A circular piece of wood containing four or five small holes, into which were fixed iron splitters, in the form of a spokes of a wheel, with spikes to run down the straw, thus placing a whole set of machines in one frame.

One pound of straw as it leaves the farmer, is calculated to make a score of plait. The straw-factor knots them, and ties them up in bundles;

these bundles are sorted by the plaiter into different parcels, according to the length of whiteness; the longest being clear straw all the length, will work eight stitches on each side and then set out, while the shortest will require setting out after the fourth turn. Good work is all made with straws of the same length of whiteness, and set in at regular distances all the while : if the straws are set in at irregular distances, the value of the plait is lessened. Plaiters should use the second finger and thumb, instead of the forefinger which is thus left at liberty to turn the straws.

The slips of straws thus formed are softened in water, and plaited with great rapidity : when the plait is finished, it is passed between a pair of small wooden rollers, called a plait mill, to make it flat and hard. When these mills were introduced in 1807, they were called box mills, and cost 7s. 6d. each. There were seven descriptions of plait in general use, from which all the rest have sprung, viz. whole Dunstaple, the first introduced, plaited with seven entire straws ; split straws, introduced in 1809 ; Mr. Frederick Brown is said to have been the first to have worked them up and to have cleared in one year, £10,000 ; patent Dunstaple, or double seven, formed of fourteen split straws, every two wetted and laid together; Devonshire, formed of seven split straws, invented in 1829 ; Luton plait (an imitation of whole Dunstaple), formed of double seven, and coarser than the patent Dunstaple ; Bedford Leghorn, formed of twenty-two or double eleven straws, and plaited similar to the Tuscan ; and Italian, formed of eleven split straws.

U

The beautiful rice straw plait, so much in favour of late years, and which ladies prefer to have for wedding bonnets, at a guinea a piece, was invented and made up by that enterprising manufacturer still living, Mr. Blackwell. It is so called simply from its colour, occasioned by working the straws inside out.

The first straw bonnet is generally admitted to have been made at Dunstaple, which no doubt accounts for the fact of the great notoriety of the town for that article. Lady Bridgewater, of Ashridge House, is said to have been the first in the neighbourhood that wore the corkscrew bonnet, so called, from the kind of plait which succeeded the laid work.

The plait is sold by the score yard, and the market is opened by a bell, rung from Lady-day to Michaelmas at eight o'clock, and from Michaelmas to Lady-day at nine. An immense number of scores change hands in a few hours, which are removed to the work-rooms, of which there are twelve in the town, but only one exclusively for hats. These factories give employment to something like 1,500 hands; here it is sewn up, which operation, Cobbett in his "Cottage Economy," thus describes, "The English straw plait is put together as boards are on the side of a barn, that is to say, the lists of plait are made to cover a part of the other, and they are sewed through and through, the needle and thread performing the office of the nails, in the case of the barn. Not thus with Leghorn hats and bonnets. In order to make them, the plait is not lapped a part of one list over another, but the lists are fastened to each other by glue; and you can no more discover the joining of the plait than you can the joining of two boards with the same material. The first bonnet ever brought over from America was joined in the same way."

The sewing employs a great number of females. It is generally the case, that laxity of conduct is the characteristic of females, who are engaged in a factory, it is not so however, in Dunstaple; and a stranger is struck with the neatness of their appearance and the propriety of their demeanour, and to their honour, be it said, collectively there are none who possess more purity of morals, or higher respectability of character.

After the sewing they are given first to the wetters, and then to the blockers, which latter is a very laborious process, and was till 1837, performed by the sewers themselves. In the year 1827, a Mr. Arnold came from London, and began business in the town as blocker, and from his superior abilities, was much sought after; and at last was permanently engaged by Messrs. Masters and Hitchman. Arnold's superior talents soon gave his employers a preference over the rest, who soon followed the example thus set, and engaged the male sex for the more laborious duties of blockers and wetters.

Hats and bonnets are sometimes made of chips, or shavings of wood, woven or plaited into the requisite forms. The preparation of the chip for this purpose is curiously effected. The wood chosen is white, and tolerably free from knots, such as willow, lime, poplar, &c. The wood is worked while it is yet green, by a double-ironed plane; one of these irons has the plain straight edge of a common plane, while the other, which is placed nearly close and parallel to it, has the edge notched with teeth: the consequence is, that while a shaving of the wood is being cut off, it is at the same time cut up into narrow slips by the teeth of the notched iron. The chips are then bleached, by steeping them in cold soapy water, containing a little indigo, after which they are dried on the grass. Chips of wood and small strips of whalebone are sometimes combined in making hats: these strips are woven with a loom into a kind of twill or diamond tissue. About the year 1795, a person named Almond, had the honour of introducing it from Dunstaple into Luton.

More recently hats have been made of Brazillian grass. At the time of its introduction, hats sold for two guineas each; now, a few pence will enable you to purchase one any market day in the season.

A large variety of fancy trimmings are now used for the manufacture of bonnets, being a composition of various materials, as manilla, straw, horsehair, cardonet and chip: many of these are worked up on a pillow, the same as lace-making.

The prevalent fashion of wearing silk bonnets, or when made of straw, the preference now universally given for Dunstaple bonnets, has caused a gradual and long-continued decline in the trade of Leghorn and Tuscany, such as seriously to affect the straw plaiters in that country. The wages earned by the straw plaiters in Tuscany need not excite the envy of our workpeople in

England; the wages of an ordinary plaiter a-
mounting only to 2s. 8d. English money.

It is much to be regretted that no public
provision has as yet been made in the town, for
the families of the poor who provide the numerous
scores of plait, which prove such a source of
wealth to their more opulent neighbours, but who
seem condemned to weave the same in hereditary
ignorance. Having no industrial school in the
town to supply the necessary statistics, on this
interesting problem, pardon me, if I introduce the
condition of one of my own schools, as a proof of
what can be done by comprising straw plaiting
with intellectual development: the thing is easy
of accomplishment, and ought to be done in the
town of Dunstaple.

The first table will show the average ages of
my children in each class, with the degree of
intellectual advancement at the period of the
Inspector's visit, June 19th, 1855, and is an
extract from his printed report. The second
shews the value of the work on an average, during
the school hours.

1855	CLASSES						
	1	2	3	4	5	6	7
Average Age of Boys	13	11	11	10	9	5	
„ „ Girls	14	11	12	10	7	5	4
Elementary Church Catechism.........	A	A	A	A	A	A	A
In Old Testament	B						
„ New Testament	B	B					
Reed's Monosyllables...........					B	C	
„ Easy Lessons			B	B	B		
„ Books of Greater Difficulty...	B	B	B				
Arithmetic, Simple Rules................	B						
„ Compound & Reduction..	C						
Knowledge of Geography	B	B					
„ Singing	B	B	B	B			
„ Industrial Work..........	B	B	B	B	B	B	
„ Needle Work	B	B	B				

The degree of efficiency is marked by the letters A. B. C. D. in the compartment under each class, and in a line with the respective subjects:— A denoting the highest degree, or very good; B good; C moderate; and D bad or deficient.

Thus it is clear, that although the children of the 4th class is earning 1s. 3d. a week, during the school hours, and from thence to 5s., and upwards, in the first; yet not one of the classes were considered bad or deficient by the Inspector, and only two cases in which the attainments were moderate. The foregoing was the table for the first half-year, exclusive of Copy Books and Dictation, while the other half, found some of this list displaced and filled up with Liturgy, Letter Writing, Bill Making, Grammar and Secular History, in each of which, they held a similar position.

Should any one looking over the table think the amount small, I would answer, that having two schools under my care, a mile and a-half apart, the result has been obtained by not more than three hours teaching per day.

The children work eight hours a day, less the time engaged with the master in religious and secular instruction, and the subjoined table shews the average of their earnings during the same period.

Children of the	s. d.			s. d.	s. d.
4th Class	3 score at 0 6	Value of Straws deduct	0 3	1 3
3rd Class	5 score at 0 8	„ „	0 7	2 9
2nd Class	6 score at 0 9	„ „	1 0	3 6
1st Class	6 score at 1 1	„ „	1 0	5 0

Out of 22 presented to the bishop for confirmation, 16 were yet scholars in the school.

In well-regulated families, children work twelve hours a day, the work done at school being considered a sufficient remuneration for board, lodging, &c., and the remainder the children enjoy as a perquisite of its own: thus a double object is secured, the child early becomes acquainted with the value of money, and acquires habits of patient and persevering industry.

In the year 1773, the rents and profits of the manor were leased to to the duke of Bedford, and continued in their possession till 1839, when the manor once more reverted to the crown. This time was very favourable to the squatters, and Peters, one of the ringers, who having got a house ready built of wood, was carried to the waste by ringers, he sitting on a rope fastened to the top of the building, and the wooden house was ever after called the " Ringer's hall." This house was the first erected by the squatters in Church street, in 1801.

Between the year 1845 and 1850, seventeen leases of portions of waste land was granted to persons in Dunstaple.

The second Baptist meeting was opened under the auspices of the late Mr. Gutteridge and others, in the year 1790, being near to where the present noble building is erected, the foundation-stone of which was laid by Joseph Tritton, Esq., on the 11th day of August, 1847. It is fitted up with seats for 800 people, and cost £21,00 in erection, one-fifth of the entire cost being paid by Richard Gutteridge, Esq. ; Mr. Clark, of London, being the architect. The entire cost of the erection was paid off on New Year's-day, 1857. During the violent storm in the spring of 1854, it sustained slight damage by the falling of a stack of chimneys on the roof. Connected with this meeting-house is a Sunday-school, having been in active operation since the 28th of January, 1807. On New Year's-day, the children of these schools are regaled with a substantial dinner of beef and plum-pudding, the annual gift of the aforesaid R. Gutteridge, Esq. After the children have partaken of the good things provided for them, the teachers sit down to a dinner, the gift of the same kind and liberal gentleman. The present pastor is the Rev. D. Gould, who was married in this meeting-house in July, 1840, the officiating minister being the Rev. Alexander Smith, of the Baptist society at Houghton. The burial ground contains a few altar tombs of the Gutteridge, Batchelar, and Chamber's families, and a neat square monument surmounted by an urn, enclosed with neat iron palisading, covers certain portions of the Osborn family.

I have endeavoured, but without success, to discover the precise date of the first Sabbath-school. I have been more fortunate as to the devoted individual conducting the same, and what is more interesting, like Robert Raikes the distinguished founder of such institutions, in 1781, was one who never failed in her devotion and attachment to the church of England. Old Nanny Burton, though at the age of eighty years still gathered the little urchins together, in her own hired school-room at the back of the premises now occupied by Mr. Rush, the brazier. This is asserted by some to have been the second Sabbath-

NEW BAPTIST CHAPEL, DUNSTABLE.

Pub.d by J. Tibbett, Dunstable.

R. TODD sc

From a Photograph by J. H. Lowe

Priory Church & National School, Dunstable.

school in the county; but I have not been able to trace that out sufficiently clear, though it is certain she had been several years labouring in this then new and interesting employment, when in 1793, she was called from her labours below, to receive her everlasting reward. The good work was carried on by her successor, Mrs. Bouse, who was the wife of the parish clerk, and removed the school to her own house in West street.

In 1802, Sir John Kightly, estimating aright the importance of Sabbath-school instruction, by a will and codicil, dated the 4th and 20th of June, 1802, gave £200 for supporting a church school in Dunstaple. This bequest now consists of £191 17s. Bank £3 per cent. annuities, and the interest is payable by the Accountant-General in the court of Chancery, in the cause of Brooks against Woodman.

Then we meet with Mrs. Hitchman, in West-street, as school mistress. At her death it was removed to the Town Hall, and subsequently, through the exertions of the late rector, to a more permanent spot in 1839.

On Tuesday, October 23rd, 1838, was laid the foundation-stone of a Sunday and Day-schools, (incorporated with the National society), on a portion of the ground adjoining the church-yard, and which from a grave found in digging the foundation, appears at one time to have formed a part of it. The Rev. Solomon Piggott, rector, churchwardens, sidesmen, committee of the Sunday-school and teachers, attended amidst the ringing of bells, and about 500 inhabitants, surrounding the foundation-stone sang the 70th

v

Psalm. The rector then laid the foundation-stone and reported that the Lords of the Treasury had granted £85 towards the erection, the National society had rendered assistance to the same amount, while the township raised £201 by subscription: the education to be given was to be religious instruction in the Holy Scriptures, and church catechism on Sunday, writing and arithmetic on week-day evenings; for which purpose, the school is open to all young persons of every denomination, on paying one penny per week; the Scriptures are to be taught in a pure and unmutilated state, not in mere scraps, to promote party purposes, and the Prayer Book is to be used for devotional exercises. This highly-interesting address was afterwards published, and a memoir added of Ann Billington, a scholar, who died the same morning the stone was laid: the erection was also commemorated by another little work, entitled "Memoirs of Teachers connected with the school in its earlier stages." During the time of my superintendence, the Sunday scholars numbered 250, taught by 10 male teachers, and 14 female, many of whom had been trained up in the Bible-class.

Subsequently the evening teaching expanded itself into a day school when under the able and judicious management of Mr. Alfred T. Smith, C.M. in 1855, the average daily attendance exceeded one hundred. He had so won the affections of his scholars and their friends, and the general esteem of the town that on his removal to a more lucrative employment, in 1856, he was presented with a very handsome and valuable inkstand,—a very appropriate present to a school master.

On the site now occupied by the school was formerly held the weekly plait market. At the right-hand corner of the Green, towards the Priory wall, were to be seen until a few years' since, three little mounds, marking the graves of as many persons who had committed suicide, and were not allowed a place in consecrated ground: others are reported to have been buried in the cross-road, opposite the " Red Lion" Inn.

In 1805, the old Town Hall was taken down and the present structure erected. Two years' later, the County Insurance Office placed an agent in the town; thus preparing the way for getting rid of the ancient custom of reading briefs in the church, in aid of those who suffered by fire. Having degenerated into a mere form, therefore comparatively speaking, little was collected, and of that little comparatively nothing went to the object intended. The only thing briefs did in latter times, was to destract the congregation in a most important part of the service.—See Rubric.

There are now several other agencies in the town, and the Albert and Times Company have a local secretary resident here.

The year 1809 introduces several pugilists to our notice, viz. :—De Gullin against Grickson; Old Dutch Sam against Cropley; Cribb against Horton. Grickson resided at the " Sugar Loaf," during his training, but so retired, that his profession was not even guessed at. The fight was originally intended to have taken place at Woburn, but on reaching that place they found a prohibition, and were compelled to return to Dunstaple.

The number of people congregated to witness their return was so great, as to render the road impassable from the Sugar Loaf to Brewer's-hill. Then the Downs was to witness this exhibition of manly strength; here again a disappointment awaited them,—the Dunstaple Volunteer Corps, 120 strong, were drawn up in the "Waggon and Horses" close, then used by them as a parade ground; from thence under their noble and gallant leader, they marched to the Downs and put an end to the preparations, which, with the exception of doing military honours over the grave of George Downman, buried in Dunstaple church-yard, and also another of their comrades in Houghton, is all that is recorded of their active service. After all, the fight did take place by permission of Sir John Seabright in Beechwood park.

The following year being the 50th year of the reign of George III., the jubilee of that event was celebrated in the town with all due honours, an ox being roasted whole on the Square, and the townspeople enjoying a sumptuous entertainment.

In 1812, we first meet with the appearance of Wesleyan Methodists in the town. They began divine worship, according to their peculiar custom, in a workshop belonging to Mr. Darley, in Church street; thence they removed to Mr. Fossey's the confectioner, in High street, a few doors from Church street; afterwards they congregated together in the Old Meeting-house belonging to the society of Friends, where, after remaining ten years, in 1831 they erected a meeting-house for themselves on the spot where the present building now stands. This was destroyed by fire in 1844 ; of the origin of which, no moral doubt remains but that it was the work of an incendiary upon the premises of Mr. Goode, farmer and mail contractor, whose premises were also entirely destroyed, but fortunately insured in the Phœnix for £2,000. The year following, the chapel was rebuilt at a cost of £2,000 and is calculated to seat 800 persons. In the first instance, no architect was employed to superintend its erection, the work being undertaken by Messrs. Barker and Bass, builders, of Toddington. After having carried the walls a certain height, they were considered unsafe ; the opinion of three different architects was then taken, they without hesitation condemned it, suggesting two means only whereby the building might be rendered safe,—either to take it down entirely and rebuild it from the foundation, or else pillars at certain distances must be erected—the latter alternative was chosen, hence the origin of those unsightly pillars under the gallery.

It is worthy of remark, that the year before they left the Friends' Meeting-house, this people held their first missionary meeting in the town, under the chairmanship of Mr. Blundell.

Dunstaple became a circuit town in 1843, when John Knowles was the first superintendent, and William Wey, second preacher. The public library which they established in 1842, now contains 400 volumes, many of them of great utility and value. In 1854, increased facilities in psalmody was given by the erection of an organ, at a cost of £120. They have a large and flourishing Sunday-school in connexion, under 4 superintendents, assisted by 76 teachers, with 400 children, who are taught on "Mimpriss' Graduated System;" they are divided into the Upper & Lower Schools, to facilitate the work of examination. In 1853, a day-school was opened on the Glasgow system, it is mixed, and contains 70 boys and 30 girls, Mr. Samuel Noall being the first master. A committee of ladies superintend by turns, the instruction in needle-work. An infant school and recreation ground has since been added. This is the second time that such an attempt has been made : the first infant school was opened in the Friends' meeting-house by one Mr. Pargetten, the same year that the Wesleyans vacated that building.

There are 18 places of worship and 34 local preachers in the circuit; and two of these places being situated so remote, a horse is provided for the use of the preachers.

Only one sepulchral monument adorns the burial ground, and is sacred to the memory of Mrs. Cooper, concerning whom, an interesting memoir of nearly 200 pages was written by the Rev. Henry Fisk, M.A.

During the rapid enlargement of our town the oft-repeated cry of the bricklayer has sounded in our ears, " Wo'nt you lay a brick?" But it remained for the 5th of July, 1858, to point out the way in which this expression might be turned to profit and advantage on that day. The ceremony of laying the foundation-stone for a new wing to the Wesleyan chapel, took place under the supervision of W. Pocock, Esq.; but with the exception of laying bricks, the ceremony did not differ from that which is common on such occasions, and therefore need not be further particularized, but the distinctive peculiarity is thus described by an eye-witness :—" All things being ready, a bottle hermetically sealed, was then produced, containing a copy of the "Dunstable Chronicle" for July 3rd,—the circuit plan of preachers—a list of the chapel trustees—and of such gentlemen and ladies as had kindly signified their intention to lay bricks. This bottle amid the plaudits of the spectators was then deposited in a hollow made expressly for it underneath the stone—mortar was spread over it, securely encasing it, after which the stone was lowered, the people uncovering and singing "Praise God from whom all blessings flow." This done, to the satisfaction of the architect, he mounted it, and with upraised arm announced "In the name of the Father, Son and Holy Ghost, three persons in one Godhead, I declare this stone well and truly laid." Many a hearty Amen and "hear! hear!" followed, when John Cooper, Esq. in a workmanlike manner proceeded to redeem his promise. His graceful and accomplished lady next stepped forward and performed her part with true feminine dignity. Miss Cooper and the younger branches of the family succeeded, and acquitted themselves with that modesty and timidity which are the glory and characteristics of youth. Mrs. Bennett next took the trowel, and seemed evidently to think that she should get on better if the partner of her joys and sorrows were standing by her side; so he was fetched off from the spot from which he was

with true christian emotion haranguing his friends,
and right nimbly did he go to work.   If our eyes
did not deceive us, we saw some very desirable
looking pieces of paper lying on the said bricks;
lawful possession of which for £9 10s. each, we
should have thought a bargain.   Mr. J. Robinson
followed in like manner.   This we mention all
the more gladly because we think we have somewhere read that prior donations of £25 each, had
been given by the three families in question.   Mr.
Howes and his family next appeared as brick-
layers, and we doubt not they got through their
duties well; but the truth is, an amusing speech
from our friend Bennett so occupied our attention
and provoked our mirth that we feel compelled to
speak with diffidence.   One thing we admired the
man for—there is nothing of the aristocrat in
him—and with a delicate regard for the feelings
of his poorer fellow-worshippers, he declared,
that "any of them should lay a brick for six-
pence."   In the excellent remarks which followed
he energetically promised to "love old Dunstaple
all the more, for supporting him so nobly that
day."   We can truly say that we rejoiced with
him, and shall love and respect *him* too, all the
more from what we saw of his mind and spirit on
Monday last.   The bricklaying over, the Sunday-
school children were marshalled on the Square,
and a few minutes allowed them to feast their
imagination on the good things in store for them.
At the right time the order to march into the
Priory grounds was obeyed with alacrity, and we
here publicly tender our thanks to Mr. and Mrs.
Hunt for their kindness in placing their beautiful

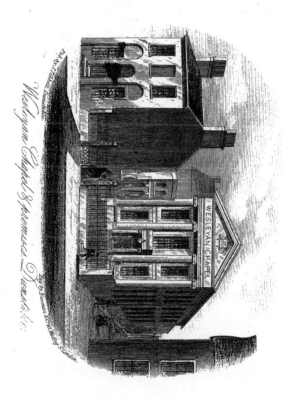

Wesleyan Chapel, Spennimoor, Durham &c.

lawn and field at the disposal of the committee.
How few travellers through Dunstable there are
who dream as they pass along our dry and dusty
streets that on the right hand and on the left
our manufacturers possess the beautiful in nature
and in art as well as the merchant princes whom
they represent. The entrances and avenues leading to the rendezvous were most tastefully
decorated, and the view about six o'clock from
beneath the noble walnut tree in the field was
beautiful in the extreme. The numerous tables
were well occupied and bountifully supplied, and
we are quite ashamed to place on record the
number of pounds of currant cake which the
youngsters stowed away. Verily a child's stomach
is a mystery. The tea over, there was a general
move towards the field from which a good view of
our noble parish church was obtained. With
much kind feeling the ringers gave us a merry
peal, a compliment which all felt and enjoyed.
Soon after seven we were summoned to the lower
end of the field to hear the Rev. Wright Shovelton
and other ministers utter " thoughts that breathe
and words that burn," and we are very much
indebted to them for their kindness in coming a-
mong us, and so eloquently setting before us
sentiments and principles which tend to our souls'
health. The choir rendered efficient service, and
their melody was listened to by a grateful and
delighted audience. We need hardly say that
the nimble fingers and gratuitous services of the
young ladies of the chapel contributed greatly to
the day's success. The following is an account
of the proceeds of the day :—

W

Stone	68	11	0
Collection in the Evening	18	10	10
Tickets Sold	57	6	5
Subscriptions Promised	52	17	0
Collected for Children's Tea	6	0	0
Total £203		5	3

The cost of tea and other expenses to be deducted."

The only circumstance of 1814 was an encroachment made on the waste land by Charles Bowstead, who erected two cottages and sheds in East street, during the month of May, as shewn by the court rolls.

The following year terminated the great war which had devastated Europe during the last 22 years, and which cost as much as would require a tax of £29 on every individual in Europe, supposing the population to be 214,000,000 souls, or near £8 on every individual of the globe; of which, Great Britain paid as much as would buy the whole territory of France, at £14 per acre. Surely the people never had greater reason for rejoicing than this return to peace. On this occasion our noble town once more displayed its loyalty by numerous decorations, and a sumptuous entertainment prepared : an ox was roasted on the Square, and tables were arranged along the High street, for the accommodation of numerous guests. The gaiety of such an assemblage, was however, sullied by the remembrance of the king's malady under which he then laboured, and from which he never recovered. Who could help wishing that our venerable king whose spirit had roused his people to maintain this struggle had been permitted to witness its triumphant close.

Fire though it is a great destroyer, is often a great restorer, and so it proved this year; for while it consumed the " Saracen's Head," opened the way for the discovery of numerous coins in gold and silver, bearing the effigy of the several kings and queens from Edward VI. to Charles I., inclusive, but none after the latter monarch. Most of them were twelve-penny pieces and half-crowns; many of the latter was of the reign of Charles I., and thus leading to the supposition, that they were buried during the period of the great rebellion, yet appeared quite fresh and new, very little injured, except where the damp had touched them. They tell a sad tale of the urgency of those unhappy times, presenting none of that neatness of finish which generally distinguishes English coinage: the impression is rough, the edges simply clipped, not rounded, proving the hastiness of their issue.

When the old stables were removed, in order to clear out the ground for a new foundation, they were found under the floor.

The last coin connected with Dunstaple in my own possession, is one of William III. and Mary II.; it was dug up in a garden near the Ladies' Lodge. The coins of this reign are interesting, inasmuch as they represent the likeness of both king and queen on the same side, with the super-scription Gulielmus et Maria, with a full-length portrait of Frances Theresa Stuart, duchess of Leonnox; on the other with the words Britannia, 1694. The original portrait was painted by Lely, and is extant, at Lethington castle, East Lothian, Scotland. It was the uncle of Mary (Charles II.) who caused this lady to be represented, and which subsequent monarch has ever continued as the emblematical figure of Britannia. The portrait represents a tall woman, with that fullness of feature and person which characterized the beauties of the reign of the "Merry Monarch."

This coin brings to our remembrance the only reign wherein the executive power in England was held jointly by two crowned heads, at the same time. By William the Protestant faith was firmly established in the land, and one of the last acts of Mary was to send pecuniary aid to the suffering Waldenses, in 1694, the year this coin was struck, and in which she died.

Obv.—GVLIELMVS ET MARIA, profile busts, side by side to the right, as usual, the king's head laureated.

Rev.—BRITANNIA. Britannia seated with spear and shield, holding an olive branch in the right hand. Date, 1694.

The emblematical figure for Britannia differs from that in present use; the upper parts of the body being bare, no helmet, the lower parts barely concealed with flowing drapery.

We must now pass over a period of nearly twenty years, during which time, we find banks and friendly societies springing up here and there. The banks are of two kinds, banks of deposit and banks of issue. By deposit is meant, that the bank takes charge of deposits of cash, which it is ready to restore on demand. Banks of issue transact all the ordinary business of banks of deposit, and in addition issue notes of their own, instead of actual cash on the notes of others; of this kind there existed one as early as the beginning of the present century, known as the Dunstaple and Luton bank, whose counting-house occupied the spot now filled up by the shop of Mr. Chambers, grocer. It is believed that there are but two £1 notes remaining in Dunstaple, of this issue,—the one in the possession of Humphrey Brandreth, Esq., and the other of Mr. Johnson, postmaster. The one I had the privilege to see, bears the date of Dec. 17th, 1802 ; its registered number is 10,800, was entered by G. Taylor, signed by D. Queenborough; payable to Messrs. Button and Son, Paternoster row, London, on Gutteridge, Butterfield and Co., Dunstaple and Luton bank.

The notes of any given bank being received purely on a principle of good faith or credit, it is of great importance that the bank should not do anything to incur the suspicion of being incapable of retaining its notes. When any suspicion of this nature arises, the public, who are ignorant probably of the true circumstances, rush to the bank for gold in exchange for its notes,—this is called a run ; and one of these panics so severely tried the banks in 1826, that only Messrs. Bassetts withstood the pressure.

Previous to 1855, such of the humble classes as were given to saving, had no proper place to deposit their spare funds, which they were obliged to keep in an unfructifying hoard, in their own possession, exposed to the risk of loss, or had to consign it to some neighbour, who though deemed safe, might turn out much the reverse.

At the same time the want of a proper place for the deposit of spare money of those who might save, but lacked one important requisite to their doing so. In this year, it occurred to some benevolent minds, that an important benefit would be conferred on these classes, by the opening of a Savings' bank to receive deposits from 1s. to £30 a-year, ending on the 20th of Nov., and not more than £150 in the whole; when the sum amounts to £200, no interest is payable. Charitable and provident institutions may lodge funds to the amount of £100 in a single year, or £300 in all, principal and interest included.

Any depositor may receive, on demand, the money lodged by him, if it does not amount to a considerable sum; and even in that case, it will be returned in a few days' notice. The savings are now received at the Town Hall.

Savings instead of being stored up in a bank, to be there constantly at command, may be deposited by a working man, in a well-constituted friendly society, as a means of insuring for himself certain contingent and fixed benefits. In some respects and for some cases, joining a friendly society may be better than becoming a depositor in a savings' bank. Sickness may come before the savings are considerable, or if continued, they may melt away by long-continued affliction; but after a certain amount is paid to a friendly society the member is secure of succour, however long his illness may continue, and a decent interment at its close. Most assuredly, the arrangements of a rightly-constituted friendly society furnishes a very considerable degree of security against some of the painful uncertainties of life. Such at least were the ideas of those honourable men,

who, on the 5th of January, 1835, originated the "Dunstable General Provident Institution," which now numbers 368 members, viz. 105 males and 263 females, having a capital of £1154 0 7½d.; the rector and several influential persons of the town forming the committee.

Previous to the year 1136, the parish workhouse, which had probably stood from the days of good queen Bess, in High street, possessing no architectural beauty to attract the eye of the passer by. It looked a cold and desolate place, unadorned by flower or shrub; the door was constantly open, admitting a current of fresh air through the narrow passage, at every season of the year. The casement windows were seldom in a sound condition, broken panes patched up as best they might be until the glazier's next visit, all looked comfortless and forlorn, and told a sad tale of poverty and disorderly habits. The house contained 13 rooms, which were seldom if ever vacant: the average number of paupers was 42, this however, was but a small proportion out of 2,000 inhabitants.

In one room sat a shoemaker, who was for ever grumbling over his hard lot, but who never in his younger days put a sixpence to the benefit club, to succour him in the time of need. He seemed to imagine, like others of his class, that the poor rates were a sort of public annuity, and every one was bound to get as large a portion of the fund as possible,—and viewed it as a laudable pursuance of his rights to outwit the parish authorities at every opportunity.

Then we met with the gentleman's servant, who being unsteady, the ale-house had proved his ruin : then poor Peggy, a poor half-witted being, always slip-shod and slatternly : another, labouring under aberration of intellect, and was hardly a fit inmate for the house. But under the old system, evils and abuses crept in at every corner, and was increasing with the population to a fearful extent, that many a landlord and tenant seemed threatened with certain ruin ; the vicious and improvident were thriving on the produce of the land, at the expense of the industrious; and hard-wrought earnings of the well-disposed portion of the community were indiscriminately lavished upon by the slothful and the profligate, whilst in too many cases, imposition was fostered and upheld by the acting and often unwilling agents of parochial management. The honest labourer who struggled through his difficulties and reared a large family by dint of his own personal exertions and perseverance, was nevertheless called upon to contribute to the support of those who were too idle and dissipated to do their duty, either to themselves or families.

Such a state of things loudly called for some reform in the system, some check to the wanton expenditure of the poor rates; and the new poor laws were devised by Lord Brougham, and coming into effect the house in High street was closed, and the paupers removed to the Union House at Luton, in the year 1836.

Since then, however, there have at times sprung up agitators, who have supposed that it would have been better to have had Dunstaple the centre of a union; and their opinion, on the 10th day of Dec. 1855, assumed a more definite form; a public meeting was held in the Town Hall, R. Gutteridge, Esq. in the chair, and resolutions were adopted which proposed the taking of the parishes of Houghton Regis, Kensworth, Totternhoe, Whipsnade, Studham, and the hamlet of Humbershoe, (the present Dunstaple district,) to form the union; and Messrs. Benning, Lockhart, and Burges, were appointed as a deputation to wait upon the Hon. W. P. Bouverie, and press the subject upon his attention. They were courteously received by him, on the 13th of the same month, but failing to show sufficient cause why the present arrangements of the union should be disturbed, the prayer of the petition was not granted.

Among the various schemes which have been brought forward at different times for improving the temporal condition of the labouring class, few possess so many recommendations or combine such advantages, as that adopted by the venerable Bishop of Bath and Wells and Lord Braybrooke, I mean that of allotment gardens. Frederick

x

Brown, Esq. perceiving these advantages, laid out ten acres in West street, in 1841, under the name of the "Victoria Gardens," in portions of not more than a quarter of an acre each: they were formerly let at four-pence per pole, but it has been found desirable to increase it to six-pence. Tenants of the estate take precedence of all others. The gardens are cultivated with the exertions of the labourer and his family, and the products of it finds him many comforts he would not otherwise have: he is enabled to keep a pig, he learns to store the manure, thus rendering the land much more productive. In addition to this, he reaps a positive enjoyment and relaxation, in noticing the crops as they are growing, and this draws him into the garden, thus thinning the frequenters of the dram shop, and converting the subject into a sober, peaceful, and industrious member of the community, and so diminishing the amount of the poor rates: his condition is thus improved morally and physically, and as he works himself in it only at those times he is not employed by his master, it arises from his making the land the savings' bank wherein to deposit his overplus labour (remember the poor man's capital is his labour,) and developing that capital of labour in over-hours, which would otherwise be wasted he improves his condition I say, both morally and physically—and this from merely having an opportunity of using that capital, which for want of it, he was unable to employ before.

These allotments, admirable as they are, are not sufficient for a man who has not fixed employment, neither were they ever intended to be so.

Two things yet seem wanting, in order to foster and cherish a love for cultivating these allotments to the best advantage: the one is, a well-regulated horticultural society, offering premiums for plants, roots, fruits of the best quality; and secondly, an addition to the public libraries of a few well-selected books on horticulture, written in a popular style, adapted to this particular class of readers.

One other circumstance connected with this year deserves especial notice. We have before intimated, that in the 15th century the choir of Dunstaple had acquired a very extensive renown, so that year its services were called forth for a benevolent object. The adjoining county of Bucks. was desirous of erecting an infirmary for the impotent and weak, and in order to raise the necessary funds, among the contrivances a series of concerts were got up throughout the county, the singers being chiefly of the choir of Dunstaple, headed by Mr. Nicholls, the then organist. These concerts were highly enjoyed at the time, and are still spoken of in the warmest manner.

Hark ! 'tis the bells of the Priory Church ;
How pleasantly they strike on the ear !
How merrily they ring!

Those Priory bells, those Priory bells,
How many a tale their music tells,
Of youth and home, and that sweet time,
Since last I heard their soothing chime.

Those joyous hours have passed away ;
And many a heart then young and gay,
Within the tomb now darkly dwells,
And hears no more the Priory bells.

And so 'twill be when I am gone ;
That tuneful peal will still ring on :
While other bards shall walk these dells,
And sing your praise, sweet Priory bells.

Ye seem to say, they rest in peace,
Where care is not, where sorrows cease :
The thought my rising anguish quells,
Repeat the strain, sweet Priory bells.

They hear no more a mortal voice,
But still in heavenly songs rejoice ;
In songs whose music far excells,
Your softest notes, sweet Priory bells.

Adapted from Moore.

In the year 1755, died Mr. Benjamin Anable,
the inventor of change-ringing, the whole art of
which is compounded of four parts, viz. : hunting,
dodging, snapping, and place-making. On seven
bells there is every reason to believe that he was
the first who produced 5,040 changes, which was
the peal of plain "bob tripple," with two singles.
He affected considerable improvement in "bob
major," which was performed on these ancient
priory bells, in 1776, by a society of college
youths, who visited Dunstaple during that year.
Again on Monday, August 21st, 1854, a first-
rate party of change ringers, selected under the
superintendence of Thomas Burton, Esq., ascended
this venerable tower, and performed in good style
the same peal of 'tripple bob major ;' the following
notice under the sanction of the rector and churchwardens having previously been issued :—"The
committee of management confidently hope that
the nobility, amateurs, and lovers of bell ringing,
will avail themselves of this series of highly in-

teresting and superior performances; trusting
that it may be a means of introducing a more
scientific system of ringing worthy of the importance of this beautiful and ancient art, upon
which our forefathers bestowed such labour and
expense, and fully relied upon after ages to carry
out with the same energy and spirit of liberality.
The change ringing will commence at twelve at
noon."

On one occasion, their iron tongues were made
to thunder forth the vengeance of an insulted
deity, under the following circumstance. On the
occasion of a marriage festival, Oct. 25th, 1837,
a poor deluded man, an open blasphemer of God,
on hearing the ringing of the priory bells, gave
vent to the most bitter oaths against them and

the church, wishing they might fall on him and
kill him if he ever entered the edifice.   Shortly
after, being in a state of intoxication, he directed
his steps to the church, and ascended the loft to
where the bells are rung, and then proceeded to
the tower.   Persons who are at all acquainted
with bells, know that when they are set, they
stand perpendicular, that is, just the reverse to
the position in which they are generally seen,
and a very slight movement brings them round
with great force.   The poor man, ignorantly or
recklesly went in among them while they were in
this upright position.

Suddenly one of the bells was heard to ring in
an unusual way, and upon going to ascertain the
cause, the beholders were astonished to find the
unfortunate man so crushed between the bell and
the beam, that three quarters of an hour after his
release, his immortal spirit took its flight to that
place from whence there is no return.

If the reader has any curiosity to know what is
on the bells, I will endeavour to satisfy him,
beginning with the first he would meet with at
the top of the staircase.

1st Bell.
"WHILE THUS WE JOIN IN CHEERFUL ROUND,
"MAY LOVE AND LOYALTY ABOUND."

2nd Bell.
"PEACE AND GOOD NEIGHBOURHOOD."

3rd Bell.
"MUSIC IS MEDICINE TO THE MIND."

4th Bell.
"ALL YE WHO JOIN WITH HANDS, YOUR HEARTS UNITE,
"SO SHALL OUR TUNEFUL TONGUES COMBINE TO LAUD
THE NUPTIAL RITE."

The great bell furnishes us with the names of

the churchwardens, and in common with the other
the date of casting: "Wm. Coles and Wm.
Eames, churchwardens, 1776."

6th Bell.
"ALTHOUGH I AM BOTH LIGHT AND SMALL,
"I WILL BE HEARD ABOVE YOU ALL."

7th Bell.
"IF YOU HAVE A JUDICIOUS EAR,
"YOU'LL OWN MY VOICE IS SWEET AND CLEAR."

8th Bell.—No Inscription.

These bells were re-cast by Pock and Chapman,
London, 1776.

The last but not the least in importance is the
"ting tang," which before the Reformation was
the "sanctus bell." For the inscription on this, I
am indebted to Mr. Mills, the present master of
the National school:—

" Ave Maria Gracia tibi."

Before quitting the belfry we take a last fond
look of the sanctus bell, and call to mind the
gorgeous ceremonial which attended its consecration. First of all, the bell was suspended from a
scaffold, having a temporary altar erected near
it, adorned with crucifix, candlestick, and pix.
Around the bell was several boys in white sur-
plices, with silver crosses and elevated lanterns.
The cure first read a long declaration of the uses
of the bell, stating that it served to call the
faithful to the service of God, and to tell the
various offices that were going on, that it communicated joyful or sad news, and would tend to
mitigate the grief caused by the latter, or to increase the pleasure of the former, and he begged

the people to unite with him in soliciting the good will of God toward the bell.

Various prayers after an established ritual were then read, and an attendant priest laved the bell with a bunch of myrrh dipped in holy water, chanting monotonously during the whole time ; a ribbon was then tied round the clapper, the bell was anointed by the curate, with oil, and under it various powders of powerful odours were burnt.

Making use of the ribbon, the cure struck the bell three times with the clapper, and afterwards a lady probably Matilda, daughter of Malcolm, king of Scotland, who was the godmother of the bell, if we may so speak, struck it in like manner. The clapper was then wrapped up in a napkin, the inside of the bell again fumigated and anointed after which, the whole party adjourned to the interior of the church to celebrate mass.

Three bells especially deserve notice. First, the " incumbent induction bell," which is only rung at the induction of a new rector. After the person empowered to induct has laid the hand of the person to be inducted upon the key of the church, and pronounced the usual formula, he opens the door and puts the new incumbent into possession of the church, who when he has tolled the bell comes forth, and the inductor endorses and signs a certificate of such induction. The last time this bell was rung, was on the first of June, 1844, being the day on which the Rev. F. Hose, the present rector, entered upon the living.

2nd.—" The pancake bell :" it is always rung on Shrove Tuesday, and was formerly the confessional bell. There is strong reason to believe that eating pancakes on this day is a relic of the adaptations of papal customs, to those of heathen converts. The Roman Fomacalia, a festival celebrated in honour of Fomax, who presided over bread-making, was celebrated on the 18th of February.

The last is the "passing bell," as its name implies, was rung originally for the benefit of the person dying, and not as now, to announce the death of the individual,—that intercession might be made, and the priest hasten to administer extreme unction. In the 67th canon it is ordered, "And when any is passing out of this life, a bell shall be tolled, and the minister shall not then slack to do his last duty."

It appears to have been used in this strict, literal sense, till the year 1714.

> That sound upon my ear falls heavily:
> It is the PASSING BELL, the deep low knoll
> Which speaks the transit of a deathless soul,
> Called from its mortal tenement to fly,
> And of the unseen world the secret try.
> A few more hours wrapt in its funeral stole,
> Death's winding sheet. That bell again shall knoll
> The body hence, in its long home to lie,
> 'Till angels' trump arouse it. Do not say
> 'Tis a vain sound, that passing spirit's sign,
> Be warned awhile, thy heart withdraw away
> From this world's toys, to heavenly themes incline;
> And think the solemn knell which now is tolling
> A brother's fate, to-morrow may be mine.
> *Musings on the Church*

Y

MONUMENTAL BRASSES.

The following observations being accidentally omitted on page 135, as they breathe a kindred spirit to the lines just quoted, are introduced here as most convenient :

> " Where brass memorials display
> The forms that long have passed away ;
> In all beside, remembered not,
> Their faith and virtues all forgot ;
> Nor prayer, nor mass, for ages said
> To cheat the world, and mock the dead ;
> Nor saints, nor purgatory's fire
> Their disembodied souls require."
>
> G. D.

E have before remarked, that Henry I. founded his priory for the maintenance of a hundred brothers of the order of Benedictines ; now, making due allowance for attendants, lay officers, choristers, &c., the number of deaths, which according to modern calculators, would occur amongst such a body may be taken as two in a year, considering that the priory retained its full complement of inmates. For about four centuries, the total number of deaths occuring within the monastery during that period, would be nearly one thousand.

Now we may reasouably seek for traces of the sepulchre of these men and also of the townsmen of the same period, in the church, and enquire as to the mode of perpetuating the memory of the departed, common at those periods.

There are at the present time visible nine tablets with representations of the deceased persons, eight stones with traces of the figures once affixed to them, and many more concealed by the flooring of the pews; so these we must add to those which have perished in the destruction of the chancel and lady chapel, most of which from their position, and the fact that they commemorated the memory of departed priors, sub-priors, and other clerical worthies, must have been of a costly and beautiful description.

We may give the following general summary of the ancient memorials of the dead, existing in this church, as far as can be ascertained :—no less than eight have been removed from their slabs and totally lost; three are partly hidden; six are more or less perfect; and eight which have been removed by the care of Mr. G. Derbyshire, have been collected and placed in the south aisle. The periods of their execution are as follows: one of the 14th century; one of the 15th; two of the 16th, and one of the 17th., thus giving a total reckoning, including those the date of which cannot be ascertained, of twenty-five. Of these, three were undoubtedly commemorative of ecclesiastics, the remainder, of laymen and their wives.

Hence we may conclude, that the present number bears but a small proportion to the original number deposited. We may account for their disappearance, in several ways,—by the zeal of the Puritan soldiers and civilians, who seldom, as in the case before us, spared the monuments of the Romish clergy ; also, by avarice and necessities of lay impropriators, churchwardens and ministers, who, to defray the expense of disfiguring the structure, frequently confined to the furnace, bells, lead, and whole batches of brasses,—brass then being of much more value than at present, as its manufacture was unknown in England.

Raised, or altar tombs, were frequently employed till the close of the 12th century. It was then found, as the principles of art were better understood, that the crowding of the interior with tombs had a bad general effect, and was practically inconvenient. To remedy this, the art of inlaying brass in slabs of stone, was introduced from the continent, probably from Flanders or Normandy, where the manufacture of brass was known, and the early and more elaborate specimens appear to have been executed ; the later are doubtless, English work, as we may gather from the similarity of dress and inscriptions.

This art, like all other branches of church ornament, had its period of development and decadency. In proof of this assertion, we have but to examine the traces of the ancient brass in the north aisle, of the 14th century, or either of those in the nave of a later date, and compare it with that of Charles I., in the nave, containing a somewhat fulsome panegyric on the virtues of

Richard Fynche, bachelor; and the inferiority of the latter, both in style and execution, is manifest.

The metal chosen was brass, of a very hard and durable nature, frequently more durable than the stone on which it was laid; on this was engraved a representation of the deceased in the attitude of devotion, either in his ordinary attire, as in some of those preserved in the south aisle, and in some lying in the nave,—or in his grave-clothes, as on the gravestone of Richard Flarey. Some were supposed to be uttering an ejaculation, which was engraved on a scroll proceeding from the mouth of the figure. Such an one, may be seen in the nave; the name and date is gone, but the figure, that of a woman remains, which has the following, " Oh God, the Father of heaven, have mercy on us." The accompanying figure of the husband, which had a similar scroll, has perished.

The engraved lines appear to have been filled up with a bituminous substance, generally black, but in some cases vermillion and other brilliant colours were used. The surface of the surrounding stone was covered with an enamel of various colours, according to the nature of the device. The figure was affixed to a hollow, with pitch and flat-headed rivets let into the stone, fastened with lead; this mode of fastening may be clearly traced in the specimen last-mentioned. In some instances, the number of surviving children is denoted by two groups of smaller figures, placed at the foot of the stone, one group representing each sex.

The stone generally chosen to form the slabs,

is that now known by the name of Purbeck
marble ; it is found in the south of England, and
is easily distinguished by its grey colour, and the
embedded fossil shells.

We shall proceed to notice separately and more
in detail, the brasses and inscriptions of interest.
In the north aisle is a slab, which though much
worn, has undoubted traces of having been ornamented with a brass of a costly and beautiful
description, to the memory of an ecclesiastic. The
size of the stone is nearly ten feet by four feet.
We may partly account for the wear this stone
has experienced by the subsequent opening of a
door into the church at that part, which is now
blocked up by a kind of monument to the memory
of Jane Cart, and the disfigurement of the church.
The deceased was represented in his habit, under
a canopy of tabernacle work, executed about the
beginning of the 14th century; the sides were
decorated with entwined scrolls and various
heraldic devices and monograms.

Here a tale migh be told of sacrilege and
violence done to the house of God, but we forbear;
suffice it to say that ignorance, prejudice, and
misguided zeal has done ten thousand times more
to destroy the costly works once in our churches
than time itself.

Two other stones, which evidently were placed
to commemorate departed priests, are to be found;
the largest is at the west entrance, just within
the church ; the smallest is placed without the
church, near to the belfry door. It was split
some years since by the clapper of a bell, which
flew out as it was being rung, and fell on the

stone. The brasses of both are gone. The sill of the west door is formed of an old coffin of Purbeck marble, the shape is clearly distinguishable. A similar stone coffin, in its original position, and once having a brass on the lid is to be noticed on entering: it is near the stove, and the date of these is the early part of the 14th century.

Passing towards the chancel, we have an imitation of the ancient monuments previously noticed. The execution, inscription, figures, &c., are worthy of record : there are three effigies,— the deceased, his father, and mother : at the foot are small groups, representing the brothers and sisters of the deceased : beneath are the arms of the Merchant Tailors, and on the margin the following doggerel, which, with the inscription are given verbatim :—

"WE NOW THOV ART NOT LOST BUT SENT BEFORE
THY FRENDES ALL LEFTE THY ABSENCE TO DEPLOARE
NOR CAN THY VERTYES EVER BE FOR GOTTEN
THOVGHT IN THE GRAVE THY CORPSE BE DED AND
    ROTTEN
FOR YEL TONGED ENVYE TO THE WORD MVST TELL
THAT AS THOV LIVEST THOV DYEST AND THAT WAS
    WELL."

The inscription has been removed, and is on the board in the south aisle :—

"Here lyeth the body of Richard Fynche, Cittizen and Marchaunt Taylor, of London, being a bachiler of the age of 81 yeares or thereabouts, who deceased ye 12 day of January, A° Don 1640, the son of Thomas Fynche and Elizabeth his wife, which Elixabeth departed the Second Day of August, 1607, and the said Thomas deceased the 26th Day of Dec. A. D. 1586." [This is a later date than any found in the church.]

Further on are to be seen several large slabs,

once ornamented with brasses. On one of these was an epitaph, so quaint and ambiguous, that it gave rise to the incredible report of one woman having had nineteen children at five births, viz: three times, three children, and twice, five at two other times. It was first recorded by "Hakewill's Apologie," page 252. Speaking of the profligacy of women in ancient and modern ages, says, "Now some others there are, namely Haurtes the author of " The Tryall of Wits," who would bear us in hand that more twins and male children were born in the first ages of the world, than there now are ; neither can I call to mind any example in all antiquity, parallel to that of a woman buried in the church of Dunstaple, who as her epitaph testifies, bore at three several times three children at a birth, and five at a birth two other times." Fuller in his "Worthies of Bedfordshire," mentions this, but in a note says, "that it was not correct, the truth being that a man at Dunstaple had nineteen children by two wives, and that the other was only a legend of the place." The error thus started, through careless reading, and the tradition of the town has ever since continued.

Upon the slab were inlaid the figures of a man and woman in brass, both dressed in gowns, with their hands in the attitude of prayer, and at their feet the inscription. Beneath the latter were two groups, one of boys and one of girls, with the types of the evangelists at the corners. The inscription was in Latin, and is as follows :—

" Hic William Mulso sibi quem sociabit et Alice
Marmore sub duro conclusit moro generalis
Fer tres bis quinos hæc natos fertur habere
Per sponsos binos Deus his clemens miserere."

which literally translated is, "One general fate has enclosed here under a hard marble, William Mulso, and Alice his wife; she is reported to have had three times three, and twice five children by two husbands, the Lord being merciful to commiserate." This conceited mode of informing the world that a woman had nineteen children, gave rise to the mistake of their having been produced at five births.

The following are some of the inscriptions, arranged according to date :—

Hic iaceut Johes Pedder qui obijt iii die Mensis Augusti Anno Dni Millaiu'cccclriii Et Margareta Matildis ac Agnes uxoies ci quos ai als piciet de ame.

I confess that to give a correct translation of this baffles my ingenuity, as well as that of several college friends, good Latin scholars. The difficulty arises not from any illegibility, but from the numerous contractions in the last sentence; so that we are doubtful whether it is a prayer at all, but simply a declaration. Three different readings have been sent me on the subject, and my own opinion agrees with the first; but I give the others out of respect to the authors.

1st ending.—"Here lyeth the bodies of John Pedder who died on the 3rd day of the month of August, in the year of our Lord, 1463, and Margaret, Matilda and Agnes, his wives: their aged remains, by reason of absolution, rest peaceably."

2nd ending.—"Whose aged remains grieve no more, the soul being at peace."

3rd ending.—"They dying honourably, in old age, for whose rest pray."

It is worthy of observation, that the rector of

z

the parish at the time of the great rebellion, was named William Pedder; and he seems to have anticipated some of the coming changes, for instead of signing the register as usual, he very early dropt the obnoxious title of rector, and conformed so far to the popular feeling, as to affix his signature, thus " William Pedder, Minister."

Here lyeth John Blurte and Elizabeth his wyf whiche John decessid the xx day of Apriell, in the yeare of oure Lord thousand ccccc and ii on whose soulus ihs habe mercy Amen.

Off yo charite py for the soule of henry flarey and Agnes his wife the which lyeth buried under this stone and the said henri deceassed the xxbiii day of December A dm Mcccccxbi.

Pray for the soules of Nicolas Purbey Elizabeth and Alys his wybes which Nicolas decessid the secunde day of January A° MDxxi.

Pray for the soules of Robert Alee and Elizabeth and Agnes his wyfes the whiche Robt decessed the iiii day of Septembre the yer of o Lord MDrliiiio o whose souls ihs habe m.

Of your chartie pray for the soules of Richard Pynfold and Margaret his wife the which Richard deceased the xxiii day of Robember in the year of our Lord God MDlxbi.

We can form but a very imperfect notion of the beauty, and richness in design of the old English brasses, from the specimens extant in the church, seeing that they were executed at the period when art was on the decline. The deceased persons appear to have been in no way distinguished either for rank or achievements to merit costly memorials. This style of memorial was succeeded by one comprising weeping cupids, urns, torches, hour glasses, and other symbolical figures borrowed from the antiquities and fables of Greece and Rome.

No other remains within the walls of this church carry even the cursory examiner so forcibly back to the past, or impart more useful information than these memorials of the departed : but few can fail on reflection, to realize vividly to themselves some of the manners, habits, feelings, skill and failings of a by-gone age.

As some of these contain a prayer, it may be well to observe, that while as Protestants we strenuously resist the Roman doctrine of purgatory, because it is a dangerous one, which we verily believe hath betrayed a multitude of souls into eternal perdition, who might have escaped hell if they had not depended upon the after-game of purgatory. On the other hand, we cannot take part with those who look upon death as only a release to those weary of suffering ; but prefer rather the teaching of the church, as shown in the book of Common Prayer, and supported by the authority of Holy Scripture, without expressing an opinion as to how far it might be desirable, or otherwise, to revive the ancient liturgies on this point. Prayers for the dead, as founded upon the hypothesis of purgatory (and we in no otherwise reject them,) falls together with it. The prayers for the dead used in the ancient church, (those I mean that were more properly prayers, *i.e.* either deprecations or petitions,) were of two sorts, either the common and general commemoration of all the faithful at the oblation of the Holy Eucharist, or the particular prayers used at the funeral of any of the faithful, lately deceased.

The former respected their final absolution, and the consummation of their bliss at the resurrection; like as that our church useth both in the office for the Communion and in that for the Burial of the Dead; which indeed, seems to be no more than we daily pray for, in that petition of the Lord's prayer, (if we rightly understand it,) "Thy kingdom come." The latter were also charitable omens and good wishes of the faithful living, as it were accompanying the soul of the deceased to the joys of paradise, of which they believed it already possessed; as the ancient author of the "Ecclesiastical Hierarchy," in his last chapter of that book plainly informs us. In a word, let any understanding and unprejudiced person attentively observe the prayers for the dead, in the most undoubtedly ancient Liturgies, especially those in the Clementine Liturgy, and those mentioned in the "Ecclesiastical Hierarchy," and he will be so far from believing the Roman purgatory, upon the account of these prayers, that he must needs see they make directly against it. For they all run (as even that prayer for the dead, which is unadvisedly left by the Romanists in their own canon of the mass, as a testimony against themselves,) in this form, "For all that are at peace or at rest in the Lord." Now how can they be said to be "in peace or at rest in the Lord," who are supposed to be in a state of misery and torment? Thus it is evident that the Popish custom of praying for souls in a state of pain, is altogether different from the practice which prevailed from a very early period, for praying for souls that rest in peace.

DURING the night of Whit-tuesday, June 2nd, 1841, an alarming fire broke out at the house of Mr. Fossey, confectioner, and was not subdued until 19 houses, forming the corner of Church-street and High-street were burnt down. During the same year the sovereign of the land paid a visit to this royal manor, a circumstance which had not taken place since the reign of Elizabeth. Triumphal arches were erected, and the staple trade of the town was well exhibited, by trophies formed of plait and bonnets. As there no longer existed a royal residence on the estate, nor a priory with its capacious rooms and extensive privileges, many of which had been granted specially with a view to accommodate the reigning monarch whenever they came this way, Her most gracious Majesty was pleased to alight for a short time at the Sugar Loaf; but that old familiar face of host and hostess who had so often welcomed her arrival when princess Victoria, was not there; another though only for a short time, occupied that post.

The Temperance Hall was erected in 1841, Mr. Stephens, of Bedford, being the architect, and Mr. Joseph Cheshire, of Dunstable, the builder. It cost £600, and though the piers are 18 inches thick, yet not being of sufficient width, they were found unable to carry the roof; hence those pillars on the side walls were added, which being screwed to the roof at one end and the floor at the other, gives increased strength, and for the like purpose as well as for convenience, the platform and room below was added.

The Bible Society which was established in this town, in 1812, have held many of their later meetings within its walls, and the grand Jubilee year of the Parent society was celebrated in Nov. 1854, with great rejoicing in this hall, Edward Burr, Esq., occupying the chair. The sum of £30 17s. 4½d., was collected, and being afterwards made up to £50, was remitted to the Parent society, free from all deductions, as the Dunstaple offering to the Jubilee fund.

Suffering humanity has here unfolded its distress to the ears of a sympathising audience. William Wells Brown and other fugitive slaves of America, here met a warm reception in 1854, and told their own unvarnished tale of the sufferings endured, and the cruel oppressions of their countrymen under the so-called " christian" government of America.

The walls have echoed often to the sound of melody and song; the Caledonian has sat with pleasure to hear the music of his native land troll forth from the throats of his countrymen and women, and enjoyed in the land of his adoption, the advantages of home. But the crowning musical effects was the adoption of concerts for the million, in 1857.

Once it was the favoured spot where Hugh Thripp and Marianne his wife kept their marriage feast, and the walls resounded with the joyous accents of the bridal day.

Here the disciples of Sir Andrew Agnew have

pleaded hard for the better observance of the Lord's-day; while a few, simple-minded, earnest men have endeavoured to stem the tide of moral evil in one direction,—one by a fierce counterblast against tobacco; another, would remove indiscriminately, all kinds of customary refreshments, while a third, enters into a lengthy disquisition on the philosophy of public-house signs : yet notwithstanding the pathos of one, and the fiery eloquence of another, with the quaintness of a third whose glory it is to appear on gala days in the very hat which covered his head in many a drunken hubbub, but still more interesting now, it being the identical one in which he signed the pledge : it became evident even to the heads of society that they had no power to move the middle and lower classes any further. Then with a perseverance, worthy of the men who had testified the sincerity of their attachment to the cause by the costly sacrifices they had made, the aristocracy were invited by circular, to attend a conference in 1856, with a view to open if possible, a fresh field in that direction.

On the 20th of May, 1856, it was thrown open to the purposes of active benevolence, and a fancy fair was held on Tuesday and the two following days, with a view to clear off the debt on the West-street chapel. It was remarkably well attended, and owing to the liberal support of the public, the proceeds exceeded the most sanguine expectations. The hall on this occasion presented a lively and elegant appearance, being decorated with a number of flags, and the stalls adorned with foliage & flowers. The proceeds realized £150.

Previous to the year 1837, candle and lantern were the only means of enlightening the street after dark ; or an occasional apprentice carrying a torch whenever his master or mistress wished to visit a neighbour. In that year, the Gas works on the outside of the town were erected, and let on a lease of 14 years to Messrs. Brothers. The mains, as they are called, are about 9 ft. in length, and pipes branching from the mains to supply gas to dwelling-houses or manufactories, are called service-pipes. The quantity of gas consumed, is told by a very simple and ingenuous instrument, invented by Mr. Clegg, and subsequently improved by Crosby, and called a gas-meter, consisting of a hollow iron case containing an inner cylinder or drum, so constructed that the gas passing through it by the pressure it receives at the Gas works, causes it to revolve on an axis. Each rotation allows a known quantity of gas to pass through the water, with which the outer vessel is partially filled, to the exit pipe ; and as the revolutions are registered by wheel-work and an index, the quantity of gas consumed is indicated with considerable accuracy. It is usually examined quarterly by a person employed by the Gas company, who charge the consumer according to the quantity indicated, at the rate of 7s. per 1,000 feet.

The rapid increase of the population, as well as the diversity of prevailing religious opinions in the town, induced certain reflecting individuals in 1843, to look upon popular ignorance as a national calamity, and yet conscientiously objecting to the only means of instruction offered, they resolved to make an effort to open a school on the

British system, for the following reasons:

1st.—Because they considered it most favourable to the maintenance of civil and religious liberty. The direction of popular education is the proper duty and inalienable right of the people themselves; it cannot be, say they, resigned to Government; it cannot be yielded to the National Establishment; it cannot be laid at the feet of ministers of religion, either of one or all denominations; it is not exclusively a religious thing; if in one respect it involves spiritual privileges, in another it distinctly includes civil rights; to possess it is a secular advantage, to be deprived of it is to be brought under a civil disability.

2nd.—Because it is best adapted to promote the extension and improvement of education; and

3rd.—Because it is most consistent with the christian character and love of the Gospel, by confining religious instruction to the sacred Scriptures, and by inculcating points which unite rather than those which divide real christians.

It presents truth to the mind of the children in its just proportions; it avoids the danger of forming sectarian partizans, instead of enlightened christians; and it prevents the growth of mere prejudices, by withholding from the young sentiments and opinions which can have no practical hold either on their intellect or affections.

It binds together by common efforts in a common cause, those who are always too prone to separate; it enables the stronger to assist the weaker, by generously bearing a portion of their burdens and by manifesting to the world the

A 1

identity of christian character, it tends to promote
the fulfilment of the Redeemer's prayer, "that
they all may be one." They saw the eminence
which schools in connexion with the British and
Foreign School Society had attained in other
places, so as to be emphatically designated "Bible
Schools." On these principles, a school for boys
was opened in the little room belonging to the
West-street meeting-house. In 1845, being found
too small, an arrangement was subsequently concluded by which they occupied the Temperance
Hall; here they continued to flourish under the
able teaching of Mr. Hopcroft, till 1850, when an
entire new room was erected at a cost of £300,
and capable of holding 200 children, being 50 ft.
long and 25 ft. wide. This however which appeared to be the only means of giving the system
a permanent footing in the town, was the cause
of its overthrow; for the treasurer's book to this
very day shows a large amount of promissory
subscriptions from £1 up to £10, that were never
paid. Thus debt was unavoidably incurred, and
at every subsequent meeting debt was the subject
of conversation, till those entrusted with its
management had no heart to move; so that on
the 24th of March, 1855, a public meeting was
hastily called, but the townspeople felt so little
interested in the issue that only three persons
attended, and into their hands the committee
resigned their trust, and in a few days arrangements were made and 65 children were removed
to the National school, on Church green, and the
doors of the new school closed.

The same year that the boys removed to the

Temperance Hall, a girls' school was opened in the room they vacated: like its forerunner, the room soon proved too small. It continued to flourish, till in 1847, the committee felt themselves justified to rent a more convenient place, where it went on prosperous for eight years. From this place they again removed in 1855, to the room rendered vacant by the closing of the boys' school, of which they took possession, under such circumstances as will ultimately secure the building to the town for the purposes of unsectarian education, for ever. Its present teacher, Miss Amelia Wootton, has been connected therewith almost from its commencement. The average number of scholars is 100.

Perhaps I cannot better show the progress of intellectual development, than by the following items obtained from the Post Office. The year that these schools were opened (1843,) the average number of letters passing through the Post Office daily, was considerably under 100. In 1858, they had increased to a daily average of from 1,100 to 1,200, and a weekly sale of postage stamps amounting to £12 worth, while money orders are issued at the rate of £5,000 per month.

When all processions were abolished at the Reformation, yet for the retaining the perambulations of the circuit of parishes it was enjoined, "That the people shall, once a-year, at the time accustomed, with the curate and substantial men of the parish walk about the parish as they were accustomed, and at their return to church make their common prayer; provided that the curate in their said common perambulations used heretofore in the days of Rogation, at certain convenient places, to admonish the people, to give thanks to God in the beholding of God's benefits, for the increase and abundance of his fruits upon the face of the earth, with the saying of the 103rd Psalm, at which time also the same minister shall inculcate this and such like sentences, "Cursed be he that trespasseth the bounds and doles of his neighbour."

This processioning after being for many years carried out in all its fulness, began to decline, and became triennial instead of annual; and from Rogation Monday was shifted to Holy Thursday, and lastly a mere holiday for the Free Boys, attended by some of the townspeople and bellman, when in the year 1844 it ceased altogether. The following is the route forming the boundary of the parish :—" From the Church to Fig's Croft, thence to Long Hedge across to Half Moon Lane, over to Sixteen Acres, down Perwinkle Lane (so called from a plant of that name which there grows wild, and nowhere else in the parish,) to Home Ground, over Chalk-dell Field, across Butts' Lane to Catch Acre, thence to Leighton Gap." Here in addition to the ceremony of pursing, which took place at each of the points, in the following manner :—First, a large cross was dug in the earth by a spade, carried for the purpose by one of the boys, and at the point of intersection a turf 9 inches square was removed; in this hole a boy stood upon his head, while he received one slap on the seat, where honours lodged, as an emblem that punishment was the just desert of those who should remove his neighbour's landmark :—then came the customary anathemas upon those who should trespass upon their neighbour's bounds, &c. This part of the ceremony being over, the Rogation bun and cheese with a small tot of ale, was distributed by the churchwarden. The procession again moved on, headed by the bellman, down Union-street to Dog-kennel Close, crossing the Park to Fig's Croft, and finished at the Church, the point of starting.

The year 1845 brought in a change of rectors. The Rev. Solomon Piggott, after a period of 20 years' ministerial duties connected with the parish, during which period he established the evening lecture, being called to rest from his labours. The following hymn was written and sung on the occasion of his death; and if to the professional eye it is found wanting in any of the essentials of good versification, yet it must be admitted that the lines exhibit traces of an earnest and affectionate mind, and may be taken as a fair estimate of the love and affection entertained by all classes of society for their pastor.

"OUR PASTOR SLEEPS."

OUR pastor sleeps in certain trust,
Of waking with the ransom'd just;
And seeing joyful face to face,
The King of saints, the God of grace !

Within the silent tomb is laid
The form, whose lips to us convey'd
The word of life, the message given,
To dying men, by pitying heaven !

Our thoughts from grief we cannot keep,
The heart will feel—the eyes will weep ;
But hope can bid the tear be dry,
And point to mansions in the sky !

O glorious day ! O happy hour !
When Christ shall come with pomp and power ;
The grave shall all its trusts restore,
The dead shall live for evermore !

He was succeeded by the Rev. F. Hose, the present rector. Considerable changes were effected, the entire parish was brought more immediately under the notice of its minister, who made large use of lay agency, a district visiting society was established, and the town divided into as many districts as then necessary. In 1855 they had been increased to 21 in number ; each visitor being furnished with a book containing the necessary instruction for the proper discharge of their duties ; and which provides certain tables to be filled up from time to time, and brought to the monthly meetings for examination. The visitors are instructed to make inquiries as to the number composing the family, with the ages of the children ; whether they attend school, or can read ; whether the family possess a bible, or any other religious books ; how the Sabbath and leisure hours are spent ; if temporary relief is required ; enquire as to the means of subsistence, whether by parochial aid, labour, charity, or otherwise ; the amount of rent, &c. ; to urge on them the duty and privilege of observing the Sabbath, of prayer, of attending public worship ;

to point out to them as occasion may require, their relative duties, and avail yourself of suitable opportunities of reproving open vice; to pay particular attention to the young, sick, and aged; to inculcate habits of industry and cleanliness, both of rooms and persons; and such I am able to testify that many of the visitors conscienciously carry out, it is presumed that all do so more or less. In order to acquire skill in the Holy Scriptures, for the conviction of the gainsayer, the instruction of the ignorant, the comfort of the feeble-minded, the healing of the backslider, and the building up of believers in their most holy faith, the visitors meet every Wednesday evening at the house of one of the seniors among their number, to study the Holy Scriptures, the internal and external evidences of Christianity, &c., &c.

As a proof, the fears expressed by Jas. Tongue, though not amounting to a prophesy, were more than fully realized. I have been favoured with the following from balance-sheets, showing the decline of the posting trade at the Sugar Loaf.

From April 9th, 1837, to April 7th, 1838.

Posting.			House Accommodation.		
£.	s.	d.	£.	s.	d.
2492	7	6½	669	10	3
			2492	7	6½
			£3191	17	9½

From April 8th, 1838, to April 6th, 1839.

Posting.			House Accommodation.		
1005	15	4½	253	19	11
			1005	15	4½
			£1259	15	4½

	£.	s.	d.
Total in 1838...	3191	17	9½
„ „ 1839...	1259	15	3½

Making a total Loss of £1932   2   6 in 2 yrs.

The road opened to Birmingham during the week ending Sept. 16th, 1838. The receipts fell that week to £22 4s. 9d. and continued to decrease until April the following year, when the loss amounted in the gross to nearly £4,000. Others in various amounts were in a similar situation; the people were panic struck, and dismay was visible in every countenance, "the hope of their gains was gone." The manufacturers suffered considerable inconvenience in the disposal of their produce; it was a fearful time, but in the depth of their difficulties, there shone forth those graces which are the genuine fruits of that deep-toned piety which forms so prominent a feature amongst society at Dunstaple;—true, on this delightful town had long shone the sun of prosperity, but it had neither weakened their graces nor enfeebled their manly strength;—but calmly and deliberately facing the evil they sought the remedy, and were prepared to welcome George Stephenson, Esq., and listen to his proposition for railway communication. A capital of £50,000 in £20 shares was required; the measure was approved by the Board of Trade, and the bill read a first time April 4th, 1845 : the parliamentary agents were Messrs. Burke, Pratt, Venables and Co.

Witnesses were called in support of the preamble

which was unopposed. From the evidence it appeared that there is an incline plane,* proposed to be worked by weights, and with this exception the steepest gradient is 1 in 73. This is at the junction of the London and Birmingham, and there is no tunnel. It is to be a single line of railway, except where the incline plane is. The profits after deducting all expenses for working the line, is estimated at 5 per cent.: the committee decided the preamble proved.

The first general meeting of the proprietors was held on Wednesday, July 30th, 1845, at Euston Square Station,—Mr. George Stephenson, Engineer, in the chair.

Considerable difficulty was experienced in obtaining the requisite number of proprietors to constitute a legal meeting.

The chairman said, that before vacating the chair, to attend another meeting where his presence was more imperatively required, he would state that being perfectly satisfied with the safety of the concern, the shareholders need not be under any apprehension of not receiving 4½ per cent. dividend, that amount having been guaranteed by the London and Birmingham, who had undertaken to lease the line, with the determination of extending it from Dunstaple to St. Albans, and St. Albans to Watford and Luton.

The proposed line would reinstate Dunstaple in its former position, as an important town on the great northern thoroughfare. He had visited Luton with the expectation of being kindly re-

---

* Between Standbridge-Ford and Sewell, which rises 1 ft. in 5.

B1

ceived, in offering to carry out the extension line, but having met with anything but kindness, he had resolved never to revisit them as long as he lived, unless for other purposes.

Mr. Hudson was then called to the chair, and said that as a sufficient number of proprietors were not present to form a legal meeting, the proprietors must adjourn to the 27th of August.

The 3rd half-yearly meeting was held on the 17th of August, 1846, at Euston Station,— E. D. Mangles, Esq., M.P. was voted to the chair, and called upon the secretary, Mr. Thos. Long, to read the advertisement convening the meeting, which having been done, the seal of the company was affixed to the register of proprietors, the minutes of the last meeting having been confirmed, the secretary read the following report :—

" The Directors have to report to their proprietors, that the bill for the Cambridge and Oxford railway has been rejected by the House of Commons. The proprietors are aware that the works of the line were delayed until the result of the Cambridge and Oxford Company's application to parliament was ascertained; and your directors are now in negociation with the London and North Western Company, with whom they trust to make a satisfactory arrangement. The usual statement of accounts to the 30th of June is appended to this report. It will be observed that the last call is considerably in arrear, but the Directors have not thought it necessary under the circumstances which have existed during the last half-year, to press the proprietors for payment of it. The Directors regret to announce the death of one of their colleagues, Mr. Johnson Masters, of Dunstaple. It is not their present intention to fill up the vacancy. The following is a list of the present Directors of the Company:—George Stephenson, Esq., chairman; Edward Burr, Esq.; John Ellis, Esq.; Henry Goude, Esq.; Richard Gutteridge, Esq.; Ross Donnelly Mangles, Esq.; Thomas Young, Esq."

General Statement of the Receipts and Expenditure of the Company, from the formation to June 30th, 1846:—

RECEIPTS.

	£.	s.	d.
Deposits of £1. 5s. per share on 2,500 shares	3125	0	0
Call of £4. per share thereon......... £10,000			
Less calls unpaid...... 3,008			
	6,992	0	0
Interest...	6	1	2
	£10,123	1	2
Balance, (in hands of Glyn and Co.,)......... £7,647	16	6	

EXPENDITURE.

	£.	s.	d.
Charges of Solicitors, Agents, &c., in obtaining Act of Incorporation	1888	5	9
Engineering charges	431	4	2
Travelling Expenses	9	17	0
Printing, Stationery and Advertising	11	15	9
Salary of Secretary	50	0	0
Interest on Calls	84	2	0
	£2475	4	8
Balance	7647	16	6
	£10123	1	2

Examined and found correct.

CHARLES ANSTEAD,⎫ Auditors.
E. S. ELLIS, ⎭

The Chairman then proposed the adoption of

the report, and said that he had no reason to doubt but that an arrangement would shortly be made with the London and North Western for the sale of this line. Mr. Ellis and himself had been engaged in negotiating the terms upon which it was to be effected. That gentleman not being present, he did not feel authorised to say more at present; but without pledging himself he had no doubt that it would be shortly concluded. The resolution having been put and seconded, that the report be received and adopted, was carried unanimously.

A proprietor enquired, whether another call would be made prior to the disposal of the undertaking?

The Chairman said, that no further call would be required. In answer to another question, he stated that £3,000 of the last call remained unpaid.

A special general meeting of the proprietors was held Nov. 14th, 1846, at Euston Station, for the purpose of considering an offer by the London and North Western Railway Company, for the purchase of the Dunstaple undertaking—George Stephenson, Esq., took the chair. Mr. Thomas Long, the secretary, read the clauses of the Dunstaple Act, which authorized three-fifths of the shareholders present, either in person or by proxy, to dispose of the company's interest in the undertaking, to the London and Birmingham Railway Company. He then read the advertisement convening the meeting, afterwards the written offer made by the London and North Western Railway Company, to purchase and redeem the rent and moiety of surplus profits made payable to the Dunstaple Company by the Dunstaple and London and Birmingham Act of 1845. The conditions of the offer were to return the whole of the sums paid by the proprietors of the Dunstaple Company, with interest at the rate of 4 per cent. per annum, up to the present time. The London and North Western also to pay all debts due, and satisfy all claims upon the Dunstaple Company, and to fully indemnify them therefrom. The Chairman asked if any proprietor wished to make any remarks?

The resolution was then read, authorising the Directors to accept the offer made by the London and North Western Company, and complete the terms of sale. Mr. Ellis moved the resolution. He said that he held shares in the undertaking, and also a number of proxies belonging to persons who concurred with himself in considering it to be an advantageous offer. He stated that when Mr. George Stephenson projected the line, he calculated upon charging 4d. per ton, per mile, for the carriage of iron; but their Act only allowed them to charge 1d. per mile, which would never pay the proprietors. The line would not give 4 per cent. With respect to the London and Birmingham Company, they could never reap a further advantage from the line than the 4 per cent., under any circumstances. The resolution was then seconded, and carried unanimously. The Chairman said that he was the largest shareholder in the undertaking; that when he projected the line, he intended to charge 4d. per ton, per mile; but the bill only authorized them to charge 1d. per ton, which of course considerably altered the prospects of the undertaking, and he was very glad, under the circumstances, to accept the terms offered by the London and North Western Company. Mr. Pritchard, C.E., said that he dissented to the sale of the line, and also that he objected to the form of the circular. The Chairman reminded him, that he had spoken too late, and that the resolution to which he now said that he dissented had been passed unanimously by the meeting while he was present.

Mr. Long in answer to a question, stated that a meeting of the London and North Western Company would shortly be held, in order to sanction the purchase. Mr. Mangles moved that the thanks of the meeting be given to Mr. Stephenson, which was seconded and carried unanimously. In returning thanks, he said that he was glad that their affairs had come to so favourable a conclusion.

The line was opened for luggage on the 29th of May, and for passengers on the 1st of June, 1848, and here again we witness in all its loveliness, the power and influence of religion. Cold, speculative men would have looked upon the Sabbath as being a day in which to reap a golden harvest, and probably they had been right when we view the dense population within an easy distance; but no, before she parted with the rail she showed her readiness to forego the mammon in order to secure the true riches,—and therefore remained firm in her refusal to have the line open for Sunday trade.

The amount of passenger trade is small compared with other lines, but the carrying trade is extensive. Various coal companies have accredited agents at its terminus, who carry on a brisk trade. Previous to the rail the town depended for its coal upon Biggleswade; and one William Hogg, Esq., in the month of January, held annually a coal feast first at the Sugar Loaf and then at the Crown opposite, when all persons presenting payment of the coal bills were regaled with a sumptuous entertainment. The cost of carriage for coal from Biggleswade was 9d. per bushel.

On the 3rd of May, 1858, a second line of railway communication was opened for passengers, running into the Dunstaple line at Brewer's-hill, by which means the town obtains an outlet for its trade in an opposite direction, passing through Luton and Welwyn, on to the Great Northern line. Doubtless the communication will be advantageous to both towns, and may be the means of removing that unkind feeling that has continued ever since the visit of Mr. Stephenson, before alluded to. In the March preceding, the line had been opened from Welwyn to Hertford; and arrangements have been made for a system of through-booking with that company and the Eastern Counties Company, to and from the Victoria Docks, Blackwall, and other places beyond Hertford.

The Hertford and Welwyn, and Luton, Dunstaple and Welwyn Railway Companies have been by Act of Parliament in 1858, incorporated into one company, under the title of " The Hertford, Luton and Dunstaple Railway."

The Priory church once more demands our attention : being in a dilapidated condition, the rector successfully aroused his parishioners to the work of restoration. A committee was formed, plans duly prepared for carrying out the object by Hope Scott, Esq., architect, of London, and in the month of August, 1851, one thousand feet of Totternhoe stone was placed on the Green for the restoration works, which commenced in September; the south aisle being entirely rebuilt and the rich vaulted or arched stone roof replaced. Originally these vaulted roofs had a second roof above them, and as the pitch of the second roof which formerly covered this aisle is still to be seen on the side wall above, it is much to be regretted that in this case that also was not replaced. The wall is pierced with eight Norman windows of Powel's stamped glass, the whole was completed at a cost of £1,600, in April 1852; but for want of funds the remainder of the building has not yet been touched, though there has never been a doubt but that each part will follow in due time.

That the corresponding aisle was similarly roofed in is certain, there being so many interesting remains which supported that roof, consisting of Norman caps and pillars, ribs of arches, mutilated figures, &c., which the reader may trace from the belfry door to the other extremity, as they protrude through the surface of the wall on the north side, and from their position admit of no other interpretation, than that they were so placed as supporters of the old Norman roof. There is every reason to believe that the nave was similarly covered in, and the stones in the possession of Mr. Fox, were probably some of the very stones or bosses of this centre roof, as they certainly belonged to some extensive system of vaulting, and the joining of the ribs are clearly to be seen upon the largest of them. Most of the churches in the neighbourhood are built and repaired from the quarries which run a considerable distance under the hills. The stone is removed on sledges with low wheels, being dug from dark pits, by the aid of lighted candles. On one occasion, a Mr. Bliss took two companions on a Sunday afternoon, to view the quarries, when by some accident the candles went out, and though they found their way back to the "Old Bottle" several times were unable to extricate themseves. Here they remained several days, until accidentally relieved by a party of workmen. The stone when first dug is soft, but hardens by exposure to the air. This stone like all other is not durable, unless placed on its natural bed, that is, on the same position of the strata of stone lying in the pit: in any other position wet will penetrate into the pores, and then by the action of frost, causes it to fly to pieces.

In "Pool's Ecclesiastical Architecture," the quarries are thus mentioned :—

"4th of June, 1363, we find William de Walsyngham engaged in the works for St. Stephen's chapel, within the palace of Westminster, and one item under date of March 19 (26 Ed. III, was paid to William Padrynton, for stone bought at Dunstaple, for making an image of St. Stephen, ten shillings."

"To the same, for carriage of the same, with two other stones bought for the images of two

B2

serjeants-at-arms from Dunstable, ten shillings."

These images probably remained in St. Stephen's chapel, until that building together with the other parliamentary offices were destroyed by fire on the 16th of October, 1834.

On taking down the wall of this aisle, between the stones were found a silver coin of the founder and endower Henry I. Whether the same fell in by accident during the erection of the church, or whether placed there as a record by some patriotic mason, we cannot now decide: it is now the property of Mr. Gostelow.

A bazaar was opened for three days for the sale of fancy, ornamental and useful articles, in aid of the funds for increasing the accommodation in the parish church, commenced on the 25th of August, 1855, under distinguished patronage. The National school room in Church-street, was tastefully fitted up for the occasion, under the direction of the rector, curate and churchwardens. The walls were lined with pink and white glazed canvas, with vandyke trimmings and rosettes; the slender cross-beams were covered with ever-greens and flowers, from which, were pendant glass baskets of beautiful design, miniature bal-loons and other ornamantal appendages. In the centre was displayed on a stand, citron trees bear-ing fruit; German trees were prettily adorned, and in a recess was an elegant stand of flowers, with vase containing gold and silver fish. The stalls presented a rich and varied collection, from many parts of the kingdom, as well as by the ladies of Bedfordshire and adjoining counties. A representation of the new aisle, in tapestry, commanded much admiration.

Cases of wax flowers, elegant brackets in leather-work, very beautiful cushions and exquisitely rich specimens of embroidery, needlework in endless variety. The Dunstaple staple manufacture was represented on a stall near the entrance, and displayed a pleasing array of elegant trifles. At the back of the building and communicating with the room, a handsome marquee displayed its dimensions forming a spacious refreshment-room and promenade, where a superior band played a choice selection of music, while the bells of the fine old priory church poured forth a merry peal during the day. The following ladies were stall-keepers :—The Rt. Hon. Lady Marianne Margaret Alford, the Rt. Hon. Lady Charles Russell, Lady Seebright, Mrs. Hose, Mrs. Flowers, Mrs. Pemberton, Mrs. Benning, Mrs. Medland, Mrs. E. Lockhart, Mrs. T. Rogers, Mrs. Elliott, Miss Warr, Mrs. Scott, Mrs. F. Farr, Miss Cartwright, and Miss Horton. Mrs. Johnson attended the refreshment room. The bazaar opened at eleven, and notwithstanding the unfavourable state of the weather the company gradually increased, and at three the room was crowded.

As the company increased matters began to wear a more cheerful aspect: great activity was manifested at various stalls, and during the remainder of the day a large amount of business was transacted by the fair and distinguished sales-women, whose gentle appeals to the smiling visitor could not be resisted, and as we gazed upon the busy scene and saw the generous efforts that were made for the restoration of our beloved church, we felt assured that this day would never be forgotten; for though no Richard de Morins should chronicle the event, still in years to come, when the musing swain at gentle eve shall wander round these ancient towers, he shall think with grateful pride on the illustrious names, and bless the memory of those who called into existence the stately column and the graceful arch.

On Friday the bazaar was opened again. The bells rang and music played at intervals during the day; there was a great number of visitors present, and at times the room presented a most animated scene. The priory church was open for inspection on each day, when that eminent and distinguished organist, Mr. Bobbett, performed some exquisite pieces. The proceeds from the sale realized £190.

In 1852, the health of the rector gave way under the weight of his accumulated duties, and the heavy responsibilities these new works brought with them. He was obliged for a time to retire to the continent in order to recruit his shattered health. On his return the Church Pastoral-Aid society granted him the assistance of a curate, under certain conditions, agreeing to pay £70 towards his salary. Thus assisted, an enlarged sphere of labour was sought for, two bible-classes were established, one for males on Thursdays, and another for females on Friday's, which are open to young persons of respectable families, from all denominations, who meet in the school-room. The cottage lecture on a Wednesday evening, in one or other portion of the town, dates its origin from this year.

Twice during the year 1853, did the small pox make its appearance in the town, on the first occasion but lightly, for although most houses were visited, yet none is known to have died from it. Not so, however, on its second attack; for death on his pale horse, beginning in Church-street, hurried many of the adult population to their long resting-place. Among the places which he visited was the old lodging-house for travellers, where crime lay concealed, vice fostered, poverty nestled, ignorance triumphed, and no man cared. There might be found the travelling tinker, tramping beggar, that had "thravelled in e'en a'most every country and sheer in England," rag collectors, wandering minstrels, owners & trainers of dogs, itinerant dealers in small wares, and a multitude of "ould Oirish" reapers, who just before harvest pass through the town in immense numbers, and spread themselves over the adjacent counties, gathering in the harvest, while not a few go as far as Kent and Sussex, finding temporary employment as hop-pickers. Of many of them it may be truly said,

"No small-tooth'd trap their locks disposes,
"Nor kerchiefs white attack their noses."

Of some whom this visitation carried off, we may hope that when delivered from the burden of the flesh they entered into joy and felicity, and they parted with their friends, not without a good hope of once more meeting them again, and when the vital spark had fled, the body was laid with becoming reverence in the silent grave; but at the lodging-house, a preliminary ceremonial was deemed necessary before the body could be removed. It was on a Monday evening, I lifted the latch of the door and entering, behind a screen without observation, I saw a number of persons in a state of almost intoxication. There sat women with their hair untrimmed, and all loose and disorderly, sipping their favourite drink, while it was almost impossible to penetrate the room for tobacco smoke, tears were flowing in great abundance down but few cheeks, and a rocking motion to and fro was given to the body, while cries and groans bespoke an amount of mental anguish and distress, which probably but few felt. There were inquiries, in doleful accents, why he left his family and friends; the wailing then continued, till it died away in a low sob. I waited for a short time, but finding it impossible to engage the attention of the motley group, I exchanged words with a few and then retired. Had I not been engaged in discharging the duty of a brother visitor, who was sick, I might never had an opportunity of witnessing such a scene, and learning the lessons it was calculated to impart.

Notwithstanding the virulence of the disease and its long continuance, the old Pest-house originally erected through the piety, wisdom, and benevolence of our ancestors, for the reception of those who fell victims to this disease, was not now available, nor can I discover the period when last its services were in requisition, or any regulations respecting its management when so used; but one thing seems beyond a doubt, that since the new road made through Dunstaple, from

Oxford to Cambridge, in 1784, it has not been used.

In laying out the ground for this new road, a considerable number of grave hillocks were levelled down in its vicinity. Both from the disorderly manner and the little depth at which they were deposited, bespeak the hastiness of their interment. I am inclined to accept the tradition, as being very likely true, "that a number of persons dying with small-pox were buried on the Downs," and that these graves contained the remains of those victims who succumbed to that fearful disease within the walls of the adjoining Pest House. The frequent communication between this town and London, occasioned the plague to be very fatal here in 1603 & 1625, but does not appear to have affected it. In 1665, the number of deaths registered that year being only 14.

During this year also, a subterranean telegraph was laid down, at a depth of 18ins. from the surface, all along the west side of High-street.

The Primitive-Methodists erected a meeting-house in Mount-street, at a cost of £300, simultaneously with a temporary building called the Tabernacle, for the use of the Independent denomination, till which time the members of this society were dependent on the kindness of various Nonconformists in the town, for religious instruction and accommodation; but in the year 1854, the present substantial building was erected, Mr. John Usher, of St. Peter's-green, Bedford, being the architect. On the 9th of August, 1853, the foundation-stone was laid by Mr. Joseph Osborn, and an address was delivered by the Rev. George Smith, of Poplar. A large company of friends assembled, and the day being fine, it was a time of great rejoicing. On the 12th of January, 1854, Mr. John Marshall, the builder, had so far completed his contract, that it was on that day opened for Divine worship and solemnly dedicated to the one true and living God.

The building is of Italian character, 58ft. long, 41ft. 6ins. wide, and 26ft. high. It is constructed of grey brick and Corsham stone dressings. The principal front has an imposing appearance, being divided into three compartments ; the two outer divisions projecting and forming staircase entrances for the gallery. The centre compartment, which is approached by a flight of stone steps consists of three doorways, with elliptical heads; above which is a spacious window, with nine distinct lights, the three centre lights rising considerably above the others. The stairs, turrets, and parapets are capped with stone, on bold ornamental brackets of frieze. The interior of the building is fitted up with flatform, in lieu of a pulpit, approached by two flights of stairs ; it is furnished with three handsome carved oak chairs, of chaste design. From the platform, and leading to the first row of seats, is an accoustic apparatus, for four deaf persons. The whole of the seats are open, with solid chamfered and rounded ends. The roof of the chapel consists of Memel timber framed into four strong queen trusses, covered with diagonal boarding as high as the straining piece, the upper portion being ceiled horizontally, and decorated with open iron work in panels and flowers, to

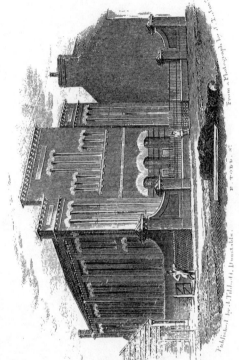

Published by A. Tibbett, Dunstable.   P. TODD, sc.

From a Photograph by J. Dunn.

INDEPENDENT CHAPEL.

assist ventilation. The timbers of the roof are supported by story posts, standing on carved stone corbeilles, descending the wall six feet. All the wood work is stained and varnished. The chapel is lighted with gas. Cost £1,400, and will accommodate 700 persons.

On the 9th of November in the same year, the Rev. James Lyon was recognized as the first pastor : the usual questions, on such occasions, being proposed by the Rev. William Robinson, of Luton.

The two first questions were put to Mr. Osborn, as to what led to the formation of the present interest, and secondly, what steps led to the selection of Mr. Lyon. The answers being satisfactory, the interrogation then required Mr. Lyon to state the way in which he had been led to take the oversight of the church. 2ndly, suggested a caution against coming among a people without a sufficient evidence of his call from God so to do. Third, to give a public statement of the principles and doctrines upon which he would proceed to feed the church of God committed to his care, and a statement of his belief.

The Rev. J. Sleigh, of Hockliffe, gave an address, explanatory of their faith and order, showing the duties of the pastor to the church, his aptitude to teach ; the deacons to look after the poor, to see the house properly prepared for worship ; and concluded with the relative duties of members.

The Sabbath-school contains 100 scholars under 20 teachers.

This year was also remarkable for the failure

cl

on the part of Mr. Samuel Sherwood Collis and others, who have during the last few years striven to revive the horse-races, for which in olden times Dunstaple was famous, and for which the elastic nature of the turf seems well adapted. The last races were held in Dunstaple park.

At the monthly district-meeting, a few nights before the races, the subject of the forthcoming races being introduced, a conversation arose as to the visitors' duty on that occasion, after which arrangements were made for the distribution of the following tracts —" Eight reasons for not going to the races;" "Evil consequences attending the race-course;" " A peep at the races;" "Sure gain." These were circulated by the district visitors in the customary visits. One of the visitors, an active young man, volunteered to distribute the handbills which were reserved for the day of the races, so that even at the last moment the votaries of pleasure might not rush into excess without having had a friendly pre-monition. One hundred of each of the following, were distributed by him at the entrance:—" The races;" " Go not;" " Drunkard's character;" Effects of drunkenness;" " One glass more."

As was expected, the distribution at such a time and place, formed the subject of many a humourous joke; but the most kindly feeling prevailed, with one exception, which arose from one deeply interested in the profits of the day, he on several occasions threatened the defenceless young man if he set his foot within the gateway, the only entrance by which the company had access to the park.

EXTRACTS FROM THE "DUNSTAPLE CHRONICLE," ETC.

THE only objects of 1855, deserving our attention are first, the establishment of a Newspaper. The government having removed many of the restrictions connected with the public Press, the township was furnished with a monthly serial under the title of "The Dunstaple Chronicle," of which the first number made its appearance on the first of June, 1855, when the proprietor at the end of the year, gave notice of a weekly issue which has continued to increase, until there is now a circulation of 36,400 annually. A few months after a new periodical was started, called "The Dunstaple Reformer;" but its existence was of short duration; and lastly, the proprietor of the Chronicle issued a third publication, once a-month, entitled "The Dunstaple Illustrated Magazine," which had an annual circulation of 4,000, and was continued for two years.

The remaining object of interest was the celebration of the fifth of November. Few towns made such a loyal demonstration as Dunstaple

did, to celebrate the great and glorious battle of
Inkerman.   Early in the morning the Free Boys
began to assemble at Mr. Johnson's, to have
presented to them a most formidable looking
personage, representing the emperor of all the
Russias.   A certain gentleman worked with his
own hands two beautiful flags, representing the
Union Jack and the Tricolor.   At nine o'clock,
the boys sallied out of the Sugar Loaf yard, with
the effigies of the Emperor and Guy Fawkes ; the
figure of the Emperor wearing a real trophy from
the battle of Inkerman, was made a present by
Mr. James McMillan, of the Scots Fusileer Guards.
After they had paraded the town and canvassed it
pretty well, they returned to their starting place
to count out the proceeds, which amounted to
3s. 6d. per boy, after paying the expenses.   In
the afternoon, they set to work to take the fuel to
the Downs, kindly granted by Lady Alford for
this pleasing demonstration.   In the evening, at
six, the band assembled together and a procession
formed in the following order :—

A man carrying a Naptha lamp, in front.

Two boys carrying flags.

Band.

The Emperor.

Field-Marshal Plummer, ⎫

Brigadier Jardine,   ⎬ with drawn swords.

Brigadier Derbyshire, ⎭

A row of the Bedfordshire Militia.

Another Naptha lamp.

After parading the town, they proceeded to the
Downs to burn the effigy.   The bonfire was a
splendid sight, and with the fireworks was a

grand spectacle. Upwards of three thousand persons assembled on the Downs.

The short and severe struggle which had been carried on against the emperor of all the Russias, was in 1856, happily brought to a close, and once more the town of Dunstaple fully prepared itself for a festival to commemorate the return of peace.

A committee was formed for the purpose of arranging the public dinner, to commemorate the return of peace, which took place on the twenty-fourth of June, 1856, under certain regulations, of which the following is a copy, printed and circulated some days before.

"The dinner will take place on the Square, and will commence at one o'clock. All persons who shall have received tickets, are requested to assemble not later than half-past twelve o'clock, at the places specified, and proceed to the Square in the following order:—

DISTRICT No. 1

Includes the inhabitants of houses in High-street, from the Gas-house to the Red Lion, with White Hart yard and other courts therein; and from the Red Lion to the last house in the Luton road, on the North side of Church-street, with Mellor's yard and all other courts. These shall assemble from Houghton stile to the Sugar Loaf, and shall proceed at the above time to the Square and enter within the ropes at the opening opposite the Priory.

DISTRICT No. 2

Includes the inhabitants of houses on the South

side of Luton-road and Church-street, Church-green, Church-passage, High-street, to the last house on Half Moon-hill, with all the streets and courts therein. These shall assemble from the Wagon and Horses toward London-terrace, and shall enter within the ropes at the opening opposite the Saracen's Head.

District No. 3

Includes the West side of High-street from Half Moon-hill, with the courts therein, Chapel-place, Back-street, Middle-row, Butt's-lane, West-street, on the South side from Icknield-terrace to Mr. C. Farr's, with all the courts therein. These shall assemble from Half Moon-hill to Mr. Joseph Gutteridge's, and enter within the ropes at the opening near Miss Baylie's house.

District No. 4

Includes the North side of West-street from the Mill to the Nag's Head, High-street, the West side to Union-street, with the courts therein; Albion-road, Edward-street, Mount-street, Union-street, the South side, and Winfield-street. These shall assemble from Union-street to Mr. Elliott's, and enter the ropes at the opening of the Priory. Each person is to come provided with plate, knife, fork and pint mug.

Stewards, two for each division (who are requested to provide themselves with wand and rosette,) will marshal and walk in front of their divisions to the Square, and will then stand at the several openings; to whom also the persons who are to partake of dinner will show their tickets as they pass on to take their seats. When all are seated, the stewards will give to each person who may desire it, a ticket entitling them to receive one pint of beer; and will during dinner walk between the tables to keep order and see the wants of all supplied.

Persons are requested not to leave their seats when once taken, as they will be supplied with all they want by waiters appointed for that purpose.

At the sound of the bugle-horn the company will keep silence while the band plays the Old Hundredth psalm tune, they will then stand uncovered and sing, accompanied by the band, as Grace before meat, the Doxology,

"Praise God, from whom all blessings flow."

The dinner being finished, the bugle-horn will again sound as a signal for silence; when accompanied by the band, and to the same tune, standing and uncovered as before, as Grace after meat, will be sung,

"We thank thee, Lord, for this our food."

After the dishes are removed, the band will play once over the tune of the National Anthem, when the company will again rise and sing,

"God save the Queen."

Those who wish may now leave their seats; but tobacco and pipes will be provided for those who desire to use them.

N.B.—The president, vice-presidents & carvers are requested to take the places assigned to them,

at a quarter before one, that they may assist in
arranging the company and keeping order, as the
several divisions arrive.

One-half the waiters are desired to be on the
ground at ten o'clock, to assist the committee in
placing the dishes, &c., on the table.

FREDERICK HOSE, Chairman."

From a very early period the summer solstice
was celebrated with peculiar ceremonies, among
which, the kindling of fires formed a conspicuous
figure. These were called bonfires, and were a
sign of goodwill among neighbours. In an old
metrical description of the customs common at
the Midsummer festival, we read,

> "Then doth the feast of John
> The Baptist take his turn ;
> When bonfire great with loftie flame
> In every town do burn."

They were a part of the heathen customs which
celebrated the summer solstice. They were intended to honour the feast of St. John the Baptist.
They were regarded as being conducive to health.
They were chosen as the place where old quarrels
might be made up and new friendships formed.
Of all the days in the calendar, that of St. John
had the greatest claim as the one on which the
peace rejoicings should be held ; the palm was
yielded to it, and for it the committee waited.
The long-expected morn at length arrived,
Tuesday, the 24th of June, and a more true
English holiday was never celebrated anywhere,
than was on this day by the loyal inhabitants of
Dunstaple. The first commencement of the day

was the firing of a salute of twenty-one guns, in honour of the occasion. About six o'clock, a.m., the Dunstaple brass band aroused the inhabitants with their music, as they paraded the town, and their performance drew forth the warmest praise from all who heard them. The bells of the ancient priory church added their music and gave forth a merry peal. Flag after flag continued to make their appearance from all the principal houses. About ten o'clock the splendid band of the Bedfordshire militia arrived and paraded the town, headed by the Free boys carrying flags & banners. Upon the arrival of the train came the London band, who marched up the town headed by the parish beadle and Free-school boys.

On the Square all was bustle in preparing the dinner for 1,000 people; and about eleven o'clock the different districts began to assemble at the places appointed for them to meet. All were soon in readiness to march to the Square, where every arrangement was made to receive them. Around the outside of the tables were flags, of various descriptions; and at the grand entrance were placed some fashionable straw hats and bonnets, in commemoration of the staple trade of the town.

At a quarter before one, the bands took their places allotted to them, and the people began to arrive for dinner; and a thousand more orderly and respectable people could nowhere be found. The sight of the Square was now one of the most splendid ever seen in Dunstaple. Ample justice having been done to the real old English fare of beef and plum-pudding, the bugle-horn sounded for silence, after which, the band again played

c2

the Old Hundredth psalm tune, and the company
returned thanks: the band then played the
National Anthem, and the waiters cleared the
tables. The streets were now crowded, and the
numbers are variously estimated; from 25,000
to 30,000 persons were assembled, anxiously
waiting for the other interesting fetes of the day,
and their patience was not long tried; for very
soon the children of the Church and Wesleyan
Sunday Schools headed by their pastors and superintendents, and the Bedfordshire Militia band;
these were joined by the Baptist schools, headed
by the Dunstaple and London bands, marching
from the Free school down to the Post Office, up
the Albion-road to the Tabernacle, where they
received another addition from the schools of that
place, and proceeding onward they came to the
Primitive-Methodist chapel, and were joined by
the school, headed by the celebrated Morfey band.
After marching round the town, the children of
the various schools to the number of 1,200, sat
down to tea on the Square, where an unlimited
supply of cake and tea was provided for them.
After the children had done ample justice to the
repast provided, they all adjourned to a meadow,
where the Militia and Morfey bands amused the
company, and all kinds of innocent amusements
were carried on. Another company, headed by
the London band, proceeded to a meadow near
the ancient recreation ground, known as the Butts,
and there spent the evening until the time arrived
for the thousands to disperse to witness the illu-
minations and fireworks.

Most of the principal manufacturers and tradesmen illuminated their houses, and amongst the most tasteful were the decorations at the different solicitor's offices, and a triumphal arch across the road, with Chinese lamps at the Sugar Loaf, and a handsome gas star joining the Market House. At ten o'clock in the evening, a splendid display of fireworks commenced which gave great satisfaction.

A few of the manufacturers gave their sewers a private entertainment the same day, and the factory yards exhibited a pleasing spectacle, being tastefully decorated with foliage and flowers; while Messrs. Munt and Brown reserved their treat for the following day, which consisted of a good tea and supper, with bands of music to play during the refreshment, so we are of opinion that all parties have been well cared for.

Toward the end of the year, the rector was again the subject of a long and severe illness, which led no less than 130 individuals, of various denominations, to give a substantial proof of their sympathy and regard in the following manner :—

DUNSTABLE, Dec. 15th, 1856.

REV. AND DEAR SIR,

Many of your parishioners sympathising with you on your late serious illness, and feeling your inability to come amongst them, both in your ministry, and in your general usefulness in any matters which concern your parish, beg to express to you their hearty congratulations on your partial recovery ; and they sincerely trust, that under God's blessing, your restoration to perfect health is not far distant. Inasmuch as a change of air and a perfect rest from your labours is strongly recommended for your recovery, they beg with all due respect to present you with the accompanying purse and its contents ; in the hope that you will be induced to take the earliest opportunity of seeking change of air, and taking such means for recruiting your health as are thought most beneficial.

They beg at the same time to express to you their full appreciation of your great usefulness both ministerially and otherwise, and of your perfect readiness at all times, to assist in any matter which concerns the benefit of your parish in which you have now laboured for upwards of eleven years.

With best wishes they beg to subscribe themselves your sincere friends and grateful parishioners, by their chairman,

(Signed) CHAS. S. BENNING.

To the Rev. F. Hose.

After the presentation, the Rev. F. Hose was much affected, and begged the deputation to tender his sincere thanks to all the subscribers for their great kindness.

Few places have suffered more from incendiary fires than the town of Dunstaple and its neighbourhood, and yet with all these fearful warnings they were never prepared for the emergency with the necessary requirements, viz :—a modern fire engine and brigade. Happily a few energetic men, who took so prominent a part in the peace rejoicings last year, seeing the importance and utility of such an establishment set to work, and on the 23rd of January, 1857, had the satisfaction to receive at the Railway Station, a first-class fire engine. A brigade was formed to take the charge and management of the engine, and Mr. James Young, superintendent of the Leighton brigade being applied to, brought his great experience to bear upon the subject, and gave them a series of rules for their guidance and direction.

The following year was held the Fire Brigade Fete and Holiday, (a most interesting and novel sight,) on Friday, the 9th of July, 1858. The morning threatened rain, but before ten o'clock the clouds dispersed and a fine day followed, and not too hot—a smart breeze making it more pleasant. By eleven o'clock, special trains from Luton and Leighton, well filled, began to make for the station, and at that hour more than four thousand persons had arrived, the number greatly increasing as the day advanced; the main streets were profusely decorated with flags, evergreens, &c.; six triumphal arches were raised and gaily decorated.

The first and most imposing one was fixed across the High-street from the residence of Wm. Medland, Esq., having festoons and flowers interwoven with evergreens, and flags flying from the tops and sides of the pillars, and hanging from the centre a beautifully-finished decoration, having thereon in large letters, *"Welcome to the Leighton Buzzard and Newport Pagnell Fire Brigades."* From Mr. Medland's windows four flags hung.

The second arch was over the entrance of the Sugar Loaf Hotel yard, and in large letters, *"Success to the Dunstaple Fire Brigade,"* and on another board, the following lines:—

"Though Commerce guards her shrine with ceaseless care,
A wandering spark may hurl destruction there,
Though in the garner lies the golden grain,
Th' incendiary comes, and lo! 'tis dust again.
Then hail to those who venture life and health,
To save their neighbours, and their neighbour's wealth."
W.H.Derbyshire.

The third arch had *"Welcome to the Brigades,"* and the fourth *"Welcome to Hemel Hempstead and Berkhampstead Brigades,"* decorated with many large and beautiful flags, some furnished by Messrs. Cooper, preserved from those provided for the last peace demonstration.

The fifth was across High-street, near to Church-street, and had hung from its centre, "*Welcome to St. Alban's Brigade.*"

The sixth across Church-street, with "*Welcome to our Luton Friends and Neighbours.*"

The seventh across West-street, leading to Hemel Hempstead; and every respectable house had either flags or banners hanging from the windows, which were crowded with elegantly dressed ladies, in fact, the town was one scene of gaiety. The bells of the parish church rang merry peals throughout the day; the shops were closed and all appeared resolved to make it a day of pleasure. At twelve o'clock, the order of the procession being completed, under the superintendence of William Medland, Esq., and other gentlemen over the various brigades, they began to move in the following order:—

First.—The Dunstaple brigade; Mr. Derbyshire superintendent. Dress, blue, with helmets, headed by William Medland, Esq., with a companion on each side of him. One of the brigade carrying a splendid blue flag, fringed with white, having in large gold letters "Success to the fire brigades." The band, 3 outriders, fire engine, drawn by 4 horses, with 12 of the brigade thereon, 8 volunteers in a splendid car, 6 ditto carrying a beautiful model of a fire engine.

Second.—The Leighton brigade. Dress, dark green, with helmets, &c., Mr. James Young superintendent, and two others on horseback, preceded by a band of music. On the engine drawn by 4 horses, were seated 12 paid brigade; the same number of volunteers were conveyed in the superintendent's splendid music car, and 6 others by another conveyance formed the superintendent's private brigade. Although this establishment thought it more prudent to bring but one engine out of the town on this occasion, it was notwithstanding, a very compact and apparently effective turn out.

Third.—The Hemel Hempstead. Mr. Cranstone, superintendent. A most imposing set out; ten outriders, band, engine with 12 of the brigade drawn by 4 horses. Second engine with 12 of the brigade belonging to the Phœnix office, London. This fine body of men, including paid and volunteers, had with them the Thame brass band; one part of the brigade wore red, with caps, the others had light blue coats, with straw hats decorated with red and blue ribbons.

Fourth.—The Berkhampstead. Superintendent, Mr. J. Wood. A great number of gentlemen outriders preceded this brigade, then followed the engine drawn by 4 horses; their dress was white, with black caps.

Fifth.—The Newport Pagnell. Mr. J. Shepherd, superintendent. One engine with 21 of the brigade, some on the engine, others in various vehicles; their dresses drab, with strong helmets; a very fine and useful body of men. The volunteers wore a dark dress.

Sixth.—The St. Alban's. Superintendent, Mr. Webster. Several outriders accompanied the fire engine, belonging to the County Fire Office, London, furnished by them to the parish of St. Albans, with their brigade.

Seventh—Was a perfect curiosity, and which it

is hoped nothing, out of the ordinary course of
time, will ever destroy, being not unaptly called
"The father of fire engines,"—an old wooden fire
engine belonging to the town, in the form of a
large oval tub, broader at bottom than top, drawn
by one horse, and said to be 283 years' old—a
striking contrast to the beautiful engines now
made. The procession went through the principal
streets with the four bands playing, after which
they entered the park, where a sumptuous dinner
was provided, of which nearly 270 partook. The
company then retired to another spacious booth,
150 feet in length, and an excellent selection of
songs and glees were given, concluding with
"God save the Queen," by the whole company,
who afterwards dispersed over the beautiful park,
some seated under the noble elm and beech trees,
others reclining on the soft turf, parties playing
at cricket, trap and ball &c., &c. Another large
booth was put up, 200 feet in length, for those
wishing to take tea; the charge was reasonable,
and it was well patronized.

The entrance to the park was under a triumphal
arch, opposite Manchester-place. The talisman
for open-sesame was for adults one shilling, and
juniors under twelve years, six-pence.

On Whit-sunday, 1859, this town was visited
by one of the heaviest storms of rain known in
this neighbourhood for thirty years, causing an
inundation in all the flat parts of the town. In
the cellar of Mr. Howes, farmer, in Church-street,
was a large vat of harvest beer just brewed; the
cellar flooded, the barrels burst doing considerable
damage. Several other houses were flooded in

like manner. The Fire Brigade, true to their post in the hour of danger, were to be seen, not at the fire but at the water, and right earnestly did they work both engines. About eight o'clock most of the water was got out of the cellars, and the town presented its usual appearance.

The following day being that fixed for the great Wesleyan bazaar, was all that could be desired. On this sunny June morning we travelled through the chalky gorge, and entered this world-esteemed locality—

> " Where Lassies smile, and Bonnets win renown,
> You there will hear of Dunstaple's old town."

The morning's market was ending, the plait buyers were leaving, and the streets were filling with persons flocking to the bazaar, opened by an address from Lord Charles Russell, in aid of the Wesleyan funds. We strolled the town, and when we reached the ancient church we rather wished for " old antiquary" to tell us more about Norman and Gothic styles; however, we mused on mouldering stone and mutilated images, and supposing six or seven centuries to have rolled since its erection, and thinking of the generations which had fled since then, Watts came to our help in musing—

> " Time, like an ever rolling stream
> Bears all its sons away ;
> They fly forgotten as a dream
> Dies at the opening day."

From the church we turned into the Priory grounds through an ornamented archway, from the centre of which was suspended an enormous

D1

straw hat, a present from **Mr. B. Bennett**, as an emblem of the staple trade of the town. Farming implements and fuel met the eye; further on, a block of coal weighing 2T. 1c. 2QRS., then a hutch of rabbits, coop of ducks and fowls, and a sack of wheat, which showed the earnestness of the contributors. We strolled the tents, looked upon Nature's best workmanship and Art's pretty manufacture, and then we found ourselves kindly asked to look into the priory, and then we were told we were standing in the very chamber where Cranmer and the commissioners signed and sealed the divorce between Henry and Catherine of Arragon. History tells the swift retribution that followed. Looking upon the groined arches, Shakespere vitalized them—

> "The archbishop
> Of Canterbury, accompanied with other
> Learned and reverend fathers of his order
> Held a court at Dunstaple, six miles off
> From Ampthill, where the princess lay; to which
> She oft was cited by them, but appeared not."

The refreshment room, under the superintendence of Mr. Hunt, assisted by Messrs. Barber and Hanchard, was admirably conducted: some 25 or 30 joints of meat were consumed on the spot, and promptitude, politeness, & reasonable charges reigned here supreme. At six o'clock a bell sounded, and in a dell or hollow of the field were assembled an effective choir of singers, under the leadership of Mr. John Robinson, who poured forth a stream of harmony which delighted the audience. Games and pastimes of an innocent nature were freely indulged in. In looking over

the subjoined table, there can be no doubt but
that the promoters of this undertaking met with
an agreeable surprise in the enormous sum received
at the stalls, remembering that the circuit is not
many miles in extent.

Stalls	£.	s.	d.
1 Mesdames Fowler and Darley....................	57	0	0
2 ,, Wilson and Ginger..................	40	0	0
3 Mrs. Cooper and Daughters.....................	42	0	0
4 Mrs. Bennett and Sons.........................	70	17	8
5 Mesdames Robinson & Cotching ......£41 }	82	0	0
5½ Mrs. Hunt and Miss Wingrave ......£41 }			
6 Mesdames C. Lockhart, Bailey, and Labrum	40	0	0
7 ,, Howes, Gibbard and Scott.........	40	0	0
8 The Misses Rudd and Mrs. George.......... ..	32	0	0
9 Mesdames Foster, Windmill, Driffill & Lester	26	0	2
10 ,, W. Cheshire, E. Horn and Turney	34	1	0
11 ,, Williams and Weatherill............	31	0	0
12 The Misses Varney............................	12	0	0
13 Miss Cutler and the Misses Beale	30	11	2
14 Mesdames Line, Beech, Pitkin and Billing...	24	7	0
15 Mrs. Pickering and the Misses Slough	22	6	6½
16 Mesdames Tibbett and Brown..................	32	5	0
17 ,, Hanchard, Underwood & Faulkner	28	10	0
18 Miss Darley and Mr. Tearle, (Confectionery)	9	12	4
19 Sunday Scholars................................	11	19	0½
20 Book Stall	2	6	2¾
Post Office	1	4	8
Refreshment Department	100	9	0½
Entrance-Fees	110	1	4
Musical Performance	25	19	6
	£906	10	8¼

MISCELLANEOUS.

Since the book was printed off, the following communications have been received in answer to the request put forth in the introduction.

Synod.—page 55.

AT this time A.D. 1251, Boniface archbishop of Canterbury was using his diligent endeavours to the utmost of his power and even beyond it, at the Roman court to bring his design to effect, namely, to obtain the power of making a general visitation of all the clergy throughout his province. The bishop of England being annoyed at this, (because it was evident to them that he did not aim at this, for the reformation of morals and religion,) assembled at Dunstaple on St. Matthias' day, to deliberate on the act of injury and oppression; for what concerned and grieved all, ought to be provided against by all. There were then present the bishops of Lincoln, London, Norwich, Salisbury, Ely and Worcester; the bishop of Chester being unwell, could not attend. After a deliberate discussion they sent their proctor to the Roman court to lay their complaint in this matter before the pope, being determined to free themselves from the visitation of the archbishop, even if it were necessary that they should expend four thousand marks (for the Roman court was usually ready to grant favour to those making presents,) the said proctor proceeded to that court and diligently set to work in the matter entrusted to him. The pope also was at this time given to understand by the said proctor or by some other enemy of the archbishop that he the archbishop, had to the great injury of the English church, collected more than eleven thousand marks, which were granted to him by the pope; whereupon the pope wrote back in reply, that they were to give him further information concerning the said transgression, and promised both of the parties who complained, with all due moderation they should obtain whatever was just.

The bishops thereupon became more calm in their minds, owing to the goodwill of the pope, and would not add more lest a multitude of complaints should give an appearance of hatred, but firmly urged their principal cause.

Assize.

The last assize held in Dunstaple, was one for the county, in 1607.

Chalgrave.—Page 66.

The chapel at Tebworth having been endowed with 36 acres of land, the inhabitants of the village endeavoured but without success, in 1277, to oblige the prior and convent in whom the rectory and advowson was then vested and who were in possession of the land forming the endowment, to provide a chaplain to celebrate divine worship in Tebworth chapel.

Seal.—Page 85.

It is worthy of observation, that an impression of the common seal of the priory, somewhat imperfect, is attached to the acknowledgement of supremacy, in 1534, in the Chapter house at Westminster. It represents St. Peter with his keys, seated, and the legend round him is:—

SIGIL ECCLIE SCI PETRI DE DVNESTAPLE.

Marriage.—Page 96.

The blunder of the Barebone's parliament in permitting people to be married by a justice of the peace in a private house, was notwithstanding the aversion of the great proportion of the women of England, revived during the last year of the late king.

In 1836, an act of parliament was passed, allowing all those who chose to consider marriage as a mere civil contract, to be entered into before any witnesses who can testify to the mere fact so to do. The first marriage under the new act in connexion with Dunstaple, was that of Mr. Jos. Gutteridge, and the contract was entered into at the registrar's office for the district, in 1840, thus four years were allowed to pass over without any couple availing themselves of the supposed advantages; although a gratuity had been offered for those who should be the first. I need scarcely add, that in the present instance it was not accepted.

Amusements.—Page 89.

Hallam in his " Literature of Europe," p. 1. c. 3, 6, 210, speaking of theatrical representations in the west, says, "The earliest mention of them, it has been said is in England. Geoffrey, afterwards abbot of St. Albans, whilst teaching a school at Dunstaple, caused one of the shows vulgarly called " Miracles," on the story of St. Catherine, to be represented in that town. Such is the account of Matthew Paris, who mentions the circumstance incidentally in connexion with a fire that ensued. This must have been within the first twenty years of the twelfth century. It is not to be questioned that Geoffrey, a native of France, had some earlier models in his own country. Roscoe thinks there is reason to conjecture that the Miracle play acted at Dunstaple, was in Dumbshoe, but in this he was mistaken. Warton in vol. 1 " Dessart," says " Geoffrey was a Norman, his scholars were the actors, the performance took place in 1110, and he borrowed the copes from the sacrist of the neighbouring abbey of St. Albans, to dress his characters."

The story of St. Catherine we find in the Roman Breviary : from it we learn that she was born at Alexandria, and died a martyr in the eighteenth year of her age, during the reign of Maximinus, in the year 305. The following is an extract therefrom relating to the miracles, and a translation in parallel columns :—

BREVIARIUM ROMANUM.	ROMAN BREVIARY.

BREVIARIUM ROMANUM.
xxv die Mensis Novembris,
Lexio vj.

" Quo tempore Maximini
uxor et Porphyrius belli dux
visendæ virginis causa carce-
rum ingressi et ejusdem præ-
dicatione in Jesum Christum
credentes, postea martyris
corronati sunt. Interim Cath-
arina educitur e custodia; et
rota expeditur crebis et acutis
præfixa gladis ut virginis cor-
pus crudelissime delacerare-
tur. Quo machina trevi Cath-
erinæ oratione confraeta est ;
eoque miraculo multi Christi
fidem susceperunt. Ipsi Maximinus in impietate et crudeli-
tate obstinatior Catherinam
securi percuti imperat. Quo
fortiter dato capite, ad dupli-
catum virginitatis et martyrii
pramium evolavit septimo
Kalendas Decembris cujus cor-
pus ab Angelis in Sina Arabiæ
monte mirabiliter collocatum
est."

ROMAN BREVIARY.
25th day of the month of November.—*Section* 6.

" At which time the wife of
Maximinus and the illustrious
general Porphry having visited
her prison for the sake of seeing the virgin (Catherine) and
believing in Jesus Christ thro'
her preaching, afterwards received the crown of maryrdom.

Meanwhile Catherine is
brought out of her prison,
and is fastened to a wheel fitted with many sharp swords,
that the virgin's body might
be most cruelly torn. This
machine was speedily broken
at Catherine's word, and in
consequence of that miracle
many received the Christian
faith. Maximinus himself became more obstinate in impiety
and cruelty, and ordered Catherine to be beheaded. She
boldly surrendered her head to
the executioner, and flew to
receive the double crown of
virginity and martyrdom, on
the 7th day before the calends
of December. The body was
miraculously buried by angels
in Sinai, a mountain in Arabia.'

Gostello.—Page 91.

Continuation of Numismotic paper by Gostello.

Abbey pieces or rosaries which North in his
remarks on Clarke's Conjectures, supposes to have

been so distinguished on account of their bearing the legend AVE-MARIA, &c., being probably not intended for money, but as Tesseræ Sacræ, for the use of monks and pilgrims, who travelled from one religious house to another.

These pieces being found often in old ruins, are mistaken for money, by persons ignorant of the coinage of the period. Among the genuine coins in his collections, found either in the town or fields adjoining, are:—

One of Claudius Cæsar, found on "Half-Moon hill,

    Obv.—Bust.
    Rev.—Full length female figure, draped.

One of Otho, found on the Downs,

    Obv.—Bust.
    Rev.—Winged Victory, wreath in right hand.

One of Adrian, found when digging for Luton railway,

    Obv.—Bust. IMP. HADRIANVS AVGVSTVS.
    Rev.—A female seated on a rock, in her right hand an image of victory; in her left, a spear; under the figure, S.C.; beyond, PONT MOX TRPO.

One of Commodus, found in Star close, under whose reign lived Lucius, the first British chieftain who professed Christianity,

    Obv.—Laureated head, COMMOD ANTON.
    Rev.—Full length figure, standing between an altar and Roman gallery; in left hand, a cornucopia; nnder the figure, S.C.

One of Probus, who reigned 6 years,—rise of the Manichean heresy,

    Obv.—Bust. IMP. C. MAVR PROBVS AVG.
    Rev.—Full length figure.

D2

Three (unknown),

First.　Obv.—Laureated head.

Rev.—Roman soldiers guarding a trophy.

Second.　Obv.—Head laureated.

Rev.—Two captives, seated on the ground under a standard, weeping.

Third.　Obv.—Bust.

Rev.—Two angels sacrificing.

Of the English series, are the following:—

Henry I.,

A small silver coin, found in that portion of the original wall of the church, near the vestry door, when the South wall was taken down, at the commencement of the restoration.

Henry III.,

Obv.—Crowned head.

Rev.—Cross molines.

Edward I., found near the Priory,

Obv.—EDW. R ANGZ. DNS. HYB.　Full faced head, with open fleury crown, the hair extending on each side of the face.

Rev.—CIVITAS LONDON, in plain cross and pallets.

Another of the same king, struck at Canterbury, CIVITAS CANTOR.

Another of the same king, struck at Bristol, VILLA BRISTOLLIE.

Edward III.,

Obv.—Crowned bust.

Rev.—Cross and pellets, CALLIS VILLA.

Henry VIII.,

Obv.—Crowned bust.

Rev.—Plain cross, with rose as Mint mark.

Elizabeth shilling, found in Mr. Joseph Gutteridge's field,

Obv.—ELISABETH DG ANG FR. HIB crowned bust with ruff.

Rev.—POSVI, &c. The shield of arms and cross, Mint mark, and a martlett.

Charles I., found after the fire at the Saracen's Head,

Obv.—CAROLVS DG MAG BRIT ET. HIBER REX. The king on horseback, as usual, underneath a view of the city of Oxford, with OXON above it, Mint mark, a quarterfoil.

Rev.—EXVRGAT DEVS DISSIPENTVR INIMICI, with a branch of olive after each word; in the area, inclosed by scrolls and similar branches, RELIG PROT LEG LIBER PARL, in two lines; above, three plumes and V; underneath, 1644.—This is one of the finest and most remarkable of the English series: it is the work of Rawlings, whose initials appear on the wall of the city.

Charles I's Shilling,

Obv.—CAROLVS, &c., profile bust, behind the head the Numerals XII.

Rev.—CHRISTO, &c., plain shield.

A piece of Maunday money of James II., of the value of two-pence,

Obv.—IACOBVS PEI GRATIA. Laureated head; neck and bust bare.

Rev.—II in the field, with crown above; 1687 under.

William III. and Mary, already described.

Anne, a two-penny piece,

Obv.—ANNA DEI GRATIA. Profile bust; hair tied up behind.

Rev.—ANNA G BRI FRA ET HIB REG. Two in the field, with cross above.

George I., a silver penny.

Obv.—Bust, &c.

Rev.—I in the field, with crown over; 1720 under.

Elkanah Settle.—Page 98, after Butler's
lines.
Again we meet with Settle, in Pope's Dunciad,
with notes, Book 1, line 90 :—

" Now night descending, the proud scene was o'er,
But lived in Settle's numbers one day more."

Settle was poet to the city of London. His
office was to compose yearly panegyrics upon the
lord mayors, and verses to be spoken in the
pageants : but that part of the shows being
frugally abolished, the employment of city poet
ceased, so that upon Settle's demise there was no
successor to that place.

Ibid, line 145.

" A Gothic library ! of Greece and Rome
Well purged and worthy Settle Banks and Broome.

Settle was his brother laureate, only indeed
upon half-pay, for the city instead of the court ;
but equally famous for unintelligible flights in his
poems on public occasions, such as shows, birth-
days, &c.   Passing on to Book iii. line 37 :—

" When lo ! a sage appears
By his broad shoulders known, and length of ears,
Known by the band and suit which Settle wore,—
(His only suit) for twice three years before :
" All as vest appeared, the wearer's frame
Old in new state, another yet the same."

Mr. Dennis tells us, " Settle was a formidable
rival to Mr. Dryden, and that in the university of
Cambridge there were those who gave him the
preference."   Mr. Welstead goes yet further in

his behalf: "Poor Settle was formerly the mighty rival of Dryden; nay, for many years bore his reputation above him."—Preface to his Poems, v. 8, p. 31. And Mr. Milbourn cried out, "How little was Dryden able, even when his blood run high, to defend himself against Mr. Settle."— Notes on Dryden's Virgil, p. 175. These are comfortable opinions, and no wonder some authors indulge them.

He was author or publisher of many noted pamphlets in the time of Charles II. He answered all Dryden's political poems, and being cried up on one side, succeeded not a little in his tragedy of the empress of Morocco the first that was printed with cuts. Upon this he grew insolent, the wits writ against his play, he replied, and the town judged he had the better. In short, Settle was then thought a very formidable rival to Mr. Dryden, and not only the town but the university of Cambridge was divided which to prefer; and in both places the younger inclined to Elkanah.—Dennis's Pref. to Roman Hom. Lastly, Ibid 283 :—

> " In Lud's old walls, tho' long I rul'd renoun'd
> Far as loud Bows stupendous bells resound,
> Tho' my old alderman confer'd the bays,
> To me committing their eternal praise.
> Their full fed heroes, their pacific may'rs,
> Their annual trophies and their monthly wars ;
> Tho' long my party built on me their hopes,
> For writing pamphlets, or for roasting Popes.
> Yet lo ! in me what authors have to brag on ;
> Reduced at last to hiss in my own dragon."

Settle like most party writers, was very uncertain in his political principles. He was employed to hold the pen in the character of a Popish successor, but afterwards printed his narrative on the other side. He had managed the ceremony of a famous Pope burning, on Nov. 17th, 1680; then became a trooper in king James' army, at Hounslow-heath. After the Revolution, he kept a booth at St. Bartholemew fair, where in the droll called " St. George for England," he acted in his old age, in a dragon of green leather of his own invention. He was at last taken into the Charter-house, and there died aged 60 years.

I have obtained a syllabus, so to speak, of this celebrated Pope burning, invented by our townsman Elkanah, and will afford a good illustration of the rest of his productions; it is entitled, "The Solemn Mock Procession, on the Tryall and Execution of the Pope and his Ministers, on the 17th of November, at Temple-Bar, 1680."

It was the practise on that day, being the anniversary of Elizabeth's accession to the throne, to celebrate the event in London by a pageant, in honour of the Established religion and in ridicule of the Pope, " the arch-traitor and the head engineer not only of civil combinations, but also of the lamentable firing of the famous mother city of our country." Elkanah apologetically observes that " Erasmus' satyrical drollery was found to be as effectual to bring down the Roman pageantry, as Luther's gravity of argument;" and proceeds to describe the show of the day, which though abridged here, is chiefly given in the words of the tract, as follows:—

First, The captain of the pope's guard on horse-back, followed by ten pioneers in red caps

and coats, in ranks, with staves and truncheons,
to make way (as whifflers) for the main body;
next a bellman ringing, and saying in a loud
doleful voice "Remember Justice Godfrey. Then
a bloody corpse representing Sir Edmund Bury
Godfrey, on horseback, supported by a Jesuit
behind, with a bloody dagger in his hand; after
this, carried by two men, a large cloth banner
painted in colours, representing the Jesuits of
Wild-house all hanging on a gibbett, and among
them " another twelve that would betray their
trust and confidence;" on the other side, Gammer
cell with a bloody bladder, and all her other
Presbyterian plot-fangers and Protestants in masquerade.

First Pageant.

In the fore-part a meal tub, Mrs. Celliers in
one corner leaning on it with her " narrative" in
her hand; at the other corner " one in black,"
bare-headed and playing on a fiddle; behind, four
Protestants in masquerade, bi-partite garments of
white and black; after the pageants an "abhorrer"
on horseback, with his face to the tail; then a
man on horseback bearing a banner inscribed
"We Protestants in masquerade usher in Popery."

Second Pageant.

Four Franciscan friars, two being Capuchins in
gray russett with a cord about the middle, and
long cowls on their heads hanging behind with a
tail; the other, two minorites, a diminutive
species of these Franciscan birds in cinnamon,
coloured habit with shorter cowls.

Third Pageant.

Two Augustine friars, in black close habits
with a leather girdle ; and two Dominican bounc-
ing friars in black and white garments, called
" Brother preachers."

Fourth Pageant.

Here strut out four Jesuits in a black hue and
garb, suitable to their manners, with high collars,
mounting up about their necks like a pasty crust.

Fifth Pageant.

Here are mounted two bishops, a sort of disciples
of Christ that pretend to take the place of ordinary
dukes and princes ; behind are two archbishops
in Pontificalibus, they differ in their crosiers.

Sixth Pageant.

Two patriarchs with two forked crosiers, in
bishop-like vestments ; and two cardinals riding
in pure scarlet vestments, being next cousins to
the scarlet whore of Babylon : next, his Holiness's
master of the ceremonies carrying the Pope's triple
cross, distributing bulls, pardons, and indulgences,
and crying aloud, " Here you may have heaven
for money."

Seventh Pageant.

Here comes Antichrist himself, arrayed in
scarlet robes, furred with ermine and covered with
gold and silver lace, with triple crown inscribed
in front " Mystery," holding two keys in his
hands, pretended to be of that place he is never
likely to get into ; two swords standing at his

right hand, one typifying excommunication, the other civil dominion over kings and princes; sprawling under his feet the emperor Frederick, on whose neck he insolently trod, at Venice; many other crowns and sceptres that he arrogates the disposal of, also at his feet. A page in white at the corner of the throne, brandishing a banner inscribed "This is the king of kings:" another page at the other corner holding a streamer inscribed "Thou art our God the pope."

Eighth Pageant.

The empress Donna Olympia, the pope's mistress surrounded by four nuns; on the pageants a streamer, inscribed "Courterans in ordinary."

Ninth Pageant.

They usher in their religion with fineries, but the sting of the Inquisition is in the serpent's tail; here is the main scene of anti-christ's cruelties. In this pageant, you see a sect of judicature, wherein sits a bishop as inquisitor-general, surrounded by monks as assistants; a poor martyr, condemned before them, environed with fagots to burn him, having a sanbenite cap on his head, all painted with devils, the space round about strewed and hemmed with racks and instruments of torture. In this fatal pomp, the procession sets out from Whitechapel-bars, and through Bishopgate, Cornhill, Cheapside and Ludgate, till it comes to Temple-bar, where the pope and his ministers being brought before the figure of queen Elizabeth receives his first sentence, and afterwards being led before the statue or tribunal of king Charles

II., on the other side, he receives his final doom and downfall, namely, to be burnt with all his fry before queen Bessie's throne : the ashes to be scattered about, that thence might never spring hereafter in England, one popish phœnix ; " and in remembrance of her happy days and for victories that God gives us in our days against the pope and his emissaries; the solemnity is closed with fuzees and artificial fires."

This procession was engraved on a copper-plate and sold by Jonathan Wilkins, at the Star, in Cheapside, near the Mercer's chapel.

An oil painting of the 9th pageant, long formed one of the decorations of the north aisle in our parish church, a fragment of which may still be seen.

Several northern and migratory birds visit Dunstaple during the autumnal and hyemal months, amongst which, are the

GOLDEN CREST.—*Regulus cristatus Ray.*

Among the birds flitting about those two gardens, remaining in 1855 on the waste lands in West-street, between Cross-street and Icknield-terrace, two lovely birds were knocked down by a stone : they were Golden Crests. The male and the female had been flitting about from bush to bush, and tree to tree, prying in varied attitudes into curled-up leaves, and into the crevices of the bark of the larger stems. Light are the actions of this little bird (the smallest of British birds,) and prompt its movements; but its flight is peculiar; it is not like that of the titmouse, nor yet like that of the common wren, to which, some Naturalists have considered it allied. There is a sweep in its ariel progression—a gliding gracefulness, which although it flits only to short distances, cannot but strike an attentive hearer. Still however, as is the habitual flight of the gold crest, still it is capable of performing extensive migratory journeys, and every winter we have an accession probably from the pine forests of Norway and Sweden, as visitors to our native birds, sometimes in great abundance.

It secures the position of its nest with great art on the under side of the foliage of the larch or pine, so as to be thoroughly protected from rain. It is composed of a thick and well-compacted outer layer of moss, intermixed with lichens, the webs of spiders, &c., and is lined with downy feathers. In comparison with the size of the bird, it is of large dimensions; the circumference of one which I have measured, being eleven inches, while the bird itself is less than four inches in total length.

WREN.—*Troglodytes Europeus.*

The wren is a bird of solitary and retiring habits, and is very generally diffused throughout the British Isles, singing its humble song the winter through, in cold and cheerless scenes, amid the icicles of trees, and even when flakes of snow come slowly down like plumes, with which to invest the streams, and woods, and fields. Its song, short, simple and lively as it is, loses nothing

from the fact of being heard when none else, save
the robin, is likely to arrest our steps as we
hasten over the frozen ground. One could hardly
believe that so loud a song issued from so small
a throat; but the bird gives us full means of as-
certaining that it does so, for it sits perched upon
the gooseberry-bush singing as merrily as if it
were summer, and apparently well pleased to have
a listener, as if it scarcely expected that we should
come abroad in January to hear it. The old Irish
song, says

" Her family is grate."

She has two broods in the season, and as many
as sixteen young birds have been found in one
nest. There must be much to do in feeding a
family like this, for in common with all other
nestlings, they are very voracious, and the wrens
are not far flyers, and must therefore seek their
food very near their home. The nest is deep and
large, and some of the young brood must be
placed at so great a distance from the aperture,
that one would fancy they must be sorely incon-
venienced for want of light and air. There however, they thrive, and as Graham says,

"Fed in the dark, not one forgot."

It was doubtless because of this dome-like and
gloomy dwelling, that the ancients termed the
wren, "Troglodytes," or dwellers in caves.

It is difficult to conjecture why, from the earliest
ages, the wren should have been called the king
of the birds, and this not merely by ancient writers
but by the peasantry of almost every land.   Our

little gold crest seems fitted by his beautiful coronal to bear the name of king-let, the synonyme of which is so general; but the wren it is small and feeble, and has withal, no robe of royalty nor the crown of gold. Colonel Vallancy, in a learned work of his remarks, "That the Druids represented it as the king of birds." He adds, "that the superstitious reverence formerly shown to this little creature offended the early christian missionaries, and their displeasure on account of it, originated the cruel practice of hunting and killing this bird on Christmas-day."

FIELDFARE.

The thrush tribe presents us with two winter visitors, viz. the Fieldfare *Merul pilaris Selby)*, and the Redwing *(Merula iliaca Selby.)* The birds frequent in troops the borders of woods, copses, tall hedge-rows, feeding on berries, as those of the hawthorn, mountain-ash, &c., to which the larva of insects, and snails dragged from their lurking places, are also added. These birds are natives of Norway, Sweden, Lapland, and other northern portions of continental Europe, whither they return on the approach of spring.

The song of the redwing is said to be very clear, and softly melodious. The flesh of both are in request, and indeed that of the fieldfare was highly prized by the Romans; we need scarcely say, that the gunner thins the flocks which take up their winter quarters with us.

KING-FISHER.—*Alcedo Ispida.*

And now the kingfisher deserves attention,

which during summer haunts Well-head brook,—
performs on the approach of winter a limited
migration. When the severity of the season drives
the fish from shallows to deep and sheltered
bottoms, freezes the milldams and coats with ice
the sluggish pool, the king-fisher wanders from
the interior to the coast, where it frequents the
mouths of rivulets, entering large navigable rivers
and dykes near the sea, especially along the south-
ern portion of the island. This habit was not
unknown to Belon (1551,) who, in his "Portraits
d'Oyseaux" gives the following "quatrain :"

> " Le martinet-pescheur fait sa demeure,
> En temps d'hyver au bord de l'ocean ;
> Et en este sur la riviere on estan,
> Et de poisson se repaist a toute heure."

which may be translated, in imitation of the old
style :—

> "In winter, by the borders of the sea,
> His brief abode the king-fisher doth make ;
> In summer, by the streams or pools dwells he,
> And evermore the scaly prey doth take."

Grey Shrike.—*Lansus excubitor.*

The cruel butcher bird has a sweet warbling
song, though its rich melody is sometimes lessened
by the intermingling of some harsh tones. He is
said to have the power of imitating the notes of
other birds; and though this is denied by some
ornithologists, yet there seems good authority for
believing that it exists. Bechstein says of our
shrike, that "it imitates the notes though not the
songs of other birds. Whether the opinion held

from the earliest times, be true or false, that the shrike lures the singing birds into its clutches by imitating its tune, we well know that the small birds, as well as various animals, have good reason to dread it, both for its power and skill in making them its prey ; and they seem terrified by its presence near their nests. It feeds on mice, shrews, frogs, lizards, and small birds ; adding to its meal some of our larger insects, as grasshoppers and beetles. Its own voracity and that of its hungry little ones, makes great demands on the helpless creatures which are its victims. The shrike has a singular habit of fixing its slaughtered animals on a thorn or on a forked branch of a tree, and so hanging them up,, as a butcher might do animals destined for sale ; hence the familiar name of " butcher bird."

During an afternoon's walk with my friend Smith, we observed the bloody thorn and several parcels of feathers, and presently heard the scream of a few small birds ; on looking we perceived their old enemy the shrike, in full chase, so that we had then no doubt but that the thorns and feathers we had seen before, was all that remained of his former victims.

A naturalist, who kept this species in confinement, says, that " when a bird was given to it, it always broke the skull, and usually ate the head first ; sometimes it held the bird in its claws, and pulled it to pieces as a hawk would do."

The great shrike is neither a resident, nor a regular visitant in our island, only coming occasionally to this country, from some portion of the European continent, over a great part of which it

is pretty generally diffused. The season at which
this bird visits Britain is usually between the
autumn and the spring. It builds its nest a great
height from the ground ; the eggs are of a greyish
white colour, spotted with brown and ash colour ;
the bird is ten inches long and a peculiar odour
proceeds from it after death, not unlike that
which arises from the explosion of gunpowder.

GOLDEN PLOVER.—*Charadrius luviatis.*

This is a bird of passage, and is met with in
Europe, Western Asia, and parts of North Africa.
The length of the golden plover is about ten inches
and a-half. On arriving in this country from
colder regions, it lives usually on heaths and
moors, and lays its eggs in a hollow in the ground.
In a nest formed of a few small twigs and stems
of grass, four plover's eggs may sometimes be
found after a careful search. Great care is taken
of the nest by the parent birds, especially the
female. She will practise many clever arts to
defend her little dwelling, and guard her helpless
young against the approaches of the sportsman
and his dog, though she herself may be enticed
within gunshot by a skilful imitator of their voice,
It is esteemed a delicacy, and weighs nine ounces.
The eggs are of a dull pale yellow with a tinge
of green, blotched and streaked with dark brown.
They are generally boiled hard and have a fine
rich taste. The plover when cooked as a wood-
cook is quite equal to that bird. The summer
plumage is elegantly variegated with a fine yellowish green, differs greatly from its winter's dress.
As winter comes on, the black of the neck and

under parts gradually fades; the sides of the head, neck and chest becomes of an ashy brown; the throat and under parts white.

BITTERN.—*Ardeola.*

Those who have walked in the evening by the sedgy sides of Well-head brook, cannot but remember the variety of notes from the different feather tribes: but of all sounds there is none so dismally hollow as the booming of the bittern. It is impossible for words, to give those who have not heard this evening's call, an adequate idea of its solemnity. It is like the uninterrupted bellow of a bull, but hollower and louder, and may be distinctly heard at the Five knolls, as if issuing from a formidable being that resided at the bottom of the waters.

The bird however, that produces this terrifying sound, is not so big as a heron, with a weaker bill and not above four inches long. These bellowing explosions are chiefly heard from the beginning of spring to the end of autumn; and however awful they may seem to us, are the calls to courtship, or connubial felicity.

The flesh of the bittern is greatly in esteem among the luxurious, for this reason, it is eagerly sought after by the fowler, as it is shunned by the peasant; and as it is a heavy-rising slow-winged bird, it does not often escape him. Indeed it seldom rises, but when almost trod upon; and seems to seek protection rather from concealment than flight. It is considered "royal game;" and under the Tudor princes fine or imprisonment was the consequence if any one ventured to touch its eggs.

CURLEW.—*Clovius.*

The curlew is a well-known bird, which in winter frequents our sea-coasts and marshes, feeding chiefly on frogs and marine insects. In summer they retire to mountainous and unfrequented parts to breed. Their flesh is rank and fishy. Curlews differ much in size, some weighing thirty-seven ounces, and some not twenty-two; the length of the largest is twenty-five inches. The upper parts of the plumage are of a pale brown; the breast and belly white, marked with oblong spots.

A very fine specimen of this bird is preserved by Baron Myer de Rothschild, in the new mansion at Mentmore.

RED SHANK.

The red shank weighs about five ounces and a-half, and is twelve inches long; the bill is two inches, red at the base and black toward the point; the head, neck and scapulars are dusky ash colour, obscurely spotted with black; the breast is white, streaked with dusky lines. When the nest is in danger, it makes a noise somewhat similar to that of the lapwing.

SKUA GULL.—*Catarractes.*

This bird is the size of a raven. The upper parts of the head, neck, back and wings are deep brown; the under parts a pale rusty ash colour. The legs are black, rough and warty; and the talons very strong and hooked. It is mostly a native of the north, though often found in England. It is a most formidable bird, as it not only preys on fish, but upon all the smaller water fowl, and even on young lambs. It has the fierceness of an eagle in defending its young.

GROSBEAK.—*Rostri adunciatus Cuiciare.*

This bird belongs to a very extensive genus of birds, including nearly one hundred species, of which not more than five are common to Europe. Among these the cross bill *(Loxia Curvirostra,)* is too curious a bird to be overlooked: it is common in all the northern kingdoms of Europe, and sometimes visits Dunstaple. Beside the singularity of its bill, it is remarked for varying its colours. The males, which are red, alter sometimes to orange; the females which are green, to different shades of the same colour. It is about the size of a lark, and feeds on the cones of pines and pippins of fruit. They are said to divide an apple with one stroke of the bill, to get at the contents.

This bird is known to breed in many parts of England and Scotland, but of which, vast flocks at irregular intervals visit us during winter, from the forest of northern Europe. From the same parts, as well as Iceland, we get the PIED, or DUNSTAPLE CROW, as it is here called, from the circumstance of its being a more regular visitant in the season than most of the other migratory songsters; and doubtless, there may be others that may have escaped my notice during my brief sojourn in the town, I will therefore close this chapter by two observations,—the one on a plant, and the other on an insect.

THE PERRIWINKLE.—*Vinca Minor.*

This flowering plant, which is said to grow wild
on one particular spot in the town, and no where
else, is more extensively used in Italy than with
us. To them, its bright eyes do not seem to have
the same joyous look as they have here; they
call it the "flower of death," because it is used
to put round the heads of little children when
they are carried to their graves.

They are not put in coffins, but dressed in
white frocks; a cross is put between their hands
upon their breasts, and with a wreath of these
blue flowers round their hair they are carried to
church and there lie, looking like wax, till the
psalms and prayers are read over them. The
perriwinkle seems chosen because it is a frail and
fading flower. It may be a question how this
plant first found its way to Perriwinkle-lane; but
certain it is, being thus associated with death, it
is the fittest emblem to keep up the remembrance,
the scenes and circumstances so many hundreds
of years ago, that were passing at that particular
spot—leprosy and death.

The *Campanula Latisolia* and the *Euriophoron
Polystachion*, are also natives here.

Lastly.—Whilst passing down Cross-street in
the autumn of 1852, my attention was arrested
by the number of GLOWORMS sparkling in the
little gardens in front of the row of houses newly-
erected. Every garden had its share, and the
greatest in any was eleven in front of No. 5.

No two insects can differ more than the male
and female of this species from each other. The

male is in every respect a beetle, having cases to its wings, and rising in the air at pleasure; the female on the contrary, has none, but is entirely a creeping insect, and is obliged to wait the approaches of her capricious companion. The body of the female has eleven points, with a shield breastplate, the shape of which is oval; the head is placed over this, and is very small, and the last three joints of her body are of a yellowish colour; but what distinguishes it from all the animals at least in this part of the world is, the shining light which it emits by night, and which is supposed by some philosophers to be an emanation which she sends forth to allure the male to her company; and the question has well been asked, "How he in his nightly rambles for food or pleasure, was to find his way back to his partner without it?"

God employed his wisdom and goodness, and enabled the female to kindle at her pleasure a hymeneal torch. Will you not love a God so kind to insects? Will you not regard them with tenderness? Will you not imitate the glow-worm and be content to shine in obscurity, if the Lord place you there? And will not young females be determined to resemble the glow-worm, and to cultivate that sweetness of temper, and that lustre of piety, which will in after years attract the attention and affection of those with whom they are connected? Let the brightness of personal religion be to you what the beautiful light is to the glow-worm!

GLOSSARY AND INDEX.

The difficult words referred to in the body of this work, are here explained by a reference to their roots, which are printed in *Italics*.

Arena	*Arena*, sand. The Roman amphitheatre was so called, because the floor was covered with sand to drink up the blood of the gladiators. We now use the term for any place in which a contest is going on.
Antiquarian Antiquity	} *Antiqus*, old.
Ameliorate	. *Melior*, better.
Accoustics	. *Acuo*, I hear.
Abberration	. *Erro*, I wander.
Aboriginal	. *Origio*, the beginning.
Bedford	. *Bedicanford*, a fortress on a ford.
Buckwoode	. *Bock*, a beech tree; and *Wald*, a wood.
Bradburne	. *Brad*, broad; and *Burne*, a stream.
Benevolent	. *Bene*, well; and *Volo*, I wish.
Bonfire	. *Bon*, good; and *Fue*, fire.
Corps	. *Corpus*, a body.
Cruciform	. *Crux*, a cross; and *Forma*, shape.
Consecrate	. *Saceo*, sacred.
Commemorate	. *Memor*, mindful.
Convent	. *Ventum*, come; and *Con*, with.
Confirmation	. *Firmus*, strong; and *Con*, with.
Cathedral	. *Hedra*, a seat.
Chapel Chaplain	} *Capsella*, diminutive of *Capsa*, a small box in which the relics of martyrs were formerly kept. From the box the term may have extended to the oratory, a part of the church in which it was deposited; and finally to the whole church or chapel, and the officiating minister.
Cornucopia	. *Cornu*, a horn; and *Copia*, plenty.
Dunstaplelogia	. *Dun*, a hill; *Stapel*, a market; *& logos*, discourse.
Druid	. *Drus*, an oak.
Diocese	. *Gicis*, a house; and *Dia*, through.

Domestic	. *Domus*, a house; and *Sto*, I stand.
Epitaph	. *Epi*, upon; and *Taphos*, a tomb.
Ecclesiastical	. *Ekklesiah*, the church.
Elbow	. *Elne*, an ell; (originally, the arm,) and *Bugan*, to bend.
Eddlesborough	. *Ethel*, a noble; and *Beorgan*, to protect.
Excommunicate	. *Ex*, out; and *Communis*, common.
Effigies	. *Fingo*, I form or pretend.
Egress	. *Gradian*, I step; and *Ex*, out.
Fosse	. *Fodio*, I dig; a ditch, *i.e.* something dug.
Garden	. *Geard*, an enclosure.
Horticultural	. *Hortus*, a garden; and *Colo*, I till.
Hospital	. *Hospes, hospitis*, a guest, host.
Incendiary	. *Candeo*, I burn; and *Dia*, through.
Induction	. *Duco*, I lead.
Intersection	. *Inter*, between; and *Secco*, I cut.
Itinerant	. *Iter*, a journey; and *Eo*, I go.
Interdict	. *Inter*, between or among; and *Dico*, I speak.
Kensworth	. *Cynge*, head or chief; & *worth*, a farm or village.
Lollard	. *Lollen*, to sing.
Legate	. *Lego*, I send.
Locality	. *Locus*, a place.
Migratory	. *Migro*, I change my abode.
Manuscript	. *Manus*, a hand; and *scribo*, I write.
Messes	. *Metsian*, to feed.
Meter	. *Meteor*, a measure.
Nonconformist	. *Non*, not; *Con*, with; and *Forma*, shape .
Premonition	. *Moneo*, I warn or remind; and *Pre*, before.
Parliament	. *Parler*, to speak.
Perversion	. *Verto*, I turn; and *Per*, over.
Primeval	. *Primus*, first; and *Aevum*, an age.
Portfolio	. *Porto*, I carry; and *Folium*, leaves.
Predatory	. *Preda*, plunder.
Pugilist	. *Pugil*, a boxer.
Psalmody	. *Psallo*, I sing; and *Ode*, a poem.
Prejudice	. *Judicis*, judge; and *Pre*, before.
Perambulation	. *Ambulo*, I walk; and *Per*, through.
Projected	. *Jacio*, I throw; and *Pro*, forth.
Pest	. *Pestis*, the plague.
Pix	. A vessel containing the Roman host.
Rebellion	. *Re*, back; and *Bellum*, war.
Retribution	. *Tribuo*, I give; and *Re*, back.
Reverted	. *Verto*, I turn; and *Re*, back.
Solstice	. *Sol*, the sun; and *Stow*, I stand; where the sun stops in its course, going no farther north or south; our summer solstice is the 21st of June, the winter the 21st of September.
Subterranean	. *Sub*, under; *Terra*, the earth.
Succumb	. *Suc*, under; *Cubo*, I bend.
Structure	. *Struo*, I build.
Succeed	. *Cedo*, I give up.
Sympathising	. *Pathos*, feeling; *Sym*, with or together.
Suicide	. *Caedo*, I cut or kill; and *Sui*, of one's self.

Sewell	.	*Soa*, a vessell; and *Gwella*, water.
Superscription	.	*Super*, above; and *Scribo*, I write.
Theatrical	.	*Theaomi*, I look at.
Temperance	.	*Tempero*, I moderate.
Thurrible	.	A box to hold frankincense.
Voracious	.	*Voro*, I devour.
Volunteer	.	*Volo*, I wish.
Volume	.	*Volvo*, I roll; *Volutus*, rolled; books in former times having been rolled up.
Winfield	.	*Win*, war, and field.

In the Charter of Henry I. occur the following words:

SAC.—The royalty which the lord of manor claims in holding plea or causes of debate among his tenants.

SOC.—The power to administer justice.

TOL or TOLLAGE.—The privilege to take any thing away.

TOIL.—Liberty to buy and sell within the precints of the manor; also custom for passage and buying.

INFANGENCTHEF.—The liberty of trying a thief, stealing and taken in a man's own jurisdiction.

HAMSOCNE.—The liberty and freedom of one's own house.

FORSTALL.—Permission to buy ware before it comes to market to enhance the price.

FLEMENSFORD.—The right to receive and relieve a fugitive.

PLEAS.—That which either party alleges for himself in court.

GELD.—Money paid as tribute.

DANGELDS.—Twelve pence paid to the Danes for every hide of land.

PONTAGE.—A contribution or toll towards the maintaining or rebuilding of bridges.

J. TIBBETT, PRINTER, ETC., HIGH-STREET, DUNSTABLE.

INDEX

Compiled by John Buckledee 2002

List of subscribers

Anne Allsopp
Dr.R.Astley Cowper
Mrs G.Berridge
Colin Bourne
Hazel Clare Blackledge
Scott David Blackledge
Chalk Hill Garage
David Clark
Barbara Cole
Ealey Conquest
Alan B.W.Flowerday
Hugh Garrod
David Goseltine
Robert P.Hawkes
Mr & Mrs A.W.Hunt
A.W. & L.Kitchin
Phyllis Luckman
Mr & Mrs A.W.Morgan
B.L.Poulton
Mr & Mrs P.D.Sharp
Brian G.Smith
Peter W.Smith
Tom Stainsby
Bernard Stevens
Anthony J.Ward
Michael G.F.Wilson

DUNSTAPLE: A TALE OF THE WATLING HIGHWAY
The legend of Dunne the Robber
A.W.Mooring

Dunstaple ... a dramatic historical romance, which will particularly fascinate anyone interested in the legends of Dunstable's past. The story is woven around the tale of Dunne the Robber, the man whose exploits were said by some to be the basis for the town's modern name.

A.W. Mooring, editor of The Dunstable Borough Gazette between 1895 and 1909, took the gist of the legend about the outlaws who infested the forests around Dunstable crossroads in the time of King Henry 1, and added a romantic tale set among the Totternhoe caverns and the ramparts of Maiden Bower.

It first appeared as a six-month serial in The Gazette in 1898 and the following year in two different hardback editions produced in the newspaper's printing works in Albion Street, Dunstable.

The Book Castle

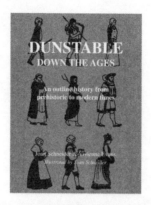

DUNSTABLE DOWN THE AGES
An outline history from prehistoric to modern times
Joan Schneider & Vivienne Evans

People have lived in South Bedfordshire for thousands of years, even before the Romans constructed Watling Street, and a town grew up where Dunstable now stands on the crossing with the Icknield Way. Then came Anglo-Saxon immigrants, and the creation of a new town and a Priory by Henry 1. There was a royal residence, and a Queen Eleanor cross was built after her coffin rested at the Priory. The decision, which ended Henry VIII's first marriage and caused England's break with the Roman Catholic Church, was taken here. Almshouses and schools were founded on the proceeds of distilling gin. Long distance coaches appeared on improved roads, and inns for travellers, but there were highwaymen too. Straw bonnets sold to travellers started the hat trade, which flourished in Victorian times. All these aspects are covered in this valuable publication, written as an introduction for all ages. Illustrated with dozens of line drawings.

The
Book
Castle

PROUD HERITAGE
A brief history of Dunstable 1000-2000AD
Vivienne Evans

Dunstable was founded by a king, had a palace, a very important Augustinian Priory and until 1600 was visited by nearly every king and queen of England. Sited on the crossroads less than forty miles from London, Oxford and Cambridge, Dunstable has been involved in many national events. Its populace has had to face economic and religious upheavals, but time after time Dunstablians pulled together, changed direction and won through to another successful era. Devoting a chapter to each of the ten centuries of the millennium, this book first sets the national and county scene in order to make more comprehensible the purely Dunstable events. Included in this book are stories about the Priory Church, Priory House, Kingsbury, Grove House, the Sugar Loaf and other inns, Ashton St Peter and other schools, Middle Row, Edward Street and other roads, the straw hat industry and the growth of the town.

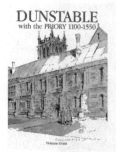 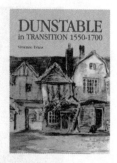

DUNSTABLE with the PRIORY 1100-1550
Vivienne Evans

This is the dramatic story of Henry I's busy and influential town with its royal palace, Augustinian Priory, Dominican Friary and thriving businesses around a major crossroads. Its rapid rise to success sees it linked to many famous national issues such as Magna Carta, the Eleanor Crosses, the Peasants' Revolt, the annulment of Henry VIII's marriage and the dissolution of the monasteries.

DUNSTABLE in TRANSITION 1550-1700
Vivienne Evans

The residents of Dunstable needed all their resourcefulness to rebuild the town's success without the Augustinian Priory.

Though disrupted by civil war, the developing coaching industry soon filled Dunstable with inns, as some new visitors brought wealth and importance to counterbalance other travellers who posed problems of poverty and disease.

The age's religious upheavals found a microcosm in Dunstable. The majority stayed worshipping at the Priory Church, but some left for America and others met in secret until reform led to the acceptance of Quakers and Baptists. Scandal punctuated this period of turmoil - the baptism of a sheep at church, the hounding of a suspected witch and the predations of notorious highwaymen. All elements of Dunstable in a volatile, transitional phase.

DUNSTABLE SCHOOL
1888-1971
F.M. Bancroft

" It was not one of the leading schools in the country... But it was a grammar school, a good grammar school, and it gave a sound all round education aligned with sporting activities of note. It taught courtesy, politeness and the home truths of life. And because of the masters over the years and a lot of the boys who went there it was a character school, with a happy atmosphere."

So, for all these reasons along with their own personal memories, though the school was superseded over a generation ago thousands of Old Boys still remember it with deep affection and gratitude.

The Book Castle

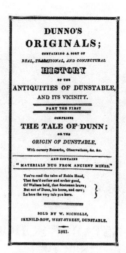

DUNNO'S
ORIGINALS;

CONTAINING A SORT OF

REAL, TRADITIONAL, AND CONJECTURAL

HISTORY

OF THE

ANTIQUITIES OF DUNSTABLE,

AND ITS VICINITY.

PART THE FIRST

COMPRISES

THE TALE OF DUNN;

OR THE

ORIGIN OF DUNSTABLE.

With cursory Remarks, Observations, &c. &c.

AND CONTAINS

" MATERIALS DUG FROM ANCIENT MINES."

You've read the tales of Robin Hood,
That fam'd outlaw and archer good,
Of Wallace bold, that Scotsman brave;
But not of Dunn, his horse, and cave;
Lo here the very tale you have. }

SOLD BY W. NICHOLLS,
IKENILD-ROW, WEST-STREET, DUNSTABLE.

1821.

DUNNO'S ORIGINALS
The First Complete Edition

A facsimile of five booklets concerning the history of Dunstable and its vicinity, including Totternhoe, Eaton Bray, Toddington, Flitwick and Flitton, first published in 1821 and 1822. Also four similar, rediscovered, and newly set manuscripts, completed by the author in 1823 shortly before his death, but previously unpublished. New introduction and glossary by John Buckledee, editor of the Dunstable Gazette.

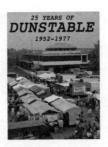

25 YEARS OF DUNSTABLE 1952-1977
A collection of photographs
Bruce Turvey

An era of enormous change in the town, 1952-1977, is commemorated in this superb collection of over 400 photographs - the best from Bruce Turvey's professional collection of over 100,000. Originally published to mark the Queen's Silver Jubilee, her Golden Jubilee seems a fitting moment for its re-issue. Changes include the disappearance of key old landmarks such as the Town Hall, the Red Lion and the California swimming pool, as well as the opening of the prestigious Civic (Queensway) Hall, the circular Catholic Church and the Quadrant Shopping Centre. Here are glimpses of other outstanding occasions, including Whipsnade's 21st Birthday party, the Pageant depicting 750 years of town history, and the granting of the Freedom of the Borough to the Herts and Beds Yeomanry - six years before the town's loss of that status in 1974. Famous visitors abound - four Prime Ministers, along with personalities like Kenneth More, Arthur Askey, David Kossoff, Brenda Lee, George Best, Mary Peters, Hugh Gaitskell and the Duchess of Gloucester. And of course there are hundreds of local people pictured in the photographs of sports teams, coach outings, dinner dances, carnival floats, retirement parties and uniformed organisations. The book opens with a snow scene and closes with a heat wave. In between are the myriad events that comprise the life of a market town during three different decades a generation ago.

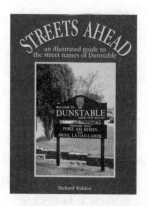

STREETS AHEAD
An illustrated guide to the street names of Dunstable
Richard Walden

Over the past 150 years Dunstable has expanded from a small rural market town with limited development beyond the four main streets, to a modem urban town of 35,000 inhabitants and over 300 individual streets. The names of many of those streets have been carefully chosen for some specific reason. Dunstable's modern housing estates in particular have been spared the all too common anonymity of poets, painters, authors and birds found in most other town. In Dunstable, developers and the local Council have taken great care to select names that record elements of the town's unique historical past and some of the characters and events that helped to shape the local community.

Streets Ahead is extensively illustrated with hundreds of photographs and copies of original documents, many of which have never been published before. The content of this work also makes it a fascinating record of the town's recent history.

Books Published by THE BOOK CASTLE

COUNTRYSIDE CYCLING IN BEDFORDSHIRE, BUCKINGHAMSHIRE AND HERTFORDSHIRE: Mick Payne. Twenty rides on and off-road for all the family.

PUB WALKS FROM COUNTRY STATIONS: Bedfordshire and Hertfordshire: Clive Higgs. Fourteen circular country rambles, each starting and finishing at a railway station and incorporating a pub stop at a mid way point.

PUB WALKS FROM COUNTRY STATIONS: Buckinghamshire and Oxfordshire: Clive Higgs. Circular rambles incorporating pub-stops.

LOCAL WALKS: South Bedfordshire and North Chilterns: Vaughan Basham. Twenty-seven thematic circular walks.

LOCAL WALKS: North and Mid Bedfordshire: Vaughan Basham. Twenty-five thematic circular walks.

FAMILY WALKS: Chilterns South: Nick Moon. Thirty 3 to 5 mile circular walks.

FAMILY WALKS: Chilterns North: Nick Moon. Thirty shorter circular walks.

CHILTERN WALKS: Hertfordshire, Bedfordshire and North Bucks: Nick Moon.

CHILTERN WALKS: Buckinghamshire: Nick Moon.

CHILTERN WALKS: Oxfordshire and West Buckinghamshire: Nick Moon. A trilogy of circular walks, in association with the Chiltern Society. Each volume contains 30 circular walks.

OXFORDSHIRE WALKS: Oxford, the Cotswolds and the Cherwell Valley: Nick Moon.

OXFORDSHIRE WALKS: Oxford, the Downs and the Thames Valley: Nick Moon.

Two volumes that complement Chiltern Walks: Oxfordshire, and complete coverage of the county, in association with the Oxford Fieldpaths Society. Thirty circular walks in each.

GHOSTLY OXFORD & OXFORDSHIRE: Marilyn Yurdan. The unexplained in all its guises in one of the country's most historic towns and the villages of the rest of the county.

THE D'ARCY DALTON WAY: Nick Moon. Long-distance footpath across the Oxfordshire Cotswolds and Thames Valley, with various circular walk suggestions.

THE CHILTERN WAY: Nick Moon. A guide to the new 133 mile circular Long-Distance Path through Bedfordshire, Buckinghamshire, Hertfordshire and Oxfordshire, as planned by the Chiltern Society.

CHANGES IN OUR LANDSCAPE: Aspects of Bedfordshire, Buckinghamshire and the Chilterns 1947-1992: Eric Meadows. Over 350 photographs from the author's collection spanning nearly 50 years.

JOURNEYS INTO BEDFORDSHIRE: Anthony Mackay. Foreword by The Marquess of Tavistock, Woburn Abbey. A lavish book of over 150 evocative ink drawings.

COCKNEY KID & COUNTRYMEN: Ted Enever. The Second World

War remembered by the children of Woburn Sands and Aspley Guise. A six year old boy is evacuated from London's East End to start life in a Buckinghamshire village.

CHANGING FACES, CHANGING PLACES: Post war Bletchley and Woburn Sands 1945-1970 Ted Enever. Evocative memoirs of post-war life on the Beds/Bucks borders, up to the coming of Milton Keynes new town.

BUCKINGHAM AT WAR: Pip Brimson. Stories of courage, humour and pathos as Buckingham people adapt to war.

WINGS OVER WING: The Story of a World War II Bomber Training Unit: Mike Warth. The activities of RAF Wing in Buckinghamshire.

JOURNEYS INTO BUCKINGHAMSHIRE: Anthony Mackay. Superb line drawings plus background text: large format landscape gift book.

BUCKINGHAMSHIRE MURDERS: Len Woodley. Nearly two centuries of nasty crimes.

WINGRAVE: A Rothschild Village in the Vale: Margaret and Ken Morley. Thoroughly researched and copiously illustrated survey of the last 200 years in this lovely village between Aylesbury and Leighton Buzzard.

HISTORIC FIGURES IN THE BUCKINGHAMSHIRE LANDSCAPE: John Houghton. Major personalities and events that have shaped the county's past, including Bletchley Park.

TWICE UPON A TIME: John Houghton. North Bucks short stories loosely based on fact.

SANCTITY AND SCANDAL IN BEDS AND BUCKS: John Houghton. A miscellany of unholy people and events.

MANORS and MAYHEM, PAUPERS and PARSONS: Tales from Four Shires: Beds., Bucks., Herts. and Northants: John Houghton. Little known historical snippets and stories.

THE LAST PATROL: Policemen killed on duty while serving the Thames Valley: Len Woodley.

FOLK: Characters and Events in the History of Bedfordshire and Northamptonshire: Vivienne Evans. Anthology of people of yesteryear - arranged alphabetically by village or town.

JOHN BUNYAN: His Life and Times: Vivienne Evans. Highly praised and readable account.

THE RAILWAY AGE IN BEDFORDSHIRE: Fred Cockman. Classic, illustrated account of early railway history.

A LASTING IMPRESSION: Michael Dundrow. A boyhood evacuee recalls his years in the Chiltern village of Totternhoe near Dunstable.

ELEPHANTS I'LL NEVER FORGET: A Keeper's Life at Whipsnade and London Zoo: John Weatherhead. Experiences, dramatic and sad, from a lifetime with these well-loved giants.

WHIPSNADE MY AFRICA: Lucy Pendar. The inside story of sixty years of this world-renowned institution. Full of history, anecdotes, stories of animals and people.

GLEANINGS REVISITED: Nostalgic Thoughts of a Bedfordshire Farmer's Boy: E.W. O'Dell. His own sketches and early photographs adorn this lively account of rural Bedfordshire in days gone by.

BEDFORDSHIRE'S YESTERYEARS: The Rural Scene: Brenda Fraser-Newstead. Vivid first-hand accounts of country life two or three generations ago.

BEDFORDSHIRE'S YESTERYEARS: Craftsmen and Tradespeople: Brenda Fraser-Newstead. Fascinating recollections over several generations practising many vanishing crafts and trades.

BEDFORDSHIRE'S YESTERYEARS: War Times and Civil Matters: Brenda Fraser-Newstead. Two World Wars, plus transport, law and order, etc.

DUNNO'S ORIGINALS: A facsimile of the rare pre-Victorian history of Dunstable and surrounding villages. New preface and glossary by John Buckledee, Editor of The Dunstable Gazette.

DUNSTABLE DOWN THE AGES: Joan Schneider and Vivienne Evans. Succinct overview of the town's prehistory and history - suitable for all ages.

HISTORIC INNS OF DUNSTABLE: Vivienne Evans. Illustrated booklet, especially featuring ten pubs in the town centre.

EXPLORING HISTORY ALL AROUND: Vivienne Evans. Planned as seven circular car tours, plus background to places of interest en-route in Bedfordshire and parts of Bucks and Herts.

PROUD HERITAGE: A Brief History of Dunstable, 1000-2000AD: Vivienne Evans. Century by century account of the town's rich tradition and key events, many of national significance.

DUNSTABLE WITH THE PRIORY: 1100-1550: Vivienne Evans. Dramatic growth of Henry I's important new town around a major crossroads.

DUNSTABLE IN TRANSITION: 1550-1700: Vivienne Evans. Wealth of original material as the town evolves without the Priory.

DUNSTABLE DECADE: THE EIGHTIES: A Collection of Photographs: Pat Lovering. A souvenir book of nearly 300 pictures of people and events in the 1980's

STREETS AHEAD: An Illustrated Guide to the Origins of Dunstable's Street Names: Richard Walden. Fascinating text and captions to hundreds of photographs, past and present, throughout the town.

DUNSTABLE IN DETAIL: Nigel Benson. A hundred of the town's buildings and features, plus town trail map.

DUNSTAPLELOGIA: Charles Lamborn. Facsimile of a well-respected mid-Victorian town history, with a number of engravings og local buildings.

DUNSTAPLE: A Tale of The Watling Highway: A.W. Mooring. Dramatic novelisation of Dunstable's legend of Dunne the Robber - reprinted after a century out of print.

25 YEARS OF DUNSTABLE: Bruce Turvey. Reissue of this photographic treasure-trove of the town up to the Queen's Silver Jubilee, 1952-77.

DUNSTABLE SCHOOL: 1888-1971. F.M. Bancroft. Short history of one of the town's most influential institutions.

BOURNE and BRED: A Dunstable Boyhood Between the Wars: Colin Bourne. An elegantly written, well illustrated book capturing the spirit of the town over fifty years ago.

OLD HOUGHTON: Pat Lovering. Pictorial record capturing the changing appearances of Houghton Regis over the past 100 years.

ROYAL HOUGHTON: Pat Lovering. Illustrated history of Houghton Regis from the earliest of times to the present.

WERE YOU BEING SERVED?: Remembering 50 Luton Shops of Yesteryear: Bob Norman. Well-illustrated review of the much loved, specialist outlets of a generation or two ago.

A BRAND NEW BRIGHT TOMORROW... A Hatters Promotion Diary: Caroline Dunn. A fans account of Luton Town Football Club during the 2001-2002 season.

GIRLS IN BLUE: Christine Turner. The activities of the famous Luton Girls Choir properly documented over its 41 year period from 1936 to 1977.

THE STOPSLEY BOOK: James Dyer. Definitive, detailed account of this historic area of Luton. 150 rare photographs.

THE STOPSLEY PICTURE BOOK: James Dyer. New material and photographs make an ideal companion to The Stopsley Book.

COMPLETELY HATTERS: An A-Z of Luton Town: Dean Hayes. Major stars and incidents throughout the good days and not so good in the club's history.

PUBS and PINTS: The Story of Luton's Public Houses and Breweries: Stuart Smith. The background to beer in the town, plus hundreds of photographs, old and new.

LUTON AT WAR - VOLUME ONE: As compiled by the Luton News in 1947, a well illustrated thematic account.

LUTON AT WAR - VOLUME TWO: Second part of the book compiled by The Luton News.

THE CHANGING FACE OF LUTON: An Illustrated History: Stephen Bunker, Robin Holgate and Marian Nichols. Luton's development from earliest times to the present busy industrial town. Illustrated in colour and mono.

WHERE THEY BURNT THE TOWN HALL DOWN: Luton, The First World War and the Peace Day Riots, July 1919: Dave Craddock. Detailed analysis of a notorious incident.

THE MEN WHO WORE STRAW HELMETS: Policing Luton, 1840-1974: Tom Madigan. Fine chronicled history, many rare photographs; author~served in Luton Police for fifty years.

BETWEEN THE HILLS: The Story of Lilley, a Chiltern Village: Roy Pinnock. A priceless piece of our heritage - the rural beauty remains but the customs and way of life described here have largely disappeared.

KENILWORTH SUNSET: A Luton Town Supporter's Journal: Tim Kingston. Frank and funny account of football's ups and downs.

A HATTER GOES MAD!: Kristina Howells. Luton Town footballers, officials and supporters talk to a female fan.

LEGACIES: Tales and Legends of Luton and the North Chilterns: Vic Lea. Mysteries and stories based on fact, including Luton Town Football Club. Many photographs.

THREADS OF TIME: Shela Porter. The life of a remarkable mother and businesswoman, spanning the entire century and based in Hitchin and (mainly) Bedford.

HARLINGTON - HEYDAYS & HIGHLIGHTS: Edna L. Wisher.

One of Bedfordshire's most historic villages, Harlington's yesteryears are seen through the eyes of one of its most empathetic residents.

FLITWICK: A DAILY TONIC: Keith Virgin. Written as a "Book of Days" containing extracts from the Flitwick Parish Magazine and local newspapers of around 100 years ago.

FARM OF MY CHILDHOOD, 1925-1947: Mary Roberts. An almost vanished lifestyle on a remote farm near Flitwick.

STICKS AND STONES: The Life and Times of a Journeyman Printer in Hertford, Dunstable, Cheltenham and Wolverton: Harry Edwards.

CRIME IN HERTFORDSHIRE Volume 1 Law and Disorder: Simon Walker. Authoritative, detailed survey of the changing legal process over many centuries.

THE LILLEY PICTURE BOOK: Betty Shaw. A picture book depicting village activities during the late nineteenth century and mainly the twentieth century.

JOURNEYS INTO HERTFORDSHIRE: Anthony Mackay. A foreword by The Marquis of Salisbury, Hatfield House. Introducing nearly 200 superbly detailed line drawings.

HAUNTED HERTFORDSHIRE: Nicholas Connell. Ghosts and other mysterious occurrences throughout the county's market towns and countryside.

LEAFING THROUGH LITERATURE: Writers' Lives in Herts and Beds: David Carroll. Illustrated short biographies of many famous authors and their connections with these counties.

A PILGRIMAGE IN HERTFORDSHIRE: H.M. Alderman. Classic, between-the-wars tour round the county, embellished with line drawings.

THE VALE OF THE NIGHTINGALE: Molly Andrews. Several generations of a family, lived against a Harpenden backdrop.

SUGAR MICE AND STICKLEBACKS: Childhood Memories of a Hertfordshire Lad: Harry Edwards. Vivid evocation of gentle pre-war in an archetypal village, Hertingfordbury.

SWANS IN MY KITCHEN: Lis Dorer. Story of a Swan Sanctuary near Hemel Hempstead.

MYSTERIOUS RUINS: The Story of Sopwell, St. Albans: Donald Pelletier. Still one of the town's most atmospheric sites. Sopwell's history is full of fluctuations and interest, mainly as a nunnery associated with St. Albans Abbey.

THE HILL OF THE MARTYR: An Architectural History of St. Albans Abbey: Eileen Roberts. Scholarly and readable chronological narrative history of Hertfordshire and Bedfordshire's famous cathedral. Fully illustrated with photographs and plans.

THE TALL HITCHIN INSPECTOR'S CASEBOOK: A Victorian Crime Novel Based on Fact: Edgar Newman. Worthies of the time encounter more archetypal villains.

HARE & HOUNDS: The Aldenham Harriers: Eric Edwards. Detailed highly illustrated history of a countryside institution.

SPECIALLY FOR CHILDREN

VILLA BELOW THE KNOLLS: A Story of Roman Britain: Michael Dundrow. An exciting adventure for young John in Totternhoe and Dunstable two thousand years ago.

THE RAVENS: One Boy Against the Might of Rome: James Dyer. On the Barton Hills and in the south-east of England as the men of the great fort of Ravensburgh (near Hexton) confront the invaders.

TITLES ACQUIRED BY THE BOOK CASTLE

BEDFORDSHIRE WILDLIFE: B.S. Nau, C.R. Boon, J.P. Knowles for the Bedfordshire Natural History Society. Over 200 illustrations, maps, photographs and tables survey the plants and animals of this varied habitat.

BIRDS OF BEDFORDSHIRE: Paul Trodd and David Kramer. Environments, breeding maps and details of 267 species, with dozens of photographs, illustrations and diagrams.

A BEDFORDSHIRE QUIZ BOOK: Eric G. Meadows. Wide ranging quizzes and picture puzzles on the history, people, places and bygones of the county.

CURIOSITIES OF BEDFORDSHIRE: A County Guide to the Unusual: Pieter and Rita Boogaart. Quirky, well-illustrated survey of little-known features throughout the county.

THE BIRDS OF HERTFORDSHIRE: Tom Gladwin and Bryan Sage. Essays, maps and records for all 297 species, plus illustrations, photographs and other plates.

BUTTERFLIES OF HERTFORDSHIRE: Brian Sawford. History and ecological guide, with colour photographs and maps for nearly 50 species.

WELWYN RAILWAYS: Tom Gladwin, Peter Neville, Douglas White. A history of the Great Northern line from 1850 to 1986, as epitomised by the five mile stretch between Welwyn Garden City and Woolmer Green. Profusely illustrated in colour and black and white - landscape format.

LIFE AND TIMES OF THE GREAT EASTERN RAILWAY (1839-1922): Harry Paar and Adrian Gray. Personalities, accidents, traffic and tales, plus contemporary photographs and old o.s. maps of this charming railway that transformed East Anglia and Hertfordshire between 1839 and 1922.

THE QUACK: Edgar Newman. Imaginative faction featuring characters in a nineteenth-century painting of a busy Hitchin market scene - especially quack doctor William Mansell.

D-DAY TO ARNHEIM - with Hertfordshire's Gunners: Major Robert Kiln. Vivid, personal accounts of the D-Day preparations and drama, and the subsequent Normandy battles, plus photographs and detailed campaign maps.

THE BOOK CASTLE
12 Church Street, Dunstable, Bedfordshire LU5 4RU
Tel: (01582) 605670 Fax (01582) 662431
Email: bc@book-castle.co.uk
Website: www.book-castle.co.uk